RUSSIAN COURT MEMOIRS
1914–1916

RUSSIAN COURT MEMOIRS
1914–1916

by
A RUSSIAN

with an introduction by
ALAN WOOD
*Senior Lecturer in Russian History,
Lancaster University*

Ian Faulkner Publishing
Cambridge · England

Ian Faulkner Publishing Ltd
Lincoln House
347 Cherry Hinton Road
Cambridge CB1 4DJ

First published 1917
by Herbert Jenkins Ltd

This edition copyright © Ian Faulkner Publishing Ltd 1992
Introduction copyright © Alan Wood 1992

All rights reserved. No part of this publication may be reproduced, stored in a retrieval system, or transmitted, in any form or by any means, electronic, mechanical, photocopying, recording, or otherwise, without the prior permission of the copyright owner.

A CIP record for this book is available from the British Library.

ISBN 1-85763-002-5

Printed in Great Britain by Billings and Sons Ltd

INTRODUCTION

by Alan Wood

THE year 1992 marks the seventy-fifth anniversary of the great revolutions in Russia which dramatically brought about the end of the three-centuries-long Romanov dynasty, the collapse of the tsarist social and political order, the end of the Russian Empire, and, in October 1917, the revolutionary seizure of political power by the Bolshevik Party and the inauguration of seven and a half decades of Soviet rule. The Soviet Union, founded on the ruins of the old empire in 1922, is itself now undergoing a process of deep economic crisis, political disintegration and territorial dismemberment which promises to be as far-reaching and profound in its effects as the 'ten days that shook the world' in 1917. One of the direct consequences of the present sea-change in domestic affairs within the former USSR has been a startling reorientation of cultural, intellectual and artistic values, including what may somewhat clumsily be described as the 'de-ideologisation of historiography' – that is, a re-examination of Russia's past, unconfined by the compulsory constraints of Marxist-Leninist or Stalinesque methodology.

However healthy this process may be, one of the dangers within it is that, in the rush to rewrite the history of the Russian Revolution and to counteract the distorting effects of so many years of communist party-dominated historical explanations, some writers may be tempted to slide to the opposite extreme and to compose a defence of the *ancien régime*, an apologia for the corrupt, inequitable and authoritarian tsarist system which an accumulation of objective and subjective factors caused to be swept away during that climactic year. There is in the Soviet Union today a tendency in some quarters – unthinkable only a

INTRODUCTION

few years ago – to romanticise the pre-revolutionary past, to reinstate fallen idols and even to revere figures and institutions which have no respectable or honourable place in a dispassionate analysis of the underlying causes for the overthrow of the Russian autocracy.

In the West, the study of recent Russian history has also undergone many changes since the immediate post-revolutionary hysteria, through the revisionism of the 1950s and 1960s, to the present more scholarly post-Cold War climate. In the early years, such was the general ignorance outside Russia of the causes and antecedents of the Revolution, of the role of its major protagonists and antagonists, of the economic, social, ethnic and political tensions which brought it about, that the majority of interested Western observers were dependent for their understanding of events on the interpretations of Russian émigré authors and publicists who had fled their homeland in the wake of the Revolution and Civil War (1918–22) to settle in various foreign havens. Many superannuated, unsuccessful and dispossessed members of the old society – politicians, generals, civil servants, aristocrats, courtiers, intellectuals and industrialists – made it their business to publish their own understandably personal and partisan explanations of the tragedy which they felt had overtaken their country and delivered it into the hands of the diabolical Bolsheviks. Some of these accounts still retain their credit as important memoir sources, penned by leading actors in the drama, whether as statesmen, revolutionaries or war-lords; others, written by self-opinionated minor spectators or peripheral spear-carriers, have a rather more dubious and ephemeral historical significance, but may nevertheless be justifiably regarded as possessing a certain bibliographical and antiquarian curiosity value.

It is to the latter category that the present work and its companion volume, *The Fall of the Romanoffs*, by the same anonymous author, belong. *Russian Court Memoirs, 1914–1916*, was written in 1916 (published in early 1917, obviously before the abdication of Tsar Nicholas II at the beginning of March of that year), and contains the thoughts, memories, diatribes and observations of an individual (identified in his(?) Preface by the initials 'B.W.') who was apparently extremely well acquainted with the inner secrets, scandals and intrigues of the Russian imperial court, and with the comings-and-goings and cavortings of Petrograd's (St Petersburg's) very high society during the last days and

INTRODUCTION

years of the doom-laden regime. In his introductory remarks (pages 3-4) the author states that it is his intention to provide the English public with an undistorted view of 'Russia as she really is' and of the 'inner life of the people' which only someone of his 'absolutely independent' and apolitical position can provide. Not mincing his words, this independent and apolitical author then goes on to declare that his 'convictions are strictly monarchical', that a British-style constitution 'with a king who reigns but does not rule' could not be adopted in Russia, and that any kind of republicanism 'is opposed to the genius of the [Russian] people'. Such views were of course typical of those of his 'social position' and of one in such obviously close proximity to the royal family and the capital's *beau monde*. However, such a clear declaration of political principle should dispel any misconceptions on the reader's part as to where 'B.W.'s' loyalties lay. It is painfully obvious that he was not only a devoted servant of autocratic government, but also an opponent of all those forces for progressive reform, constitutional rule, parliamentary democracy, for the pristine principles of 'liberty, equality and fraternity' in whose name the revolutionary struggle – whatever its ultimate outcome – was fought. The major interest in the following account therefore lies in the peculiar insight it gives us into the mentality, psychology and antiquated value system of those who shared the author's atavistic *Weltanschauung* and whose inability to adapt to the economic and political demands of the early twentieth century proved to be a central factor in their ultimate destruction.

The author's main concern is twofold: to paint a rather sad portrait of Russia's royal family, court entourage and metropolitan society during the first two years of the First World War, and to lay the blame for that war squarely at the feet of the German government and the 'hated Teutons', for whom he displays an almost pathological, racialist loathing. Much of his material is of an anecdotal nature, uncorroborated by any kind of documentary or evidential support, and seemingly based on rumour, hearsay and high-life tittle-tattle. He displays a touching reverence for the last of the Romanovs, his 'beloved Emperor', Nicholas II, and offers a spirited and sympathetic defence of the royal consort, Empress Alexandra – the 'German woman' – whose distressing unpopularity with Russian society he puts down to misunderstanding which was a consequence of the Tsarina's 'painful shy-

INTRODUCTION

ness' and 'based on misconception and prejudice against her German origin' (page 00). (After the February 1917 Revolution which forced the Tsar's abdication, the author was to change his tune and with a pen dipped in xenophobic and misogynic venom ascribe the dynasty's destruction exclusively to the evil machinations of the Empress and her *éminence noire*, the lecherous Rasputin – see *The Fall of the Romanoffs, passim*.) Despite his earlier deep respect for the imperial couple, the writer nevertheless bemoans the fact that court life under Nicholas II now lacked the splendour, gaiety and exemplary leadership of St Petersburg's high society which it displayed during the previous reign of Alexander III – 'the only real national Sovereign... a true Russian in all respects' (page 71). Rather than an annual season packed with balls, banquets and glittering soirées, 'for the past twelve years life at the Imperial Court has been reduced to the limits of family life' (page 25) – that is, the close and intimate family of Nicholas, Alexandra, their four daughters (the Grand Duchesses Tatiana, Olga, Maria and Anastasia) and the apple of everybody's eye, the Tsarevich Alexis, the latter appearing not as the author attempts to portray him as a bright young lad pluckily struggling against his unfortunate haemophiliac condition, but as a thoroughly spoiled and precocious little brat.

Apart from a stream of stories and anecdotes about these and other members of the Romanov family – dowagers, Grand Dukes, lesser Princesses, and a crew of counts, cousins and suitors of the European royal houses – and apart from his splenetic attacks on Germans and those of German ancestry still in Russian service ('every German is at heart an executioner': page 155), the author attempts, rather unsuccessfully, to provide his readership with some understanding of the historical tradition and cultural context within which the subject of his memoirs is set. 'By recalling some historical facts,' he says, he hopes to 'explain the psychological state of the Russian mind at the present time' (page 60). Unfortunately, like so many of his other observations, his account of Russian history from the time of Peter the Great (r. 1696–1725) to the First World War (Chapter V) and his characterisation of the 'mystical fatalism' of the Russian peasantry and of *fin de siècle* literature and society (Chapter IX) are embarrassing in their naïvety, their gross imbalance and their unbearably snobbish pomposity. Not only that: they are also inaccurate. It is hoped, therefore, that the following paragraphs will arm the modern

INTRODUCTION

reader with some rather more reliable information concerning the history of the regime whose demise our chronicler was about to witness.

Nicholas II was the last of the Romanov dynasty founded in 1613 with the election of Tsar Mikhail Fyodorovich to the Muscovite throne. His election solved a political crisis born of nearly two decades of revolutionary turmoil and domestic upheaval, usually referred to as 'the Time of Troubles' (1598–1613). The dynasty that died in revolution was therefore also born of one, and the continuing antagonisms and tensions between an increasingly autocratic government and an alternatingly submissive and rebellious Russian people was to remain the major leitmotif of Russian history for the next three hundred years. During the seventeenth century the autocracy consolidated its political power, enserfed the Russian peasantry, expanded territorially to the Pacific littoral and exercised its authority through a powerful military and the centralised bureaucracy. At the same time, the century was also one of popular opposition, mass uprisings and religious schism, culminating in the great cossack and peasant revolt led by Stenka Razin in 1670–71.

During the eighteenth century the same pattern and processes were continued, particularly during the reigns of Peter the Great and Catherine the Great (r. 1762–96), but with an important difference. Peter's establishment of Russia as a major European power following his victory in the Great Northern War against Sweden (1700–21), and his brutally enforced domestic policies of westernisation, which included a whole battery of military, administrative and fiscal reforms, succeeded in exacerbating those divisions and confrontations within Russian society that he had inherited from his Muscovite forebears. The symbol of his Europeanising zeal was the new capital of St Petersburg, designed by foreign architects, built by conscript and convict labour on the swamps and marshes of the Finnish Gulf, and inhabited by the serf-owning service nobility now forcibly educated and attired in the contemporary learning and style of Western Europe. Peter in fact created a fatal dichotomy in Russian society. Despite the social antagonisms of the seventeenth century, old Muscovy had experienced a certain amount of cultural and religious homogeneity, largely untouched by outside influences. After Peter, there were now two societies – the world of the Europeanised nobility, not only socially but also culturally divorced from the masses, and

INTRODUCTION

the world of the ignorant, superstitious and periodically starving peasant serfs. The only bond between the *barin* and the *muzhik* was henceforward that of ownership – the former owning the latter.

Despite her professions of adherence to enlightened principles, Catherine the Great did little to alleviate the plight of her people, and her policies were almost entirely designed to protect and enhance the social, economic and cultural interests of the nobility on whose support she initially relied to retain her throne. (At this point in the author's narrative there occurs a noticeable lapse in his Germanophobia, and, despite the Empress's origins as a petty German princess and her usurpation of the throne from her murdered husband, he describes her reign as 'in all respects glorious' (page 65) and the lady herself as fully deserving the accolade 'Great' – though he does concede in an aside that 'her private life could not bear microscopic investigation'!). Catherine's reign, apart from being the 'Golden Age of the Russian nobility', was also marked by two portentous manifestations of anti-government opposition. The first was another massive popular uprising, verging on a full-scale peasant war (1773–75), under the leadership of Emelyan Pugachev which seriously threatened the security of the state; the second was the publication in 1790 of a critical attack on the despotism, hypocrisy and corruption of Catherine's regime, written by a highly educated member of the Russian nobility, Alexander Radishchev (1749–1802). While the forces of popular rebellion and intellectual opposition individually represented by Pugachev and Radishchev were kept in isolation from each other, the imperial system managed to survive intact. But when, in the early twentieth century, Pugachev and Radishchev conjoined, Romanov fell.

The author's brief account of nineteenth-century Russian history is remarkable mainly for its spectacular omissions. In particular, there is hardly any mention of the growth of revolutionary opposition to the tsarist regime, even though suppression of that movement was one of the government's constant domestic preoccupations. The Decembrist revolt of 1825 which sought to replace autocratic government with a constitutional or republican regime is dismissed in a couple of lines; the emancipation of the Russian serfs in 1861 – once described as the greatest single piece of legislation in Russia's entire history – is totally ignored, as is the ambitious programme of local government, judicial, social and

INTRODUCTION

military reform undertaken by Alexander II (r. 1855–81); no attention whatsoever is paid to the dramatic growth in practical revolutionary activity during the 1860s and 1870s which culminated in the assassination of the Emperor by populist terrorists in 1881; the growth of capitalism and the whole process of industrialisation at the turn of the century is used merely as an excuse to launch yet another barrage of gratuitous abuse at German factory owners, than whom 'no more hard, overbearing and gruff task-masters exist' (page 72), and so on.

But it is in his treatment of the immediate background to the period he describes that our author is at his most cavalier. In 1905 the Russian Empire was shaken to its foundations by a whirlwind of industrial strikes, popular demonstrations, military mutinies, and social, political and economic upheavals which, in retrospect, may be seen as a full dress rehearsal for 1917. However, according to 'B.W.', 'The importance of the strikes and riots of 1905 have been grossly exaggerated... Russia is not a revolutionary country' (pages 11–12)! True, the revolutionary events of 1905 did not succeed in toppling the monarchy, and there was no profound change in the structure of society or the ownership of property, but they nevertheless marked an extremely important watershed in Russia's political development which is pitifully underestimated by this supposedly close and intimate observer of Russian reality.

During the decade between 1906 and 1916, as a direct consequence of the crisis of 1905, Russia enjoyed a brief period of quasi-constitutional government and legalised political activity unprecedented and unrepeated in her history. The Emperor never relished this experiment with quasi-parliamentary politics, and even regarded his own appointed ministers as 'unavoidable and necessary evils' (page 7). Much worse, however, were the representatives of the people elected to the four state assemblies (Dumas) which met during this remarkable decade. The first and second Dumas were dismissed; the franchise was illegally re-jigged in 1907 to favour the wealthy classes; and the government came increasingly under the corrupting influence of the religious fanatic, Grigory Rasputin, who was finally murdered by a cabal of courtiers in December 1916, four months after the following memoirs were completed, and two months before the revolutionary anger of the masses swept the 'beloved Emperor' from his throne. The circumstances in which this occurred were later

INTRODUCTION

addressed by the author in his own curious account of *The Fall of the Romanoffs*.

By the time *Russian Court Memoirs* was written, Germany and Russia had been at war for exactly two years, with devastating consequences not only on the battlefields, but also on the fabric of Russian society and the Russian people. The initial popular patriotism and mass enthusiasm to defend Holy Russia had soon worn thin; industry was in chaos; incompetence reigned at front and rear; government and society were totally divided, and the royal court and family which our author so fondly describes were held in almost universal contempt. It is this which gives the present book its peculiar fascination. Aware of the ruinous military reverses, the political turmoil and the economic shambles; in the face of police reports forecasting imminent revolutionary explosion; witness to the death agonies of a discredited dynasty and a social order which was crumbling around his ears, 'B.W.' still manages to cling on to a vision of a world in which loyalty, respect for secular and religious authority, glorious military victory over the 'ferocious savages' to the west, humility and faith in God, Tsar and country will triumph over the dark forces of liberalism, popular 'education without breeding' (page 126), democracy and the subversive teachings of dangerous intellectuals such as Leo Tolstoy, obviously a renegade to his class, who is singled out for surprisingly vicious abuse. Reading these memoirs is like entering a lost world. If, as the author says, his own political, ethical and spiritual values were typical of 'nearly all the people belonging to the same social position' as himself, then one may understand why that world – like that of the dinosaurs – was unable to survive.

RUSSIAN COURT MEMOIRS 1914–16

WITH SOME ACCOUNT OF COURT, SOCIAL
AND POLITICAL LIFE IN PETROGRAD
BEFORE AND SINCE THE WAR

by
A RUSSIAN

MCMXVII

THE EMPEROR NICHOLAS II IN HIS CAMPAIGN UNIFORM

PREFACE

MY English friends constantly complain in their welcome letters to me that they know so little of Russia and the Russians, and this gave me the idea of writing a book that should tell of social and official life in Petrograd, and also contain stories and personal particulars of those who are responsible for guiding our country through these terrible times.

It is time that English people should know Russia as she really is, without any attempt to magnify her defects or to embellish her good qualities. This real knowledge can scarcely be acquired by an English writer who has studied the country only during his travels, and who writes under the influence of casual impressions. The conclusions arrived at about matters concerning the inner life of the people depend mostly on the trustworthiness and degree of culture of those who gave him the indispensable explanations. Nor can this knowledge be imparted by a Russian politician (too often a refugee who has emigrated from his country), who sees everything in a distorted light through the glasses of a narrow party prejudice, and who writes with the deliberate object of reviling all those who do not share the opinions of his party, especially those whom he suspects of trying to prevent these ideas from dominating in Russia.

Absolutely independent, I belong to no party and do not busy myself with politics. My convictions are strictly monarchical, as are those of nearly all the people belonging to the same social position as myself. But I am not averse to progress, and acknowledge the urgent necessity of reforms for the enlightenment of the Russian people. I also believe in the strengthening of the country's economic position. I feel deeply convinced that Russia, vast in dimensions and strong in spirit, must preserve its traditions and not break with the historical association of centuries. The British constitution, with a king who reigns but does not rule, could not be adopted in Russia, and any attempt to make her republican would be almost suicidal, for it is opposed to the genius of the people.

The object of this work is to speak only the truth and to describe facts and circumstances as they appear to my mental vision; the shadows I point out are those which I see myself. I am perfectly aware that the author of this book will incur innumerable reproaches from various classes of Russian society for choosing this way of making his country known to foreigners. To this criticism I offer the ready retort that in writing this book I do not wish to be agreeable to anyone. By their attitude towards us during recent years the English people have acquired the right to claim from Russia the truth about Russia . . . and like an honest ally I pay my debt in the best way I can.

B.W.

PETROGRAD, *August*, 1916.

CONTENTS

CHAPTER		PAGE
	PREFACE	3
I.	THE TZAR AND HIS FAMILY	7
II.	THE IMPERIAL COURT	25
III.	HOW PETROGRAD GREETED THE WAR	40
IV.	RUSSIAN WOMEN DURING THE WAR	50
V.	SHADOWS OF THE PAST	60
VI.	SHADES OF THE PRESENT	73
VII.	THE TZAR AND HIS GENERALS	84
VIII.	THE TZAR'S DAUGHTERS AND SOME OTHER MEMBERS OF THE IMPERIAL FAMILY	100
IX.	CHARACTERISTICS AND IMPRESSIONS	120
X.	THE RUSSIAN FOREIGN OFFICE	129
XI.	THE WAR	139
XII.	CAN RUSSIA FORGET?	145
XIII.	THE PRESS	156
XIV.	SOCIETY OF PETROGRAD	163
XV.	LOOKING FORWARD	193

Chapter I

THE TZAR AND HIS FAMILY

THE first mention in a book such as this must be of our beloved Emperor and those dear to him. Nicholas II is not only a monarch, but also a gentleman. A short time ago such a statement would have appeared an unnecessary impertinence; but recent events have unfortunately proved that an Emperor can be far from that.

During the last two years the Tzar has so endeared himself to his people that he now possesses not only their respect and veneration as their Emperor, but their love and devotion as a friend whose first thought is of them and of their welfare.

Nicholas II did not receive the education that the future monarch of such a vast Empire as Russia should have received. Many of the qualities, which he undoubtedly possesses, were left dormant, instead of being developed, as they should have been. Kind, generous and shrewd, clever, but not intellectual, His Majesty gets easily tired of political discussions, and he dislikes his ministers to be long-winded. It takes him some time to come to a decision, or to make any change, but this is only outward hesitation, the outcome of his unwillingness to inflict pain, or hurt the feelings of others. In his mind he knows what should be done, and gradually enforces his will.

He is not personally attached to any of his ministers, and looks upon them as unavoidable and necessary evils. He particularly disliked Count Witte, whose tact was not his strong point. He was rough in his speech and inclined to be overbearing. Still, as long as he found it necessary, the Emperor tried to bear with him. Stolypine, on the contrary, was sympathetic to the Emperor, but then Stolypine was a man of refinement, birth and breeding, belonging to a very old boyar family. He had soft engaging manners and, when he wished to do so, knew how to exercise a personal charm that always had the desired effect on his listeners. Stolypine's great virtue in his Sovereign's eyes was that he never wearied him, never exceeded the length of time allotted to business. What he had to say was said clearly and succinctly, without causing the Emperor either fatigue or irritation.

Count Kokowtzoff endeavoured to follow on the same lines. Very talented and eloquent, he impressed the Emperor by his reports. Still the Sovereign is said to have felt no personal sympathy with Count Kokowtzoff: he never gave him his entire confidence. A few days before his resignation a curious scene took place, when Kokowtzoff in the presence of the President of the Council of the Empire, the late M. Akimoff, who in prospect of an anticipated triumph Kokowtzoff had specially requested to be present, read to the Emperor his new project for enlarging the Government's exchequer, but would inevitably have ruined the people.

The Emperor was sitting in an armchair at his desk drawing squares and circles on a sheet of paper. He listened attentively to the report, never lifting his eyes from the paper and making no interruption. Kokowtzoff ceased reading, glowing with exultation. Not one single item of the project had been gainsaid or criticised by the Sovereign. This was a triumph indeed! The Emperor rose, intimating that the audience was at an end. In shaking hands with the Prime Minister he said, 'I must tell you that I don't agree with your project at all.' The blow was unexpected. M. Akimoff felt uncomfortable and wished he had not come. As to Kokowtzoff his feelings can easily be imagined.

For three days following this episode, the Emperor expected the Prime Minister's resignation, but when it was not forthcoming the Tzar was obliged to take the initiative and write to Kokowtzoff giving him his dismissal. The pill was duly gilded by the title of Count which was granted to him.

Though considering that Kokowtzoff unfortunately has no son this consolation was rather a barren one.

There is a feeling that the Emperor is distrustful and suspicious of everyone. It is true that few among his most intimate circle possess his full confidence. The proverbial loneliness of kings seems to have fallen heavily upon him. Some regard him as lacking in frankness, and that, like his ancestor Alexander I, his

THE TZAR AND HIS FAMILY

amiability is not equal to all occasions. However well or ill founded this report may be, he is a devoted husband and parent, and in particular he adores his son. His private life is that of a rich country gentleman rather than that of the Tzar of All the Russias.

The spring and part of the autumn the Imperial Family spend in Livadia, a lovely place they have in the Crimea. Summer is always spent in Peterhof. During the hot weather they do a lot of cruising along the coast of Finland. The Imperial Yacht *Standart* is beautifully equipped, and has comfortable accommodation for the Imperial Family as well as for numerous guests. The same set is mostly invited to these yachting parties. The Emperor is at his best at such times, for he loves the sea and enjoys his freedom.

The suite, as well as the yacht's officers, have their meals with the Imperial Family. The Emperor presides at breakfast (the Empress only appears at lunch), and is most attentive to the wants of all present, making a point of remembering the different tastes of his guests. At one o'clock lunch is served, at five o'clock an elaborate afternoon tea, with hot cakes, sandwiches, etc. This is followed by dinner at eight o'clock, after which games fill up the evening. At about eleven o'clock everyone retires.

The Emperor is a good sportsman. He likes hunting, is a fairly good shot and an excellent tennis player. His pet recreation, however, is motoring.

One of the Tzar's favourite pleasures is to dine at mess with one of the regiments of the Guards quartered at Tzarskoe Selo. On such evenings he is the regimental guest. The military band plays alternately with one of the fashionable orchestras. A chorus of Gypsies is specially engaged. Music and singing go on all night and the Emperor returns to the Palace in the small hours. Etiquette is suspended for the time, and the Sovereign behaves like a comrade of the officers, who are all devoted to him. Occasionally such regimental dinners take place in Petrograd.

At exhibitions, specialists have often been surprised at the knowledge and deep interest manifested by the Emperor in all sorts of new inventions. At such times he will spend hours listening to the minutest explanations and going into the most intricate details.

The personal charm of the Emperor's manner impresses everyone who sees him for the first time. His best features are his large, dark, velvety-soft eyes, inherited from his mother, with her lovely expression. His courtesy never fails him; he is very reserved and exercises great self-control, seldom showing annoyance or irritation. He manifests his displeasure by completely ignoring the person who is in disgrace, but never gives way to violent outbursts.

He has the gift of elocution. His speeches are always well composed, short and to the point. He delivers them in a steady, clear voice. When the occasion is an exciting one he becomes very pale. This is the only outward sign of nervousness he exhibits.

The Empress Alexandra Feodorovna is a beautiful woman, very intellectual, with high ideals, but unfortunately she is frequently misunderstood. She is hampered by a painful shyness towards strangers, and is often thought cold and even haughty.

Loved and respected by intimate friends, the Empress has, however, not endeared herself to the general public, to whom she gives the impression of not endeavouring to make herself popular. This is no doubt due to her shyness. She leads a most secluded life, seeing only the members of her family and her most intimate circle of friends. The fact that her husband and children adore her should be the best answer to her critics.

The morbid tendency of her nature causes her to magnify troubles and misfortunes. When she came to Russia, young and lovely as she was, everyone was sorry for the sad circumstances attending her coming to this country and her marriage.

Everyone admired her and was prepared to love her. But she did not appear to understand the homage that was offered her. This was interpreted as want of appreciation on the young Sovereign's part, and the unbounded homage and admiration were replaced by criticism.

The Dowager Empress Marie's attitude towards her daughter-in-law did not ingratiate the latter with the public. People took sides, and most of the sympathies were given to the Dowager Empress, who up to the present day has retained the popularity she always enjoyed in Russia.

The Empress's intense desire to give an heir to the throne was thwarted five times. This was a sore disappointment, and, when the crucial moment approached, she was in such a state of nervous excitement that those around her were afraid to apprise her of her infant's sex.

To his wife the Emperor never showed disappointment. He was touchingly good to her, doing all in his power to comfort her grief and give her courage. The Empress was beginning to despair when, ten years after her marriage, the Grand Duke Alexis was born. The joy this event created in the Imperial Family is beyond description. Everything centred in the Imperial baby-boy. All political developments seemed to lose their importance; the reverses during the Russo-Japanese war were hardly felt. At Court all was gladness and jubilation. Then came the reaction.

It is said that those of the Dowager Empress's entourage were not as enthusiastic over the birth of the Tzessarevitch as the rest of Russia. It was a disappointment to their hopes of seeing the Grand Duke Michael remain the heir to the throne.

When Alexander III died, his second son, the Grand Duke George, was proclaimed the Heir Presumptive and received the title of Tzessarevitch, which he would have retained even if a son had been born to the Tzar. The Tzessarevitch George died in 1899, five years prior to the birth of his nephew. By the Laws of Heredity, the Grand Duke Michael became the Heir Presumptive, but the Emperor declined to let him bear the title of Tzessarevitch. This was a dire offence to the Dowager Empress and deeply hurt the feelings of the Grand Duke. In acting thus, the Sovereign, so it was whispered, was carrying out the desires of his wife. A coolness ensued between the brothers, and during these five years the Grand Duke Michael avoided appearing at any public function in the official position of heir to the throne.

The importance of the riots and strikes of 1905 have been grossly exaggerated abroad, where everybody believed that Russia was the scene of a genuine revolution. It is true there was a great deal of mismanagement. If the Emperor had not been so taken up with the birth of his heir, measures might have been taken in time and the whole movement stopped. All was falsely represented to him and unwise counsel was given. Foreign papers and books have suggested that the Imperial Family was obliged to flee before the masses who flocked to the Winter Palace led by the priest Gapon. This is absolutely untrue, for at the time the Emperor and his family were in Tzarskoe Selo. It was all the more unwise of the authorities to allow the populace to approach the Palace.

The tragic fate of the Emperor's uncle, the Grand Duke Serge, who was assassinated, was a great blow and made a deep impression on the Emperor and Empress. Married to the Empress's eldest sister, the Grand Duchess Elisabeth, the Grand Duke Serge had great influence with the Tzar, and the intercourse between the two couples had always been a very cordial and friendly one. His death was felt as a great loss, and the horror of the circumstances accompanying it left a depressing effect.

During that disquieting period Count Witte played a somewhat equivocal part, which has never been completely elucidated. However, Russia is not a revolutionary country, and therefore as soon as M. P. N. Dournovo, a man of strength and energy, sincerely devoted to the autocracy, was appointed Minister of the Interior, the revolutionists saw that the hour had produced the man, and order was quickly restored all over the Empire.

On the Empress's mind these events left an indelible impression. She was not afraid for herself, but she feared for the safety of her boy. She could hardly bear him out of her sight and always thought he was in danger.

In the course of one of their annual yachting cruises the Empress had a terrible fright, which left a lasting influence on her nervous system. An accident occurred to the *Standart* and the Imperial Family had to leave the yacht. In the excitement of the first moments it was thought that the accident had been caused by a criminal attempt. The Empress rushed to the nursery-cabin, intent on carrying off the baby son. To her dismay, she found the cradle empty, and in her terror she imagined he had been kidnapped . . . The little Tzessarevitch, meanwhile, was perfectly safe, for someone had warned the nurse before the Empress had time to reach the cabin, and the boy had been carried to a safe place. After due investigation it was discovered that there had been no foul play, and that the accident had been caused by unpardonable neglect. Nevertheless, the unfortunate Empress lived through the most miserable moments of her existence, and the shock she received has proved harmful to Her Majesty's health.

A few years later came the Tzessarevitch's illness – that was a terrible grief and continues to be a great anxiety. The Empress suffers deeply. No wonder she has neither the wish nor the energy to play up to her part as Empress of Russia.

The Empress, who is essentially a devoted wife and mother, has always disliked state functions and ceremonies, and for ten years there have been no balls or receptions at Court. An Empress of Russia belongs not only to her home circle, but to the nation, and her people expect to see her often in public. A few yearly receptions at Court, which would be accessible, not only to a small

THE TZAR AND HIS FAMILY

number of courtiers, but to society at large, would do much to bring the Empress and her people nearer together. Such balls would be a boon to commerce and have a salutary influence on society. At present Petrograd society resembles a ship that has lost its helmsman and drifts in different directions according to each change of wind.

When the Imperial Family is in Livadia the Empress becomes more social. At the annual naval bazaar in Yalta she has her stall, and, assisted by her daughters, takes an active part in the sale. Every Sunday after church a gay luncheon-party assembles at the Palace. Not only the suite is bidden to these luncheon-parties, but invitations are freely issued to the most important residents of Yalta and the neighbourhood. Dances are arranged to amuse the young Grand Duchesses.

These are considered quite unofficial and etiquette is banished for the time.

During the Romanoff Jubilee the Petrograd nobility gave a magnificent ball in honour of the Sovereigns. The question of the Empress's presence at the ball raised a good deal of talk. 'Would she or would she not appear?' was for days discussed in all circles. The Empress finally decided to attend the ball. She looked extremely handsome in the Crown diamonds, but she only remained a short time, refused to stay for supper, was very unbending in her demeanour, and gave the impression of being bored and ill at her ease, proving once more that she does not possess that magical quality that attracts the masses.

At this ball the Grand Duchess Olga made her first appearance in public as a grown-up young lady. She was beautifully gowned in a becoming evening dress of pale pink, with a ribbon of the same hue tied round her beautiful hair, and she looked as sweet as the dawn of a lovely summer day. Her enjoyment was evident, and she was so loath to be taken away by her mother that she was allowed to stay on under her grandmother's chaperonage.

Since her arrival in Russia the Empress has made a serious study of the Russian language and her laudable efforts have been crowned with success, for she speaks Russian fluently and has a very good accent. In this respect, the contrast between the two Empresses is decidedly in favour of the Empress Alexandra, for the Dowager Empress Marie has never attained a good knowledge of the language of her adopted country.

The Imperial children are delightful. The two elder, the Grand

Duchess Olga and the Grand Duchess Tatiana, are the embodiment of bright unaffected girlhood. They are charming to look at, are always well dressed and carry themselves most elegantly. The Grand Duchess Olga, from a plain child, has become a pretty girl with lovely blue eyes. The Grand Duchess Tatiana has a small piquant face and looks provoking. The third, Grand Duchess Marie, will be a beauty. Of Anastasia, the youngest, little can be said, as she is only a child of thirteen.

During their childhood the Imperial children were allowed to run rather wild, and only a few years ago both the elder Grand Duchesses Olga and Tatiana were veritable tomboys. This education was much criticised by the Dowager Empress and her friends and partisans. But the ultimate result proved the Empress to be right, for no more charming healthy-minded girls exist than the two elder Grand Duchesses.

The little Tzessarevitch Alexis, on whom Russia's hopes and his parent's idolising love are centred, is a handsome bright boy, clever and sharp-witted. He used to be a veritable small autocrat. Adored by his father and mother, and very much spoilt, he lorded it over his sisters and his immediate attendants, but since he has been staying with the Tzar at Headquarters he has much improved both physically and mentally, and the discipline which surrounds him, and to which he necessarily must submit, has a salutary influence on the development of his character. Many droll anecdotes are related about him.

Once when the Emperor was busy with a minister, the little Grand Duke burst into the room with some complaint. His father reprimanded him, saying that when the Sovereign was occupied with State affairs a little boy had no business to interrupt in such an unceremonious manner. A quarter of an hour later the Tzessarevitch reappeared, this time in full military uniform, had himself announced, and standing at attention before the Emperor, said: 'I have the honour to report to Your Imperial Majesty that Her Imperial Highness the Grand Duchess Anastasia Nicolaïevna has been naughty and has refused to play with me.'

Russian naval officers are not supposed to wear boots with buttons; nevertheless, they nearly all do wear them. One day the Grand Duke Alexis, when he was about seven years old, noticed that the late Captain Tchaguine of the Imperial Yacht *Standart* was in buttoned boots. The Tzessarevitch went up to him and drew his attention to his nether limbs, saying: 'I, as your chief [the Tzessarevitch from his birth belongs to the Guards-Equipage], reprove you for this incorrectness.' The Emperor, being near, witnessed the scene, and, quickly approaching the assembled group, he added: 'And I, as your father, send you into the corner.'

The Tzessarevitch takes a keen interest in M. Purishkevitch, the Bessarabian member of the Duma, belonging to the right faction. M. Purishkevitch is a clever man and one of the best orators in the Duma. He alternately carries away his audience by his brilliant eloquence, or sends his auditors into fits of laughter by his sallies, but he can use very forceful language, occasionally calling forth violent disturbances. On the whole M. Purishkevitch is considered the 'enfant terrible' of the Duma, and one is never sure of his next move.

During the Imperial visit to Bessarabia the Emperor and Empress made a short stay in Kishineff.

Whilst the official pageants were going on the little Tzessarevitch was left in the Imperial train. One of the local dignitaries, attracted by the little boy's wistful face looking out of the carriage window, approached him saying: 'It must be tedious for Your Imperial Highness; could I do anything to relieve your dullness?' 'Oh, please show me Purishkevitch, I do so long to see him.' The amused gentleman started in quest of the member of the Duma and returned a few minutes later accompanied by M. Purishkevitch, who good-naturedly walked up and down the platform before the delighted gaze of the Tzessarevitch.

Since then the Grand Duke Alexis has had the opportunity of making the personal acquaintance of M. Purishkevitch, for the Emperor took him to visit the hospital train, which is directed by the well-known member of the Duma, and the Tzar and his son were shown over by M. Purishkevitch himself.

The Tzessarevitch is an ardent patriot and takes the deepest interest in the development of the war. Soon after the declaration of war from Kaiser Wilhelm, the little Grand Duke told a lady that he had collected the photographs of all his German relations and connections and torn them up. He only hesitated about 'mamma's brother'. That was a dilemma he could not solve by himself, so in the contingency he applied for the opinion of Nastia (the Grand Duchess Anastasia, the sister nearest to him in age). Nastia's verdict was: 'Never mind his being mamma's brother, he is a German, tear him up with the rest.' 'So,' continued the Tzessarevitch, 'we tore them all up into the tiniest bits and then we trampled on them.'

The state of the Tzessarevitch's health has been a source of great anxiety to his adoring parents. Though much stronger at present, he is still surrounded by precautions. When he was a small boy of five he took a violent fancy to one of the sailors of the *Standart*, Derevenko, who has since been attached to the Grand Duke's service as a combination of male nurse and valet. Derevenko is devoted to his young master, carried him about when he was not allowed to walk, and never lets him out of his sight.

Many reports are current as to the Tzessarevitch's disease, but the real truth is known to a very few. The illness is caused by tubercle of the pelvis-femoral joint in the left leg. When quite a baby it was noticed that every knock or fall produced an uncalled-for swelling of the knee and leg, but no great anxiety was felt as the child looked such a healthy, sturdy little fellow, always gay and full of high spirits. The accident which brought on the crisis happened in Livadia when the Grand Duke Alexis was seven years old. He was playing with a boat on the bank of the lake situated at the end of the park. In trying to push off the boat he overbalanced and fell, causing the rupture of several blood-vessels, resulting in a *hoemotum* that spread over the whole leg, up to the hip and threatening the groin. Peritonitis set in and brought the child to the very jaws of death.

The best doctors were called in, and after a skilful treatment of five or six days the danger abated. Absolute quiet was recommended for a certain length of time, all movement was strictly forbidden, and for a long while the Tzessarevitch was not allowed to walk. For such an animated boy this was a terrible restriction. When all was going on favourably a second fall produced another crisis. The cure of immobility had to be recommenced all over again. The greatest care has since been taken of the boy on whom so much depends. Five years have passed, and the Tzessarevitch has grown much stronger; he takes long walks, plays with other children and has become active and independent, but wild romps are avoided, and a slight stiffness in the left leg is noticeable. Doctors differ in their opinion. Some of them hope he will completely outgrow this weakness, and if carefully looked after during his youth may enjoy fairly good health in the years of his manhood. Others, on the contrary, consider that the critical time of such diseases is when the patient has attained the age of from eighteen to twenty. The feelings of the parents can be imagined. They worship the boy, he is the central interest of their lives, and they live under the continual fear of the sword of Damocles.

The fact that the Grand Duke Alexis is allowed to stay with his father at Headquarters, and that he accompanies the Sovereign on his journeys is a convincing proof, however, that the doctors consider his health in a much better state. He shares the Emperor's bedroom, and goes out with him daily in the motor-car, but he takes his walks with his French tutor or Russian master. He enjoys going to the town garden and watching the children play. One day he saw two cadets of about his own age; going up to them he somewhat shyly invited them to play with him. When it was time to separate, the Tzessarevitch, after previously consulting his tutor, invited the cadets to spend the following afternoon with him. Since then they have become great friends, and the cadets very often share the Tzessarevitch's games, and one meets the Imperial car occasionally excursioning in the neighbourhood of Headquarters with the Tzar and the three boys chatting and laughing and looking merry.

The Empress and her daughters pay frequent visits to the Emperor at Headquarters. All family anniversaries are invariably spent together, and never were the Imperial couple in the whole course of their connubial existence on such tender and affectionate terms as at the present time.

Not very long ago the Tzessarevitch, escorted by his faithful attendant Derevenko, went out for a walk in the park of Tzarskoe Selo. Their walk had lasted longer than usual, and Derevenko, fearing that fatigue might harm the little Grand Duke, hailed an 'isvostchik' (cab) to take them back to the Palace. Arrived there, the Grand Duke took out his purse containing only twenty copecks (about sixpence) which he handed out to the cabman. Derevenko remonstrated, saying it was much too little. 'Well,' answered the Imperial boy, 'if you are so rich, pay him yourself.'

The Dowager Empress is one of those happy creatures at whose birth a benevolent fairy presided. Without giving herself the least trouble she commands love, admiration and popularity. From the first day she set foot on the Russian soil the Princess Dagmar gained the hearts of all her future subjects. Her beautiful eyes, her lovely smile and wonderful charm of manner were the principal cause of her immense popularity. When she smiles she seems to single one out of the crowd, and each separate individual appropriates her smile as personally intended.

On a bright winter's day, when she was still the Tzessarevna, her radiant figure wrapped in priceless furs was eagerly watched for during the hour of her daily drive down the Neva Quai, and everyone tried to catch her eye.

After the tragic events of 1881, when she became Empress, her popularity increased. The Imperial couple led a model life; everybody looked up to and respected them. This was attributed to the Empress's influence. She liked to enjoy herself; dancing was one of her favourite amusements, and during the reign of Alexander III the receptions in the Winter Palace were very gorgeous. The Emperor loved to follow with his eyes the graceful form of his Consort gliding through the brilliantly lighted ballroom. She was a perfect hostess, though she could be strict, as was shown by sleeveless dresses and those cut too low in the neck being tabooed at Court. Even now the Dowager Empress maintains her own ideas about fashions, and no lady was ever omitted to her presence wearing a tight-fitting skirt opening up the front.

In all emergencies the Dowager Empress seems to know by intuition what is the right thing to be said. Gifted with a retentive memory for faces, she is particularly gracious at presentations, and puts such pertinent questions to the ladies who are being presented as show the interest she takes in the circumstances of everyone's life. She sympathises with people's grief and rejoices in their gladness.

The Dowager Empress was always very strict as regards morals. When her son, the present Emperor Nicholas II, was about to undertake a long voyage round the world, it came to her ears that the commander of the squadron that was to accompany the Tzessarevitch lived with a woman who was not his wife. The Empress Marie insisted on his marrying her before they left Cronstadt, saying that otherwise she could not confide the safety of her son – the future monarch – to a man openly leading an immoral life. The marriage took place a few days before the squadron sailed.

For the last twenty years, since the death of the Emperor Alexander III, the Dowager Empress has led a retired life and spends a great part of the year abroad. At first, and not unnaturally, she found it very hard to be obliged to give way to her young daughter-in-law, but, having the knack of doing everything gracefully, she remained true to herself, and her withdrawal from public life was effected in a quiet and unobtrusive manner; many people felt a deep regret at the impending change.

A Russian Dowager Empress does not give up all her prerogatives. She remains at the head of all the institutions, as she was in her husband's lifetime. The Dowager Empress Marie remained the Patroness of the Red Cross Society, as well as of the institutions founded by a former Empress Marie (the Emperor Paul's widow, Maria Feodorovna). These include numerous colleges for girls (called institutes) spread all over Russia, homes for widows, schools for the deaf, dumb and blind, etc. The Dowager Empress's activity was limited to an annual duty visit to one or two 'institutes', on which occasion she would win the hearts of all present by her smiles and a few kind questions.

This sphere of activity would have been highly congenial to the young Empress. She would have taken a practical interest in the methods of bringing up a new generation. Having a genius for organisation, the supervision of these various institutions would have filled up her time. But this occupation was denied her, and as long as the Dowager Empress lives she can take no part in them.

At first the Empress's activity found vent in the foundation of workhouses. She also took a lively interest in the 'Maternity Society,' and owing to her initiative and under her guidance a model 'nursery' was established in Tzarskoe Selo where infants find healthy, hygienic treatment, and at the same time women and girls are trained to nurse their own and other people's children. The Empress frequently visits her pet nursery, stays there for hours sometimes, instructing the nurses how to handle a baby. Many an unsuspecting infant has been bathed and swathed by the fair hands of Russia's Empress.

During the Russo-Japanese war, the young Empress having nothing to do with the Russian Red Cross Society, a separate committee was founded – 'The Committee of the Empress Alexandra Feodorovna' – to give help to the wounded. The Emperor assigned two millions of roubles out of his private purse for this committee. The principal depot was in Kharbin. Continual conflicts arose between the officials of the Red Cross and the new committee; instead of helping each other there seemed to be a certain amount of rivalry between these two organisations. This was not the fault of either of the Empresses, it was only the result of over-zealous and tactless officials; but the general impression was strengthened of an established hostility between mother and daughter-in-law.

At that time the Empress gained a great deal of popularity. She established work-rooms in the halls of the Winter Palace, and for a time she made it a custom of coming daily and remaining hours, busily stitching at a sewing-machine. The Empress is a splendid seamstress, and she set an example to all the ladies present by the skilful way she accomplished her work. Her usual shyness and reserve completely vanished during these working afternoons. She felt at her ease amongst these simple surroundings, and her manner was natural and cheerful. Unfortunately this phase lasted a short time only. Summer took the Imperial Family to Peterhof. In July the Tzessarevitch was born and the ladies' workshop in the Winter Palace saw her no more.

There is no bond of sympathy between the mother and the daughter-in-law. And those about the Dowager Empress do not restrain their criticism of the actions of the Empress. The Emperor is a devoted son, and outwardly everything seems smooth enough, but still his marriage has greatly alienated him from his mother. The Empress naturally brooks no interference in her home circle, and the intercourse between the two Courts is correct, but does not err on the side of cordiality.

During the life of Alexander III the Empress Marie's name-day (July 22nd, old style) was habitually celebrated in grand style. The Court was generally at Peterhof on that day. The whole town was gorgeously decorated with flags, and in the evening there were magnificent illuminations. The Palace, the fountains, the parks, in fact all the way down to the sea, was a mass of scintillating coloured lights. It was like a scene from fairyland. People came to Peterhof specially to see this sight, and foreign royalties arranged their visits with a view to taking part in the celebration. When Alexander III died all this was changed, and the Dowager Empress Marie now tries to be absent on this day, which is for her naturally full of sad memories.

It so happened that one summer the Dowager Empress remained in Russia later than usual. She was at Peterhof on her name-day. As a rule anniversaries in the Imperial Family commence with a church service held in the Palace chapel. The Emperor motored over to his mother's summer palace, and all the members of the Imperial Family arrived to be present at the

THE TZAR AND HIS FAMILY

religious service, after which the Dowager Empress received the congratulations of all present and invited them to luncheon. The Empress pleaded ill-health, and was absent from this family gathering; but in spite of her indisposition she took a long drive with her children all through the most frequented roads of Peterhof, showing herself everywhere, as she never does on other occasions. At the time this occurrence gave rise to much gossip. It may, of course, have been pure chance, but it certainly was most unfortunate.

Since her widowhood the Dowager Empress has given up all social entertainments. She seldom invites anybody, except to dinner-parties. Three years ago, when Lord Marcus Beresford was in Petrograd, he dined several times at the Anitchkoff Palace. Last season the Empress gave a dance – the first for many years – for her granddaughter's amusement. She also honoured one or two parties by her presence.

It is always a delight to the Dowager Empress to take her place by the side of her Imperial son at any Court ceremony at which the Empress is unable to preside. Her taste in dress is irreproachable, and she looks much less than her age, having retained her slender graceful figure.

Of all her children the Grand Duchess Xenia is her favourite. The Grand Duchess Olga is too independent to be thoroughly approved of by her mother. The Grand Duke Michael's marriage, and residence abroad, is a drawback to his intercourse with her; but her eldest daughter is her mother's consolation, and her children are a constant source of interest and loving care to their grandmother.

Until quite lately the influence of Her Majesty's elder sister the Grand Duchess Elisabeth Feodorovna was paramount at the Imperial Court. Inclined to mysticism, she encouraged the same tendency in her sister's mind. Occult science absorbed the Empress for several years and enhanced the original morbidness of her disposition. After her husband's terrible death,[1] Elisabeth Feodorovna became a deaconess. It was she who introduced clericalism in Court circles and drew the Sovereign's attention to all kinds of priests, monks and 'startsi'. I don't believe people in the Western countries have the least notion of what a Russian

---

1 The Grand Duke Serge was killed in Moscow in 1905 by a bomb thrown by an anarchist named Kolaeff.

{21}

'staretz' is. It is a man, generally a simple peasant, who, having attained middle age, endeavours to give himself a venerable aspect by growing his hair and beard in flowing manes. Such men make wandering their calling, making continual pilgrimages from one monastery to another, sometimes extending their journeys to Mount Athos and the Holy Land. Provided with a staff and a knapsack, they tramp all over the country, finding shelter and food in the different convents they visit, and are gladly welcomed on their way through villages and small towns. The peasantry look upon such 'startsi' as men devoted to saintliness and asceticism; even the merchant classes – especially the womenfolk – have a great predilection for these wanderers. They invite them to their houses, ply them with food and countless glasses of fragrant tea, listening with open-mouthed wonder to their stories about their wandering life, their adventures and the miracles they have witnessed at different sacred shrines. Scarcely ever do they leave a house or an 'isba' (cottage) without some substantial proof of the veneration they inspire. Coppers from peasants and more valuable gifts from their wealthier admirers fill their purse. Some of these 'startsi' have gained a wonderful reputation for sagacity and prognostication.

It stands to reason that this calling leaves a wide range of possibilities to the idle who prefer a roving life to honest labour; and in their midst are numerous impostors, black sheep and ne'er-do-wells.

It seems preposterous to imagine such an uncouth individual amongst courtiers close to the steps of one of the most powerful thrones wielding an influence on the developments of State events. Yet one of Her Majesty's greatest favourites is a 'staretz' named Rasputine.[1] I have never seen the man, but I have heard he has something mesmeric in his eyes. To all accounts he must be a dreadful old reprobate. He has succeeded in convincing the Empress that her son's welfare depends on his (Rasputine's) presence. The extraordinary part is that on the several occasions when Rasputine was sent away, back to his birth-place somewhere in the wilds of Siberia, each time something happened to the boy's health. The strangeness of this coincidence has led to the strengthening of the Empress's superstitious belief in Rasputine's power.

1 Rasputine was murdered since this book has been in type.

THE TZAR AND HIS FAMILY

Many people are convinced that the German Government has bribed Rasputine to play into their hands and advocate the urgency of peace being speedily concluded. These rumours, implicating the Empress, give rise to no end of scandalous reports which reached their climax at the reopening of the Duma, and found vent in several impertinent speeches, completely undermining the prestige of Her Majesty.

At the present moment the country and the monarch's wife are distinctly at cross-purposes, based on a complete misunderstanding of each other's motives. As an impartial chronicler, I am bound to admit that a great part of the Empress's present unpopularity is based on misconception and prejudice against her German origin. She is supposed to be devotedly attached to her fatherland, but that has never been manifested. She is credited with intentions of enforcing peace before the opportune moment has arrived. But people forget that in doing this she would be endangering the safety of the dynasty and thus jeopardise the future welfare of her son – the worshipped idol of her heart. The Empress cannot help her German origin. The Queen of the Belgians is by birth a German princess likewise, yet no one seems to remember it. During the twenty-two years of her life in Russia, the former Princess Alix has had time to merge her nationality into that of her husband and children. If Her Majesty had been more accessible to the public during these years, less enigmatical in her attitude and more natural in her bearing towards people, these doubts would never have arisen at the present crisis.

One of the greatest problems of a Sovereign's life is to remain uncriticised by the people. When Her Majesty visited Iver a few months ago, intent on inspecting the local war hospitals, her carriage was followed by the crowd's murmur of 'Niemka iedet, Niemka iedet' (There goes the German). History repeats itself, and one is reminded of the old French cry: 'l'Autrichienne' which followed the unfortunate Marie Antoinette.

In the course of a visit to Headquarters the Empress told one of the dignitaries that she was delighted to have left Petrograd and its everlasting gossip. In saying this Her Majesty scarcely realised that it is she herself who unconsciously gives rise to evil rumours being spread. It is unwise for a Sovereign to live in seclusion and shroud herself in mystery.

It would not be difficult for the Empress to put a stop to this gossip that disgusts her, and thus regain the confidence of the

Russian nation. If she would only sweep the Court clean of its undesirable elements, let the Staretz Rasputine, who is a thorn in everybody's flesh, be definitely removed from Petrograd and eliminate some of her other favourites. Let her use her influence over her husband only to make him happy in his domestic circle, but not to interfere with Government nominations and political decisions. If this could be attained misapprehension and calumny would cease.

'Calomniez, calomniez il en reste toujours quelquechose' is an aphorism that every monarch's wife should bear in mind.

This crisis could be the turning-point of the Empress's existence. The Russians are, on the whole, a loyal nation. They would feel gratified to give their monarch's wife the tribute of golden opinions. A small effort on the Empress's part would suffice to bring her husband's subjects to her feet. Let her only be a *Russian* Empress and show her *Russian* feelings to the *Russian* people.

The following is one of the last stories about the Imperial Family. On the way to Kiev the Imperial train stopped at one of the stations. An ordinary passenger train stood parallel with the Imperial one. The Emperor approached the window and saw a priest, Father Eustache Ivlenitzky, looking at him. When the priest saw the Tzar's eyes were turned toward him he made the sign of the cross in blessing. The Emperor smiled and inclined his head. His Majesty then called for the Empress and together they stood at the window. The priest again made the sign of the cross in the Empress's direction. Her Majesty bowed and turned away. A few minutes later the Grand Duchess Tatiana entered the passenger train, and, going up to the priest, handed him an exquisitely bound New Testament and a small silver ikon. 'Mama sends you these,' said the Grand Duchess simply, and left the carriage after receiving the priest's blessing. Some time afterwards came a Court official, and by the Empress's orders took the name and address of the priest and the name of his parish.

Chapter II

THE IMPERIAL COURT

FOR the last twelve years life at the Imperial Court has been reduced to the limits of family life.

The Winter Palace stands empty and the Imperial Family never live in Petrograd (the only exception having been made for the Romanoff Jubilee days). They come over from Tzarskoe Selo, or Peterhof, when their presence is required, but as a rule no functions are held at Court, except, on very rare occasions, a State Dinner-party in the halls of the Palace.

It was hoped that this domesticated mode of life would be changed when the two elder Grand Duchesses grew up, and that balls and parties would be given to amuse them; but these expectations were doomed to disappointment, for the Grand Duchess Olga's seventeenth and eighteenth birthdays passed without the monotony of the usual routine of Court life being relieved in any way. Then came the war, and of course no entertainments could be thought of.

Singers and artists occasionally perform before the Sovereigns, and they sometimes command a private view of a remarkable cinematograph film; but such artistic evenings are not official, and no one is admitted except the family, the indispensable courtiers and one or two guests.

About five or six years ago, the necessity of periodical social gatherings at Court was so strongly felt that the matter was duly considered in high quarters. But the Empress did not see her way to act as hostess, and the outcome of these deliberations were entertainments by the Mistress of the Robes in the State apartments of the Winter Palace, which took place every Wednesday, as long as the carnival lasted. Official invitations from the Imperial Court were issued for these functions; but they had no success and were not renewed the following year.

The Mistress of the Robes of the Empress is Madame Narischkine, by birth a Princess Kourakine. Her position gives her great influence in society.

From the early days of her youth Madame Narischkine has been accustomed to Court life. She was the first maid of honour attached to the service of the Empress Marie Feodorovna after her arrival in Russia as Princess Dagmar. Subsequently, after the death of her husband, she resumed her Court duties and became the Mistress of the Robes of the late Grand Duchess Olga Feodorovna, and now she exercises the same function for the Empress Alexandra and has the rank of Lady of Honour.

Madame Narischkine is considered *the* authority upon Court matters in Petrograd, for she has been familiar with all the intricate rules of etiquette since her girlhood. It is a standing joke among the courtiers that, if Madame Narischkine were suddenly roused in the middle of the night with a question about some Court ceremony, her answer could be taken as a pronouncement.

This wonderful knowledge of etiquette is the great point in her favour. Like her predecessor Princess Golitzine, she never interferes with any vagaries that may be going on at Court. She has never tried to gain undue influence over the Empress, and confines herself strictly to the fulfilment of her official duties.

Madame Narischkine's receptions are always officially correct and rather glacial in consequence. Guests have been known to feel relieved when they are over. For her own particular circle, however, Madame Narischkine has a charming smile. The rest have to be content with an attitude, the correctness of which her worst enemies cannot question.

Her energetic activity and patronage of charitable intentions are remarkable. 'The Ladies' Prison Committee' in particular owes a great deal to her initiative and efficacious support. Unfortunately Madame Narischkine has not time to attend to everything personally, and her assistants do not always justify the confidence she places in them.

It has always been a sore point with the Russians that the Imperial Court should be chiefly composed of Germans and courtiers and officials of German origin. Count Fredericks, Count Benckendorff, Baron Meyendorf, von Grünwald, Baron Korff and von Drenteln are high officials in the Imperial Household. They may be ever so devoted to their Sovereign; still it hurts the Russian national feeling to see the Tzar surrounded by foreigners and those of foreign extraction.

The following anecdote is attributed to the late Prince Menshikoff, a renowned wit of the earlier part of the last century, and shows how acutely this German supremacy was felt. The Emperor Nicholas I wished to show the Prince some distinction; he asked him what favour he would like to obtain. 'I should like to be promoted to be a German,' was the reply.

Since the war this ill-feeling towards the German courtiers has intensified and is daily increasing. Displeasure is felt that the Emperor is surrounded by Germans. Even the common people murmur. The Emperor knows of the feelings of his subjects regarding Count Fredericks, but he is loath to dismiss him; his kindness and sense of justice prevent him from making a change that would break the old man's heart; for after all Count Fredericks is German in name only, he is devoted to the Tzar and for over twenty years has been at the head of the Imperial Household. The first place among the courtiers belongs naturally to Count Fredericks. He is a charming man, with the manners of a courtier of olden times. His courtesy never fails him, even in the most trying circumstances. He has aged much of late, which is not to be wondered at, considering that he is nearly an octogenarian. He was never considered a brilliantly clever man, but most decidedly he is a man of refinement and culture. Handsome, with an upright, stalwart figure, a delicately outlined profile, a high-bridged nose, which is considered the surest outward sign of aristocratic descent, and an imposing moustache, he is magnificent when in full uniform. People with wicked tongues aver that he owes his brilliant career to his effective exterior, which always attracted notice.

At Court ceremonies, Count Fredericks is invaluable, but he takes very little active interest in his office, as he has a very able assistant in the Chief of his Chancery, General Mossoloff.

Countess Fredericks seldom appears in society, although she is seen at Court, and enjoys all the privileges of her husband's high position and has the rank of Lady of Honour.

Count Fredericks is very rich, and he and his wife live in a beautifully appointed house, but they have never entertained on a large scale, limiting their receptions to select but informal dinner-parties.

At Easter the Emperor presented Count Fredericks with the miniatures of three monarchs: Alexander II, Alexander III, and himself, set in diamonds, to be worn on his breast when in full uniform. When this was known the public was not pleased, which was very foolish, as the Tzar's act was one of kindness to a Minister who had served him loyally. Some regard it as a mistake on the Sovereign's part not to listen to the voice of his people at such a serious crisis, marked by so much bloodshed and untold suffering caused by the Germans. Others say that Count Fredericks should appreciate the awkwardness of the monarch's position and tender his resignation, which would solve the difficulty and would be the greatest proof of devotion he could give to his Sovereign and his country. The venerable courtier has attained the pinnacle of all earthly honours; he can rise no higher. It is argued that it would be dignified for him to retire into private life, leaving the Emperor free to fulfil the general wish of the country to see a Russian nobleman appointed to this confidential and intimate post.

Count Fredericks's predecessor, Count Worontzov-Dashkoff, had surrounded the Imperial Court with a halo of grandeur. Court nominations were granted with such discrimination that they really became a distinction. Many high officials never obtained a 'Court-charge', as such appointments are called in this country. Count Worontzov-Dashkoff knew perfectly how to draw the line between government officials and courtiers.

In Count Fredericks's time this system has been completely changed. He is far too kindly and generous, and Court appointments are as plentiful as blackberries in autumn. To become a Gentleman of the Chamber is as natural and easy in these days as for a boy to be breeched, and the very facility of obtaining the rank of Chamberlain or Equerry depreciates the honour attached to it. Formerly such appointments were mostly the appendages of members of noble or ancient families. Now, on the contrary, it is quite an ordinary occurrence to find Gentlemen of the Chamber or Chamberlains amongst Messrs. Ivanoff, Petroff or Sidoroff (the equivalent to the English Smith, Brown and Robinson). Possibly this will be explained as the march of democracy.

When Peter the Great transformed the Russia of olden times into a civilised country, the change was so sudden that the first results could only be superficial, and consisted chiefly in the boyars cutting off their long beards and exchanging the caftan for

THE IMPERIAL COURT

the doublet. Feeling acutely the deficiency of his own education, the Tzar Peter was too wise not to understand this. To ensure the education of the succeeding generation and to encourage the boyars to educate their sons, he introduced into Russia the system of 'tchin', adopted from Germany. The Tzar made it a rule for every nobleman to serve his country, either as an officer, or as a 'tchinovnik' (official in the civil service); but examinations had to be passed before a young man obtained his first 'tchin', or was promoted to be an officer. There are several degrees of 'tchin'. To be admitted at Court in Russia a man must have attained the rank of an army general, a colonel of the guards or that of an 'actual councillor of state', which according to the table of the ranks and classes is equivalent to the rank of a general. Even now only the wives and daughters of men in such positions have the privilege of being received at Court. In this respect birth gives no prerogative. It is a system that offers a wide range of possibilities to self-made men, according them the opportunity of attaining the summit of their ambition by force of intellect and luck.

A Court appointment also gives a man the entrée to Court. Such appointments were bestowed upon men of high birth to equalise their positions and secure their right of entry to the Court and of being present at Court functions.

Of late the prestige of these Court nominations has completely vanished. In consequence of the lavish way in which they have been bestowed, members of the aristocracy have ceased to appreciate them. No matter what is said about the democratic tendency of present-day society, these appointments diminish the prestige of a powerful monarch's Court, giving to the State pageants the wrong tone.

During the Romanoff Jubilee a grotesque incident occurred on the day of the ladies' presentation to the Empresses in the Winter Palace. A lady of high birth, with a title that dates back to the ninth century, had an altercation with one of these mushroom courtiers about precedence. The lady insisted on her rights, the man blustered, manifesting a most uncourtier-like rudeness. At a dinner-party soon after the Jubilee this incident was most amusingly narrated by the victim. 'But what can one expect,' the lady wittily concluded, 'of a man who in matters of quarters [quarterings] only knows the one in which he lives.'

The Imperial Court of the present day differs totally from those of the Tzar's forefathers. Alexander II had intimate and devoted friends among the courtiers that surrounded the throne. The Minister of his Court, Count Adlerberg, was a contemporary of the Sovereign, the playmate of his childhood and the friend of his youth. Naturally the tie between him and the Emperor was a very close one.

The courtiers that surrounded Alexander III were likewise chosen from among valued friends and those whom the Sovereign knew intimately, and to whom he was sincerely attached. Both the Emperor and the Empress Marie Feodorovna were very constant in their friendships and their affections. The courtiers chosen from some personal motive became fixtures at Court.

The Imperial Household of Nicholas II and his Consort seems to have been formed by chance or accident. The Emperor has no real friends among the men that constitute his Court. His Majesty will let a courtier go as easily as he attached him to his service. Through all the courtesy and amiability that characterise the Sovereign's relations with the members of his household, this indifference is felt and is an effectual bar to any strong affection or unbounded devotion. Were the courtiers chosen as of old this would be impossible.

When Nicholas II became Tzar of Russia, the Minister of the Imperial Court was the late Count Worontzov-Dashkoff. The Count knew the Emperor from his infancy and sometimes he forgot the Tzar in remembering the intimate. Henceforth this could not be tolerated, so when Nicholas II ascended the throne of his ancestors, His Majesty decided to make a change. Not wishing, however, to hurt the feelings of his father's faithful friend, a golden bridge was constructed for the Count's withdrawal, over which he passed as Governor-General to the Caucasus, with the title of 'Viceroy'; a title which since the time of the Grand Duke Michael Nicolaïevitch had been in abeyance.

When the Chief Marshal of the Imperial Court, Prince Alexander Dolgorouky (intimately known as Sandy Dolgorouky), died, Count Paul Benckendorff, the brother of the late Russian Ambassador in London, became his successor. Up to that time Count Benckendorff had been Marshal of the Court, so he now ascended one step higher on the hierarchical ladder, while his stepson, Prince Basil Dolgoroukoff, succeeded to his vacant office. This was done at the suggestion of Count Fredericks in favour of his friend Count Benckendorff.

THE IMPERIAL COURT

Prince Basil Dolgoroukoff's nomination was highly approved. He belongs to an old historical Russian family, and by his personality is eminently fitted to fill this distinguished position.

A few months ago Prince Orloff left the Imperial Court and was attached to the service of the Grand Duke Nicholas in the Caucasus. His sudden removal from the Emperor's suite was a nine days' wonder and caused much heart-burning and gossip. Tongues wagged unceasingly for at least a week and the most absurd stories were circulated.

Prince Vladimir Orloff was the Director of His Majesty's 'Campaign-Chancery', and accompanied the Sovereign in all his travels. He was a very important personage and used to be considered one of the principal candidates for the post of Minister of the Imperial Court, should Count Fredericks ever resign. Prince Orloff was one of the very few courtiers whom the Emperor liked and esteemed, and with whom the monarch relaxed his habitual reserve. The atmosphere of the present Court is rather peculiar; it completely lacks the unity which characterised the Courts of the Emperor Nicholas II's predecessors on the throne of Russia. The courtiers seem to be playing a continual game of leap-frog, and the unacknowledged deity of the Palace is Madame Vyrouboff. The latter wields great influence over the Empress, and is considered one of the most important personages about the Imperial couple. Her wishes are studied and she is much courted, even by Count Fredericks and Madame Narischkine. Prince Orloff, however, was an exception. From the very first a feeling of antagonism seems to have sprung up between him and Madame Vyrouboff.

The Empress is said to disapprove of Prince Orloff. A few years ago the Imperial Family was preparing for a pleasure trip in their yacht on the shores of Finland. Prince Orloff, who, in his official capacity, and as one of the Sovereign's intimates, was always taken to the cabin allotted to him on the *Standart*, arrived on the pier at the hour fixed for departure, the Empress perceived him, and pretended to mistake him for one of those who had come to see the Imperial Family off. She approached him with an alacrity she seldom exhibits, saying pointedly: 'You will be glad of a holiday during this hot weather. Where have you settled to spend it?' Then, in token of farewell, she shook hands with the Prince and proceeded to take a gracious leave of the discomfited courtier, who in face of the Empress's words could do nothing but acquiesce, and he and his valet were left on the pier, but the luggage could not be got off in time.

Prince Vladimir Orloff's lineage dates back only about two centuries. He is a descendant of Gregory Orloff, who helped Catherine II to become Empress of Russia, and was subsequently created Prince by his grateful Sovereign. She loaded him with gifts consisting of vast estates, large sums of money, priceless jewels and beautiful silver. The enormous fortune of the Princes Orloff and their wonderful heirlooms are in a great measure due to this ancestor.

Prince Vladimir Orloff was the youngest son of the late Russian Ambassador in Paris and in Berlin. His elder brother, Prince Alexis Orloff, always lives in the French capital. The vast fortune left to them by their father was equally divided between the two brothers.

Prince Orloff has the reputation of being a straightforward, honest-minded man. To some this straightforwardness seems often to border on the brusque. In spite of this, however, and the fact that in general he is not a popular man, he has many friends and adherents. Well educated and a perfect linguist, he is undoubtedly a personality.

His wife, Princess Olga Orloff, by birth a Princess Belosselsky-Belosersky, is the most elegant and the best-dressed woman in Petrograd. Although not a beauty, she has breeding and is an aristocrat to the tips of her fingers. Endowed with the lovely blue 'Skobeleff eyes' (her mother was a sister of the famous 'White General'), she has a graceful willowy figure. In her early married life she was very thin, too thin in fact, though it suited her style. On the other hand the Prince is decidedly stout. At a Court ball, as the Prince and Princess Orloff were entering, the State chamber, a wit remarked to his neighbour: 'Behold the Prince and the Princess Orloff in flesh and bone.' The next day this epigram spread all over the town, and since then it has clung to them.

Dress is the Princess's pet weakness. She spends fabulous sums to gratify her passion for chiffons, and seldom wears a gown twice. Sometimes she orders several frocks for some special occasion, and dons the one that finds favour in her eyes, while the rest are discarded. Some of her gowns are perfect triumphs of the dressmaker's art. She is unanimously recognised as society's leader of fashion, and at important receptions everyone is interested as to what 'creation' Princess Orloff will wear.

One day, not very long ago, this supremacy in matters of toilette was put to a severe test. At an evening-party in one of the smart private houses of Petrograd, a bevy of ladies in marvellous evening-dresses, scintillating with their family diamonds, together with men in brilliant uniform, or in faultless evening-dress, were assembled. Enter Madame Polovtsoff – a handsome woman on a large scale, whose husband is very wealthy – in a lovely evening-gown from a famous firm that is the fairy-godfather of all would-be well-dressed women in Europe and America. Madame Polovtsoff is instantly surrounded, complimented and becomes the cynosure of all eyes, when the folding doors open again to give admittance to the Princess Orloff, who, with a view to securing an effective entrance, always arrives late. To the consternation of everyone present, the Princess Orloff's dress is identical with the one worn by Madame Polovtsoff. Material, colour, intricacies of trimming, diamond-studded osprey of a particular shade, every item exactly alike . . . !

By some fatal error the same model had been sent to two clients moving in the same set. The two ladies looked like twin sisters. The onlookers felt expectant, the hostess looked uncomfortable . . . A moment's ominous silence reigned. But the innate breeding of the Princess helped her to carry off the situation triumphantly. She approached Madame Polovtsoff, exclaiming: 'It is only since I see my dress on Madame Polovtsoff that I really begin to admire it'; she then boldly sat down next to that lady and spent some time in amicable conversation with her, in full view of an appreciative audience.

Princess Orloff belongs to the smart set of Petrograd society, and is on intimate terms with several members of the Imperial Family. Hostesses are keen to secure her presence at their parties, as it gives to them the patent of smartness.

The receptions given by Prince and Princess Orloff in their luxurious house on the Moika Quay are always very elegant and organised with a refined lavishness which is possible only to a very few. They never have brilliant festivities to which crowds are bidden, their invitations rarely exceed a hundred, and their gatherings are always very select.

For the last few years the Princess has become extremely up to date, taking up the 'Tango' and other ultra-modern dances; and the Tango is not at all her style.

From her infancy Princess Orloff was carefully brought up by

English nurses and governesses; she even speaks her own language with an English accent. All her tastes and customs are English.

No one knows exactly the cause of the breach between the monarch and Prince Orloff. The Orloff-Belosselsky set attributes the Prince's downfall to the intrigues of a certain faction. With his friends, the Prince frankly discusses his loss of favour posing as the victim of Court intrigues. The only one who maintained dignity in this crisis was the Princess Orloff. She carried her head higher than ever, was as cheerful as usual and no one heard her make stinging or bitter remarks. On the contrary, she appeared to be delighted to go to the Caucasus, 'A beautiful country she had heard so much of, but where she had never been.'

Princess Orloff remained in Petrograd to be present at her parents' golden wedding. After that event she joined her husband at Tiflis, but only for a short time. Her only son, Prince Nicholas Orloff, who was on the point of joining his regiment, contracted measles, and his mother was summoned to Petrograd, which she has not left since.

General Vladimir Nicolaïevitch Woyeikoff belongs to an old family of Russian boyars. His official position is that of Chief of the Administration of the Palace in Tzarskoe Selo, and at present he is *l'homme du jour* at Court.

General Woyeikoff is a clever and ambitious man. He knows what he wants, and goes for it direct. All his actions are calculated, and so far they have been successful. He is married to Count Fredericks's daughter, which from the first gave him a hold in Court circles, and he certainly owes his present position not a little to this alliance. But the General is not only a man of ambition: he is a thorough man of business.

A few years ago he suddenly discovered a spring of mineral water on one of his estates. He sent for experts, and the water of this source was extolled as something wonderful. The papers were full of the most alluring advertisements. This new mineral water, called 'Kouvaka', contains, so the experts declared, all sorts of ingredients of great therapeutic value, which make it advisable to imbibe it at meals. 'Kouvaka' is sold all over the country and brings the General a very good income.

The story goes that, when General Woyeikoff accompanies the Sovereign in his travels, he makes a point, during stoppages at important railway junctions, of rushing up to the buffet and loudly demanding, 'Kouvaka for His Majesty'; or saying: 'Our supply of Kouvaka is out, how many bottles can you let me have for the Tzar?' The consequence is that at all the stations 'Kouvaka' is kept in abundance, and the people who hear of the Emperor's predilection for this water hasten to make it likewise their daily beverage.

I tell the story for what it is worth, but I must add that it seems strange that an Emperor should trouble a General of his suite to fetch anything for him from a railway buffet. His Majesty has a sufficient number of servants for that, and there is a special Imperial caterer, whose business it is to replenish diminishing supplies of food or drink.

Suavely affable, the General's method is to inquire the object of an applicant's desired audience, and when he is cognisant of the reason he adds in a confidential way: 'You know the Emperor is so very busy, I am loath to venture an interruption at such a serious time, but I believe I could arrange the matter in which you are interested to your entire satisfaction.' The General keeps his promise and if possible arranges matters without the monarch having been troubled.

It is believed, now that Prince Orloff is out of the way, that General Woyeikoff will step into his father-in-law's shoes and become the Minister of the Imperial Court when Count Fredericks resigns.

General von Grünwald occupies the post of Master of the Horse and Chief Equerry, and at all open-air ceremonies he rides close to the Empress's carriage and has the appearance of being very German in his views and sympathies.

He has continually been considered a substantial pillar of the barons of the Baltic provinces, and in the event of any important occurrence they always apply to him to have their requirements successfully attended to.

When the Dowager Empress returned to Petrograd from Sandringham, where she had been staying with her sister the Dowager Queen Alexandra, after war had been declared by Germany she passed through Berlin, and, though the Kaiser had sanctioned her passage through his territory, Her Majesty was subjected to no end of ignominy during her short stay in the German capital. Naturally she returned to Russia highly incensed and full of indignation against the Germans. One day, soon after her return, the Empress at luncheon related some of her adventures, describing the insolence to which she had been subjected in Berlin. A general discussion followed of the horrors Russian travellers had to endure in the land of the Kaiser. General von Grunwald, who was one of the guests, is said to have stood up for the Germans, warmly taking their part, stating that all accounts of German atrocities were exaggerated. The Dowager Empress, very offended, turned to her lady-in-waiting with the remark: 'It seems we are telling untruths.'

Another point against General von Grünwald is the correspondence he continued to keep up with General von Helius, the former German Military Plenipotentiary in Petrograd. He is said even to have thought fit to allude to this correspondence in society, relating that he had received a letter from his friend von Helius (a great musician and very good violin player) expressing keen anxiety concerning the fate of his precious 'Stradivarius', which in the haste of departure he had left at the German Embassy in Petrograd.

But the following incident brought him under the indignant general notice. It is forbidden all over Russia to speak German in public places, shops, etc. Notwithstanding this strict prohibition, General von Grünwald, wearing the Imperial aigrette, in passing through one of the principal streets in Tzarskoe Selo, held an animated conversation with a friend who was accompanying him in the tabooed language. A lady approached, remarking: 'It is forbidden to speak German.' 'What business is that of yours?' angrily retorted the General. An altercation ensued, people assembled, the police had to interfere, and when the names were given the belligerent General turned out to be von Grünwald.

This incident was very much spoken of at the time. It was expected that, after such a public manifestation in the worst possible taste, General von Grünwald would be obliged to send in his resignation but Count Fredericks is said to have used his influence in favour of his friend, General von Grünwald. The only result of the incident was that the general indignation towards the 'German Courtiers' increased.

Colonel von Drenteln used to be considered a great favourite of His Majesty, who had known him years ago when both of them were officers in the Preobrajensky regiment. The Colonel was attached to the Imperial Household, and the vista of a splendid career loomed before him.

Colonel von Drenteln represented a serious rival to General Woyeikoff. They were, both of them, two clever to be opponents,

THE IMPERIAL COURT

but a secret antagonism was only veiled by the appearance of cordiality.

A few months ago, Colonel von Drenteln was appointed commander of the Preobrajensky regiment, a highly flattering nomination, which however alienated him from the Emperor's intimate environment. It characterises the Tzar, Nicholas II, that when he sees fit to have someone removed from his Court he is careful to provide the doomed courtier with a good position.

People were surprised at the Colonel's suddenly leaving the Court. It was whispered that von Drenteln did not fall in with some matrimonial plan devised for him in high quarters, and that his removal from Court was due to his 'insubordination' to these wishes.

An important figure at the Imperial Court is that of Adjutant-General Baron Theophil Meyendorf, attached to the Emperor's person, and it would be difficult to find a better man or a more honest and loyal one to whom a mean, dishonourable action would be an impossibility.

His family originate from the Baltic provinces; his tastes, inclinations and ideas are decidedly German, though his deep and sincere devotion to the Emperor and the Imperial Family is beyond doubt.

Without fortune or exceptional talent, Baron Meyendorf made a brilliant career owing to his family, the different members of which were in great favour during the reigns of Nicholas I and Alexander II. He would never have shone as a statesman, and he is too advanced in years now to have gained laurels as a warrior, but as a courtier his influence can only be beneficial. During the war he has had a great deal to do with the Red Cross, and his activity is most useful.

Baron Meyendorf is remarkable for his family life; he is married to a Countess Schouvalov, and they are the most devoted couple imaginable, without giving rise to the least ridicule. They have had thirteen children. After they had their eleventh child it was a standing joke amongst their friends that they must complete the dozen. The twelfth baby was expected, but to everyone's consternation twins were born . . .

One of the sons, Baron Paul Meyendorf, is married to a very pretty English girl, Miss Stella Whishaw, the daughter of an English merchant in Petrograd. She is very much liked and admired in society. As an amateur actress she is invaluable.

During the season last winter she achieved great success as a dancer in character dances.

A favourite of the Emperor is Admiral Niloff, who occupies the post of Flag-Admiral, and always accompanies the Sovereign in his voyages and changes of residence. Admiral Niloff is devoted to the Emperor, and, when in men's society, he can be very amusing and has a remarkable fund of funny stories.

Always known as a woman-hater, his unexpected marriage some years ago caused no little amazement in society. His chosen wife, Princess Kotchoubey, who was no longer a young woman, had been for a short time maid of honour to the Grand Duchess Maria Pavlovna senior.

A prospective candidate for the post of Minister of the Imperial Court is Prince Victor Kotchoubey. When the Emperor was still the Heir Apparent, Prince Kotchoubey was his aide-de-camp and accompanied him in his travels round the world. He got on in the most satisfactory way with His Imperial Master and the Emperor has a great liking for him. At present Prince Kotchoubey is at the head of the Imperial Apanages. He belongs to an old Little-Russian family, and is a direct descendant of the famous Oukraina-Hetman in the reign of Peter the Great.

Prince Kotchoubey is very rich and besides several estates owns an imposing mansion in Petrograd.

One of the high officials at the Imperial Court is Prince Jules Ouroussoff; he is a widower with an only daughter married to Count Ignatieff. His Court title is 'Ober-Vor-Schneider'. These German titles date from Peter the Great's time, it having been his aim to modify the old Russian Court after German and Dutch fashions. One of the consequences of the war will probably be the abolition of such titles.

Prince Ouroussoff owes this flattering nomination to his illustrious descent, being a descendant of Rurik dating back to the ninth century, as well as to his magnificent commanding figure. Dressed in his gold-embroidered uniform it would he difficult to find a more imposing courtier.

The most Serene Prince Dmitry Golitzine (not all Russian Princes have the right to the title of Serene Highness; not even all the Princes Golitzine possess it) is the Imperial Master of the Hounds, and all hunting and shooting parties, at which the Emperor or his royal guests take part, are organised by him. Prince Golitzine in his youth was an ardent sportsman, and is still

THE IMPERIAL COURT

one of the greatest authorities on all matters concerning the hunting field. He is very much valued on that account.

There are other courtiers belonging to the Imperial Household, but I have named the most important; the rest are of little account and have no influence on the developments of Palace policy. Her Majesty's present maids of honour are likewise very unimportant factors in life at Court.

Chapter III

HOW PETROGRAD GREETED THE WAR

THE season was over. Even the dowagers do not remember such a brilliant season as that of 1914. Balls and receptions followed one another, each more resplendent than the last. Magnificent festivities were organised; dinner-parties were sandwiched in between an at-home and a rout. Smart people got such numbers of invitations to parties that they could not accept all. It was a continual rush, as if there were an undefined presentiment current that the particular season was the last for many a gallant officer joyfully taking his part in the vortex of worldly gaiety, and that it would be a long time before such a merry crowd assembled again, perhaps indeed never again under quite the same conditions – for many faces would be missing, many gaps would be left.

Fortunately for human felicity no one really had a premonition of the woe and misery looming in the distance, no one foresaw the possibility of the coming bloodshed. All was joy, gaiety and brilliance. The motto of that last season ought to have been, 'Eat drink and be merry, for tomorrow you die.' Mercifully this knowledge was withheld by a wise Providence. The Petrograd season is held during the winter months, and differs in many ways from that of London, which takes place in the spring and early summer, when nature is at its best, when flowers are in full bloom and the air is warm and balmy. In Petrograd, on the contrary, it is generally bitterly cold during the months of worldly amusements, and the contrast between a hot, brilliantly lit-up ballroom, full of the loveliest flowers, and the snow, cold and darkness without has a peculiar charm for the senses.

HOW PETROGRAD GREETED THE WAR

But at the time I take up my narrative the season had closed. Easter, with all its festivities, had passed, and Petrograd was revelling in lovely spring weather. The town was still full, and the neighbourhood of Petrograd, such as Peterhof, Strelna, Tzarskoe Selo, Pavlovsk and Gatchina, was more crowded than usual. A pleasurable excitement prevailed. The British Squadron was to visit Petrograd in June, the King of Saxony was expected, and the French President, M. Poincaré, would arrive in the first days of July (old style). Numerous festivals were being prepared, and the animation, which usually slackens during the summer months, was sustained by these expected events.

The arrival of the British Squadron was welcomed with enthusiasm, and many were the entertainments prepared to welcome our friends and future allies. This feeling of gladness in welcoming the friendly manifestation of Great Britain to Holy Russia was not confined to the higher classes of society; it was shared by the whole nation, and the populace greeted the 'Anglichane' (Englishmen) as heartily as the more cultured inhabitants.

It must be admitted that up to now Russia had not been spoiled by friendly overtures from England. Queen Victoria was always prejudiced against Russia; she disliked the Emperor Nicholas I – one of the noblest and best-intentioned monarchs – whom she completely misjudged. Her sympathy with the succeeding Russian Sovereigns was tepid. Yet she was a great advocate of an alliance between her grandchild, Princess Alix, and the present Emperor, and when the young couple visited her at Balmoral she was very gracious to her grandson-in-law, and the young Tzar made a favourable impression.

In politics we distrusted each other. The late Lord Beaconsfield was steadfastly hostile to Russia, and by frustrating the Treaty of San Stefano he weakened Russia's influence in the Balkans and brought to naught any advantage won in the Russo-Turkish war of 1877–78. Germany did everything to widen the breach between the two countries that Nature herself intended to be friends.

In Russia, however, putting aside political doubts and complications, a great feeling of admiration and sympathy was always felt towards the English. English customs were assimilated, Russian children's education was confided to English tutors and governesses, English literature admired, English sports adopted, English tailors became the fashion, and the Russian book-market overflowed with products of English fiction. In fact life in Russia amongst the higher classes was modelled on English life. Could any higher tribute be offered?

Political refugees and slanderous books are largely responsible for the feeling of prejudice that reigned in England against our country, for they succeeded in spreading incongruous and malignant tales about our Imperial Family and our countrymen. Fortunately this misunderstanding is over, and both countries having thrown off the thraldom of German supremacy will, it is to be hoped, continue to be true and loyal friends.

Grand festivities were held in honour of the British officers. The Grand Duchess Victoria Feodorovna gave a garden party in the grounds of the Summer Palace in Tzarskoe Selo, to which Admiral Sir David Beatty, Lady Beatty, Lady Geraldine Churchill, who had come over to Petrograd in Lady Beatty's yacht, and some of the British officers were invited to meet a brilliant selection of the highest circle of Petrograd society. The Mansion House gave a magnificent reception in honour of the English guests. Official dinners were given at the British Embassy by the members of the English colony in Petrograd; a lunch was given on the *Lion* by the Admiral to the Emperor and Empress. The closing act of this momentous visit was a magnificent ball given by the Admiral and the officers of the British Squadron as a return for hospitality received and all the tokens of welcome that had been lavished on them in Russia.

The ball was organised on the battle-cruisers *Lion* and *New Zealand*, joined together for this occasion. About seven or eight hundred guests were present, the Grand Duchess Victoria Feodorovna and the Grand Dukes Cyril and Boris being among them. Steamers and yachts were continually going backwards and forwards between Cronstadt, Petrograd and Peterhof. The sight of Cronstadt harbour on the night of the ball was grand and picturesque. A beautiful clear night, such as is only seen in northern climes, five immense naval giants standing well out in front of the harbour brightly illuminated and decorated with flags.

The principal gangway on the *New Zealand* was surmounted by an archway with the word 'Welcome' in large letters at the summit. The British officers were charming hosts; they had thought of everything to make their reception attractive. The supper was abundant and excellent; champagne flowed the whole night, the different bands playing alternately all the time. The ball was a tremendous success.

HOW PETROGRAD GREETED THE WAR

I must relate an amusing story which was told to me by one of the English officers. Whilst the Squadron was in Cronstadt there were crowds of people who came daily to visit the British ships. Prince George of Battenberg was an officer on one of them. Nearly every visitor inquired after Prince George, wishing particularly to see him. Now the Prince was not in Cronstadt: he had paid a short visit to his aunt the Empress in Tzarskoe Selo on the day of his arrival at Cronstadt, and had gone on to Moscow to visit his other aunt the Grand Duchess Elisabeth Feodorovna. But the English officers were loath to disappoint their Russian visitors, so they always held in readiness an officer who personated the Prince, and the people are firmly persuaded to this day that they saw the Prince.

Writing of the British Fleet reminds me of a story of one of our Allies' admirals. A few years ago, when Admiral Lord Charles (now Lord) Beresford was staying at the Hôtel d'Europe during his visit to St. Petersburg, as our capital was then called, a reporter called to interview the Admiral.

His Lordship's English valet was informed of this, but when he had taken stock of this representative of the Russian Press he decided it was not worth while disturbing his master, and he himself answered the questions that were addressed to him in broken French. The entranced reporter was none the wiser, and before leaving requested permission to take his Lordship's likeness. The amiable valet assented, threw himself with alacrity into a becoming pose and a snapshot was made. The beaming reporter then withdrew with many expressions of respect and gratitude.

The next day the paper appeared bearing in large letters, 'Interview with Admiral Lord Beresford', and, to the everlasting amusement of those who knew Lord Charles, the article was headed with his valet's portrait. Petrograd enjoyed a hearty laugh at the journalist's expense.

The King of Saxony's visit was an ordeal. The Saxon monarch was dull, pompous and sleepy after meals. He made a very ungracious impression, and what most struck the Russian courtiers, used to the courtesy and urbanity of our Imperial Family, was the fact that he did not offer to shake hands with any one of the Emperor's suite who were presented to him, not even making an exception for the Minister of the Imperial Court, Count Fredericks, who had to content himself with a slight inclination of the royal head. This ungraciousness was not confined to the Russians, for the King disappointed and offended his own countrymen by refusing the reception organised by the members of the German colony in Petrograd. This was planned to take place at the German Embassy after the dinner-party given by the Count and Countess Pourtales in honour of the King. His Saxon Majesty left the Embassy directly the repast was over.

The next event was the visit of the French President. One festivity followed another. The most interesting of them was the ceremony 'Zaria', held in the camp of Krasnoe Selo, where the Guards regiments are quartered in summer.

It was a rare and imposing sight on that lovely summer day to see the wide plain with thousands and thousands of soldiers; the Emperor and all the Grand Dukes accompanied by Court and military officials on horseback; the Empress with the French President at her side in an open carriage drawn by four white horses, with the Imperial Equerry General von Grünwald riding beside the equipage. There followed all the ladies of the Imperial Family in open carriages, likewise drawn by four white horses, making the round of the camp and greeting each separate regiment. Arrived at the Imperial tent, everyone alighted and entered, where rows of comfortable armchairs were prepared. On both sides of the Imperial tent tribunes were erected for those who had come to witness the ceremony. In the front row sat Madame von Helius, the wife of the German military plenipotentiary, and all the members of the German and Austrian Embassies were among the onlookers; the military attachés swelled the suite of the Tzar.

The Imperial band played several pieces, ending with the 'Zaria'. The senior sergeant-major stepped out – all heads were bared – and in a loud, distinct voice declaimed the Lord's Prayer. The ceremony was over. The Emperor, his Consort, the French President and all the members of the Imperial Family repaired to the camp residence of the Grand Duke Nicholas, the present Viceroy of the Caucasus and the Commander-in-Chief of the Caucasian Army. Here a dinner for ninety guests was prepared, and the suite was likewise invited.

This was about the last public festivity in Petrograd, for the clouds gathering on the political horizon were becoming threatening. Agonising days of misgiving were at hand, which have now become historical.

In the last days of the negotiations between the Russian,

HOW PETROGRAD GREETED THE WAR

German and Austrian Governments the general public in Petrograd did not share the anxiety felt in higher spheres. Everyone firmly believed in Kaiser Wilhelm's peaceful intentions and in the efficacy of his powerful mediation, and were convinced that he would intervene at the last moment. The Kaiser's vaunted love of peace seemed a guarantee. Where the news spread in Petrograd that war had been declared against Russia by Germany it was as if a thunderbolt had suddenly fallen from a sunny sky. It seemed incomprehensible, but the revulsion of feeling was instantaneous, and the indignation against the Germans became as intense as had been the absolute trust in their Kaiser.

Once it was known that war was to be, the public accepted the fact unflinchingly. Everyone knew that the Emperor Nicholas and his Government had done everything in their power to avoid the outbreak, and felt grateful to the Tzar for his firmness in not giving way to Germany's insclence or letting Russia play a humiliating part.

No concession, however, on Russia's part would have availed. Germany had decided that the time for war had come and that the present moment was opportune.

The incident of the ultimatum is an eloquent proof that nothing would have appeased the Kaiser's thirst for glory.

The ultimatum contained Germany's declaration of war against Russia if the mobilisation of the Russian army were not stopped in twenty-four hours. In delivering this ultimatum to M. Sazonoff, the flurried German Ambassador, Count Pourtales, inadvertently handed over a second paper containing a declaration of war, adapted to the case of Russia's giving in to the Germans' demands. Such a diplomatic mistake seems incredible, but it is a fact, and the two documents remain to give the German Government the lie when it avers that Germany did not want the war.

A burst of patriotic enthusiasm shook the whole country to its very foundation. All other considerations were put aside, political strife forgotten. The strikes on which the Germans based such hopes, and which cost them so much, stopped at once, and the strikers became the warmest partisans of the coming war. Endless patriotic demonstrations and processions marched through the streets of Petrograd. Cheering crowds gathered in front of the British and French Embassies as well as before the Belgian and Servian Legations. The respective ambassadors and ministers received ovations. Thousands of students, working men, college boys with flying flags, carrying in front of them the portraits of the Tzar and the Tzessarevitch, singing alternately the national anthem, patriotic songs and hymns, went through the streets towards the Winter Palace. Here at the foot of the Alexander Column facing the Palace windows all the processionists fell on their knees singing 'Boje Tzaria Khrani' (God save the Tzar) and shouting 'Hurrah!' It was a general intoxication which had exalted all classes. These were days that have become historical and will never be forgotten.

Never during the twenty years of his reign had the Emperor been so beloved, so respected, so popular in the eyes of his subjects as at that moment. All hearts went out to him, all hands were stretched out in help to ward off this national calamity. Portraits of the monarch were in all the principal shop windows, and the veneration was so deep that men lifted their hats and women – even well-dressed, elegant ladies – made the sign of the cross.

On July 20th (o/s), the day following the declaration of war, a grand levée was held in the Winter Palace and the manifesto of the war was read. It was one of those solemnities that occur once in a country's history and make a mark in one's existence. No one who witnessed the scene will ever forget it. The Palace was filled with courtiers, officers and ladies. All the members of the Imperial Family – except the Dowager Empress who was in England, the late Grand Duke Constantine, his wife, and the Prince Alexander of Oldenburg, who at the time were at a German health resort – were present. A *Te Deum* was sung by the Court clergy, after which the manifesto was read. It was acknowledged by a burst of enthusiasm and loud cheering. The Tzar blessed the officers present for the approaching campaign. It was a most touching scene. All fell on their knees to receive the monarch's blessing. The Emperor was deeply affected, women kept back their tears with difficulty and even the men had a moisture in their eyes. Never yet had the walls of the Winter Palace witnessed such a tribute to a sovereign, such hearty cheering, such loud acclamations as those that greeted Nicholas II after the ceremony of giving out the manifesto. The enthusiasm was boundless; restraint, courtly demeanour, well-bred reticence were all forgotten in a general outburst of loyal feeling. The Emperor was positively mobbed, the greatest, most high-born ladies, the reserved as well as the exuberant, old and young, all rushed forward, eager to catch a look from the Sovereign, to touch him, to kiss a fold of his uniform. The exaltation rose to such a pitch that it seemed as if an electric touch had united the Tzar and his people and made them one in heart and feeling. It was a moment that will for ever remain a sacred memory to all those who were present.

Dowagers who still remember the reading of the manifesto of the Turkish war in 1877 in the reign of Alexander II assert that the enthusiasm manifested in that instance was as nothing compared to that of 1914.

When the Tzar stepped on to the balcony and showed himself to the people assembled in thousands in the open space in front of the Palace they all dropped on their knees, and the 'hurrahs' thundered through the air, shaking the walls of the Palace as if a hurricane had suddenly swept over the place.

The Emperor, visibly moved, stepped back to bring the Empress forward, who likewise was enthusiastically cheered. The majestic solemnity of the moment was all the more intense because of the sincerity of feeling which inspired it, felt alike by high and low.

Many motor-cars of foreign diplomatists had assembled on the outskirts of the square, their owners on the top of them, trying to get a bird's-eye view of this wonderful sight. Every one of them was deeply impressed.

The feelings of the members of the German Embassy, who did not leave Petrograd until the next morning and were fully cognisant of all the manifestations of loyalty and patriotism, must have been very disheartening, overthrowing all their preconceived notions of Russia's inner life. This staunch rallying round the supreme chief of all the Russians in the moment of danger to their country and their Tzar had a fatal significance for the representatives of the German Government, and was their first bitter disappointment.

The next morning the German Ambassador, Count Pourtales, his wife and the whole staff of the German Embassy, about sixty people, left Petrograd by a special train on their way to Stockholm. Eye-witnesses affirm that Count Pourtales appeared aged and worn, he was very pale and looked unhappy and nervous. The Countess wept, and the secretaries looked grave. It was a painful moment. The departing diplomats were shown the greatest courtesy. At the Finland station the Imperial rooms were kept open for them; an official of the Foreign Office, a gentleman of the chamber, M. Radkewitch (brother of the member of the Duma who has lately visited London with the Russian deputation from the State Duma and the Upper House) was delegated by M. Sazonoff to conduct the German Ambassador and his staff to the station and see them depart unmolested. How utterly differently did the 'highly cultured' Teutons comport themselves in connection with the Russian Ambassador, M. Sserbeeff's, departure from Berlin.

A few days afterwards this same M. Radkewitch was commissioned to see the Austrian Ambassador, Count Szapary, and his staff leave Petrograd, and later on it was he that conducted the Turkish *Chargé d'Affaires* to the Finland station, by which all the foreign diplomatists belonging to the belligerent countries left Russia. This gave rise to many jokes in the Foreign Office. It was said that hitherto there had always been an Ambassador's inductor, but that M. Radkewitch had immortalised the novel function of an Ambassador's exductor. A very amusing caricature was drawn representing a reception held in an elegant drawing-room; ladies and gentlemen were assembled engaged in conversation when a liveried footman ushered in a new arrival, M. Radkewitch. At the sight of him all the foreign diplomatists present looked startled, and some of them flew to hide behind curtains and furniture.

The departure of the Austrian Ambassador was attended by a slight incident. Austria declared war on Russia about a week later than Germany; the mobilisation of the Russian army and the preliminary preparations for the war were made whilst Count Szapary and his staff were in Petrograd. The Austrian military agent, Prince Hohenlohe-Schillingsfürst-Waldenburg, did not lose time. He took to driving assiduously about town in his motor-car, and was frequently seen close to the mobilisation quarters. He collected a great deal of precious material, made many sketches and plans. But the police had an eye on his doings, although to avoid a scandal he was left unmolested. On the day of the Austrian's final departure, when the Embassy left their house on the Sergnierskaïa in a long procession of motor-cars, the one containing a subordinate official of their chancery, M. Lessner, to whom all documents and important papers had been confided, was turned into a by-street and taken to the Secret Police instead of to the Finland station. Here all implicating papers were confiscated and M. Lessner conducted to the station to depart by a later train.

Naturally M. Lessner and his precious documents were missing when the Ambassador was leaving Petrograd. His disappearance created a flutter of anxiety amongst the departing Austrians, and Count Szapary turned as white as a sheet when he saw that he was obliged to leave without the missing official.

The days following the grand demonstration in the Winter Palace were full of parting, grief and foreboding to many broken-hearted mothers and loving wives; but to the honour of everyone be it said that no murmurs were heard. All recognised the seriousness of the calamity, and were proud to sacrifice their nearest and dearest at the shrine of patriotism.

The Guards were the first to leave Petrograd. In all the regimental mess-rooms *Te Deums* were sung by the regimental chaplain in the presence of the assembled officers, headed by the commanding general or colonel, the wives, mothers and sisters of the officers and all those who had at some earlier period served in the regiment.

The Standard and Imperial flags were blessed, so was each separate officer and soldier. It was a sort of farewell to Petrograd, to their families and their barracks, combined with prayers to the Almighty to grant them success and victory.

The *Te Deum* in the mess-room of the Chevalier Guards was a very touching one. Count Alexander Dmitrievitch Scheremeteff, a former officer of this regiment and the father of two sons who were going to the front with the Chevalier Guards, presented the regiment with an old and valued *ikon*, an heirloom of the family, which had always accompanied their ancestor, Count Scheremeteff, in the reign of Peter the Great, on all his successful campaigns, and was with him during the battle of Poltava.

The officers looked so brave, so eager to fight for their country, so full of energy and confidence in Russia's might and right. Some of them quite boys, with such bonny young faces. The women, though very collected, looked extremely sad; they fully understood the coming peril for their dear ones, and involuntarily the thought was uppermost in every mind that many of them would be seen no more.

A week later the supreme Commander-in-Chief of the Russian army, the Grand Duke Nicholas, left Petrograd.

Chapter IV

RUSSIAN WOMEN DURING THE WAR

THIS was the time for the Russian women to show their mettle. The noble example given by the ladies of the Imperial Family incited others to action.

The Empress was in her element. She organised a model hospital in Tzarskoe Selo, which she visits daily. The principal surgeon of this hospital is Princess Hedroitz, one of the most skilful in Russia. The Princess spent five years in Switzerland as the favourite assistant of Professor Rose, of world-wide fame. During the Russo-Japanese war she achieved a well-deserved renown by her wonderful operations.

Her Majesty appointed the Princess to be at the head of the Court hospital, and for the next few months the Empress and her two elder daughters, the Grand Duchesses Olga and Tatiana, diligently attended the lectures of the surgeon-Princess and under her tuition went through the appointed course as practical probationers, finally passing the examination that qualified them as sisters of mercy.

I have heard Princess Hedroitz express her deep admiration of the Empress's aptitude for nursing. 'To work with Her Majesty,' the Princess declares, 'is a delight; she never loses her presence of mind, remains calm and collected under the most trying circumstances, and when she assists at an operation she is positively wonderful, giving her unswerving attention, handing the right instruments at the right moment, and all the time so calm, so gentle, so unobtrusive.'

The Tzar's sister, the Grand Duchess Olga Alexandrovna,

likewise went through a course of surgical lectures and practical probation before she went out to Galicia as a hospital nurse. She worked there for several months, revealing rare self-abnegation and zeal. When Livoff was evacuated in the summer of 1915, the Grand Duchess returned to Petrograd for a short rest, but is now again at work on the Austrian frontier.

The Grand Duchess Olga is a true Russian and the most warm-hearted woman imaginable. She is clever and talented, and her water-colour drawings have often been exhibited or given for sale to charity bazaars. Her unconventionality frequently gets her into trouble with her family. She does not like to be reminded of what is due to her position. Everything she does is done in the most natural, unaffected way. When she wants to render a service she will go out of her way to do so; when she accepts an invitation to a ball she does not condescendingly take a few turns, but dances the whole evening, frankly showing that she is enjoying herself. She is a perfect skater, an excellent tennis player, a good horsewoman, and always remains her charming little self. When she is staying at her husband's country-seat 'Ramone', she insists on visiting the cottages and talking to the peasants, who adore her.

The Grand Duchess has a small face illuminated by large soft brown eyes which are full of expression, and she has a delightful way of speaking to everybody, no matter what his or her social position. Very Russian in all her views and ideas, the Grand Duchess Olga was always averse to marriage with a foreign prince, which would have entailed her leaving the country. However, when quite young she married Prince Peter of Oldenburg, who will inherit his father's enormous wealth.

In the hour of her country's trial the Grand Duchess Olga Alexandrovna faced trouble bravely and rallied to the real workers. She does all in her power to alleviate the sufferings of the wounded. Taking her work seriously, she does absolutely everything that is required of the average hospital nurse, and never permits her rank to secure her privileges that are not shared by the rest of the hospital staff. 'Sister Olga', as she is known in the hospital, is indefatigable in her zeal and is worshipped by her patients.

An officer, severely wounded in the knee, was taken half unconscious to the hospital where 'Sister Olga' worked. In a sort of dazed condition he noticed a small, unobtrusive-looking nurse who brought in a basin of hot water and commenced bathing his wound, preparing it for the coming operation. When he regained consciousness he was in the officers' ward lying in bed with his operated knee comfortably bandaged and the same nurse tending him. She brought him food, gave him a composing draught, and was coaxing him to go to sleep.

'Sister,' said the wounded warrior, 'tell me is it true that the Tzar's sister works in this hospital?'

'Yes, it is true,' was the answer.

'And does she really nurse the wounded like any other hospital sister?'

'Certainly she does, but why should that be so surprising?'

'The Tzar's sister, to demean herself to such lowly work! What a wonderful woman she must be!'

'Hush, you must not talk, go to sleep or you will delay your recovery.'

'I shall go to sleep instantly, Sister, if you will do me a favour?'

'Well, what do you want?'

'Do show me the Tzar's sister, I do so want to see her, just one glimpse of her and I shall immediately go to sleep as you tell me to do.'

'But what can it matter to you if you see the Tzar's sister or not?'

'How can you say such things, Sister,' retorted the wounded man indignantly. 'I should love to see her and thank her for all she is doing for us. Please, dear Sister, point her out to me when she comes into the ward.'

'But she is in the ward now.'

'Oh!' The officer started up, forgetting his wounded leg. A restraining hand was laid on him.

'For Heaven's sake don't excite yourself. I will show you the Tzar's sister if you promise to be quiet and go to sleep.'

'I promise.'

'Well, then, look at me. I am the Grand Duchess Olga, but here I am called Sister Olga,' and Her Imperial Highness gave her hand to the wounded man, which he reverently raised to his lips.

Another time the principal surgeon was making the round of the hospital. In the surgical ward he stopped at the bed of a seriously wounded soldier.

'Which sister bandages your wounds?' queried the doctor.

'That snub-nosed little one standing over there,' pointing with his finger towards the Grand Duchess Olga.

RUSSIAN WOMEN DURING THE WAR

The surgeon looked discomfited, but 'Sister Olga' laughed gaily at the wounded soldier's ingenuous designation.

One soldier told her she could not possibly be the 'Tzar's sister', for she looked like an ordinary hospital nurse, and worked as hard as any village girl. He was sure she was deceiving him, imposing upon his credulity. He appealed to the doctor, and when the latter confirmed Sister Olga's identity the poor man looked quite disconcerted, murmuring, 'Wonderful! I am being nursed by the Tzar's sister', and a tear trickled down his weather-beaten face.

Sister Olga's simplicity, endurance and cheerful temper have made her the idol of the hospital.

Another Imperial lady who has entirely devoted herself to hospital nursing is the Grand Duchess Marie Pavlovna junior, a charming woman, not exactly pretty, but with a clever, interesting face, and a figure slender, graceful and straight as a dart. Carefully brought up by her aunt, the Grand Duchess Elisabeth Feodorovna, she is possessed of intellect, will and lofty ideals. An excellent sportswoman before the war, she divides her time between outdoor exercise and more serious occupations. Kind-hearted and high-spirited, her sunny disposition endears her to everyone who comes into close contact with her.

When hardly out of the schoolroom, she was married to the Duke of Sudermanland. The marriage did not turn out well. The stiffness and the old-fashioned etiquette of the Swedish Court was a continual stumbling-block to the Princess. The result was that this most pure-minded Princess was accused of all sorts of indiscretions, and eventually she sought her father's protection, which ultimately ended in a divorce.

As soon as the war broke out the Grand Duchess decided to become a sister of mercy. She worked for a long time under the superintendence of Professor Walter (a well-known surgeon in Petrograd) and Doctor Schwartz in one of the hospital barracks; and after this thorough training Her Imperial Highness left Petrograd as one of the nursing staff of the Marble Palace Hospital train, whose destination was the Prussian front. The young Princess had to endure no end of hardships, for to work under such circumstances was difficult indeed. The close vicinity of strong forces of the enemy, uncertainty as to what might happen from hour to hour, the daily appearances of Zeppelins dropping bombs in the region of the hospital, and the continual increase of war victims required strength of will, self-abnegation and indefatigable labour.

When the train received orders to leave Insterburg, the Grand Duchess returned to Petrograd and became an inmate of the 'Eugenie Community' for sisters of mercy. She lived in a small, simply furnished room close to the matron's apartment. She refused the services of a maid as being against the rules for a sister of mercy, and she did not wish an exception to be made in her favour. Directly after her arrival she insisted on resuming the duties of an ordinary hospital nurse in the overfilled hospital. She worked in the ambulances, dressed the wounds of soldiers and officers in the surgical ward, and sat at the bedside of the suffering, consoling and encouraging, reading, writing letters and doing her utmost to lighten the burden of those around her. Her pretty caressing ways and soft manners, the dexterity of her beautiful hands when bandaging, and her bright personality inspired everyone with admiration. The soldiers worshipped and the officers reverenced their Imperial nurse.

She spent most of her evenings in the matron's sitting-room. She had no visitors except her grandmother, the Dowager Queen of Greece, and she dined out on three occasions during the whole time she remained in Petrograd: once with the Emperor and Empress, once with her father the Grand Duke Paul Alexandrovitch, and once at the Marble Palace with her grandmother.

When it became known in the community that the Grand Duchess was leaving for Pskov – where she has worked ever since – the convalescent officers craved the favour of her dining with them in the hospital refectory on the last day of her stay. The invitation was accepted. Before the meal commenced, the officers expressed their deep gratitude to the august sister of mercy, and presented to their deeply moved guest a lovely bouquet of flowers, tied with a wide white satin ribbon bearing the inscription in gold letters: 'To our beloved Sister, from the wounded officers.'

The Dowager Empress is at the head of the Red Cross Society in Russia. Her Majesty has established a depot and a workshop in the Anitchkoff Palace. The latter is principally attended by dowagers, the belles of former generations, who were young when the Dowager Empress reigned supreme in society, who danced at her balls and are personally known to the Sovereign and in touch with her views and opinions.

RUSSIAN WOMEN DURING THE WAR

The Dowager Empress and her elder daughter, the Grand Duchess Xenie, have their own war hospitals and hospital trains. Among the hospitals to which the Dowager Empress has given her name is the one for officers organised in the Imperial Alexander Lyceum. Her Majesty frequently visits this establishment, and has sent her own huge tent to be placed in the beautiful garden of the Lyceum. On fine days in summer the convalescent officers have their meals in the tent, and spend most of the time there. Being the honorary Colonel of the Chevalier Guards regiment, Her Majesty is likewise particularly interested in the hospital organised in the barracks of this regiment.

The Dowager Empress never spares herself, and frequently undertakes long journeys to different provincial towns to inspect war hospitals and visit the wounded.

Next to the hospitals of the members of the Imperial Family, the Youssoupoff Hospital is one of the best organised in Petrograd.

The Princess Youssoupoff gave up her palatial mansion on the Liteinaïa. A small fortune was spent in adapting the beautiful suite of apartments to its present use. The stuccoed, sculptured walls had to be disinfected and encased in lincrusta painted white. The ground floor is given up to soldiers, while officers occupy the first floor. Luxurious and cheerful sitting-rooms filled with hot-house plants and flowers, a music-room, a reading-room and a superb dining-room, all white and gold, do not give one the impression of being in a hospital. The large, lofty ballroom on the ground floor, which takes up all the centre of the building and reaches up to the height of two storeys, finishing at the top with a gallery that runs round the room, is fitted up as a ward for soldiers and holds seventy beds, though it could easily contain many more. The operating-room with all the newest surgical instruments and apparatus is wonderful. At the top of the house is a chapel, where divine service is regularly held. Workshops have been installed and instructors engaged to teach the invalided soldiers some occupation which will help them in future to earn their living, by giving them a thorough training in some trade. Each invalided warrior on quitting this hospital gets a complete outfit of clothes.

The owners of the hospital took each small item into serious consideration, and every detail has been wonderfully thought out.

One of the apartments is reserved as a sitting-room for the use of the members of the Youssoupoff family. When Princess Zéneide

Youssoupoff is in town she scarcely lets a day pass without visiting the place: indeed, she spends most of her time there.

The Princess knows all the inmates, takes the keenest interest in the nursing, and lavishes every attention on the wounded under her care. The Princess's daughter-in-law, Her Highness Princess Irene Youssoupoff, is equally assiduous in attending the hospital and providing benefits for the suffering soldiers.

The immense wealth of the Princess Youssoupoff naturally facilitated the carrying out of her generous plans, but no money could supply the atmosphere of love, delicacy of feeling and kindness of heart that reign in the Youssoupoff Hospital.

The Princess Zéneide Youssoupoff must be considered as one of the greatest ladies in Russia. Her exceptional position, enormous fortune, illustrious lineage and great humanity all combine to give her this position.

The Princess bears the name and title in her own right. Her father, the late Prince Nicholas Youssoupoff, had no son and only two daughters; the youngest of them, Princess Tatiana, died unmarried at the age of eighteen, and thus Princess Zéneide became the sole heiress of her father's large fortune and vast possessions. The young Princess was considered the richest prize in the marriage-market. Amongst the numerous aspirants who hoped to gain her hand were several Princes belonging to the reigning houses of Germany, but Princess Zéneide loved her country too well to consent to quit it for a foreigner, even though he were a Royal or Serene Highness.

The young Princess had her own ideas of marriage, and preferred to follow the impulse of her heart in the choice of a husband. Her engagement was inspired entirely by love; her choice fell on an officer of the Chevalier Guards, Count Felix Soumarokoff-Elston, and their union has been one of the happiest.

When Princess Zéneide's father died the title would have become extinct had it not been passed over by Imperial permission to the son-in-law of the deceased, who was known henceforward as Prince Youssoupoff, Count Soumarokoff-Elston. The two sons that were the issue of this marriage bore the title of their father, Count Nicholas and Count Felix Soumarokoff-Elston.

The Emperor Alexander III, ever quick to discover and appreciate noble and pure-minded people, was a great friend and admirer of the Princess Youssoupoff. A point in her favour is that, in spite of those with ill-natured tongues who like to sneer and backbite, the breath of scandal has never in the slightest degree touched her fair fame.

Since her great sorrow, caused by the untimely death of her eldest son, Count Nicholas Soumarokoff-Elston, the Princess Youssoupoff leads a retired life and never goes to parties. Count Nicholas Soumarokoff-Elston was killed in a duel by Count Manteuffel, an officer in the Horse Guards. The mere sight of an officer of this regiment is unbearable to the bereaved mother, and she has vowed that not one of them shall ever pass the threshold of her house.

All the hopes of Prince and Princess Youssoupoff centred henceforth in their youngest son, Count Felix, a very handsome young man, full of talent and capacity. He spent several years in England at Oxford University.

A year ago the Count married a member of the Imperial Family, the lovely Princess Irene, only daughter of the Grand Duke Alexander Mikhailovitch and of the Grand Duchess Xenie Alexandrovna, granddaughter of the Dowager Empress, and great-niece of Queen Alexandra of Great Britain. The bridegroom was twenty-six and the bride eighteen. It was a brilliant marriage, as well as a love match. Count Felix Soumarokoff-Elston received on this occasion by an Imperial 'ukase' the right to the title of Prince Youssoupoff for himself and any children who might be born to him.

The Emperor Alexander III and his Consort, as well as the reigning Imperial couple, have often been the guests of the Prince and Princess Youssoupoff in Coreise.

In the newly constructed palace of the Emperor's only surviving uncle, the Grand Duke Paul Alexandrovitch, in Tzarskoe Selo, work goes on unceasingly under the personal supervision of the Grand Duke's morganatic wife, the Princess Olga Paley (formerly known as the Countess Hohenfelsen). The Princess is very active, all her afternoons are devoted to her depot – indeed, she discloses rare energy and ability in the help she generously lavishes on the wounded and their families.

One of the first victims of this most distressing war was the sister of mercy, Countess Catherine Ignatieff; she died in Warsaw of pneumonia, a few months after leaving the Community of the Trinity to go to the front in one of the field-hospitals.

For years Countess Catherine had known hard work, privations and sorrow. She had been a hospital nurse in China at the time of the war following the rising of the Boxers; she nursed the wounded in Manchuria during the Russo-Japanese war, and in the interval she worked unceasingly in the Community of the Trinity, of which she had become an inmate. The wonder is she kept alive for so long, for she was quite worn out, and had become the emaciated ghost of her former brilliant self. She scarcely took any food, and did not know what rest meant. When the war with Germany commenced, Countess Ignatieff was one of the first to leave Petrograd for the front, but her health was undermined, she had no stamina, no strength of resistance, and a few hours' illness ended her existence, which had been a blessing to so many. Perhaps she was glad to give up a life that had brought her only sorrow, misunderstanding and disappointment.

It would be impossible to enumerate all the Russian women who have become conspicuous either by their heroism or their generosity. Two years of terrible war have proved that the old vigour and moral courage still exist in the Russian nation, and the times have shown us Russian women surrounded by a new halo of glory.

It would be difficult for any woman belonging to the Russian race not to be an ideal 'sister' to the wounded soldier, when from those who stand on the steps of the throne down to the poorest village girl, who carries the only jug of milk she possesses to the nearest trenches, all are full of compassion, of self-abnegation. In common justice one cannot help asserting that Russian women of high rank never hesitated for a moment to follow the dictates of their hearts. They were foremost in July, 1914, when the first shots of the Germans were fired, to undertake a labour to which they were hitherto unaccustomed, and to fill the war hospitals with efficient and devoted nurses. Several of them, as intrepid as their husbands and brothers, gave up life itself; many helped the surgeons to succour the wounded in positions quite close to the enemy, showing their grit in the most trying circumstances. Many up to the present still continue to give their labour, knowledge, care, organising capabilities and sometimes considerable means, to mitigate suffering.

The Russian great lady, accustomed, so it seemed, to live in the most refined conditions of comfort and luxury, to shine in costly clothes and family jewels, to fascinate by her beauty and charm, in this hour of trial to her country threw off all that was conventional in her nature, showing that her mind, like that of her sisters from the people, was accessible not only to the joys and pleasures of life. Her hair concealed by the white regulation kerchief, the symbolic cross on her breast, she boldly took her place at the operating-table or by the pallet of the dying soldier, and in this new role she has inspired faith in her powers and made everyone respect her strength of purpose and endurance.

Chapter V

SHADOWS OF THE PAST

NO one can understand Russia without knowing something of her past. I hope, therefore, that my English readers will forgive me if I make a slight digression by recalling some historical facts which will explain the psychological state of the Russian mind at the present time.

Peter the Great, in search of civilisation and culture, took Germany for his model. The Russian Court was organised after the fashion of the German Courts. Even the distinctive ranks of the courtiers were introduced from Germany and retained their German names, as, for instance, 'Ober-Hofmarshall, Ober-Hofmeister, Jaegermeister, Kammerherr, Kammer-Junker', etc. The principal Court functionaries are so named even at the present day, with the only difference that the Russian pronunciation has somewhat softened the hardness of the German words. The table of ranks for the Government officials likewise proceeds from Germany, but in acting thus Peter the Great thought only of introducing beneficial reforms into his Empire. He remained a true Russian, and the unlimited love he bore his country and his constant solicitude for its welfare were amongst the great qualities of this monarch.

The fear that after his death all that he had done for Russia would be undone by his son and heir persistently haunted him. The Tzessarevitch Alexis, the son of his first marriage with Eudoxia Lopoukhine, whom he repudiated, was a sore disappointment to the great reformer. Alexis was weak in mind and body. Under the influence of his mother, who had become a nun, and of the discontented clergy, who regarded the Tzar's innovations as sinful (they particularly objected to the shaving of men's beards, which used to be their pride), Alexis became an adherent of the opposition party. He hated his wife, a Princess of Wolfenbüttel by birth, with whom he had not a single idea in common. The Tzar was cognisant of these facts. The Sovereign had a son, Peter, and two daughters, Anna and Elisabeth, by his second wife Catherine Skavrousky. Peter was a bright boy, and it was his fond father's dream to leave the throne of Russia to his youngest son. Unfortunately the death of this boy frustrated these hopes and plans. Alexis was aware of his father's feelings towards him. He had no affection for his parent, who inspired him with terror. He therefore sought safety in foreign lands, but he was lured back, and some time after his return he was accused of taking part in a conspiracy against the Tzar, was arrested and died somewhat mysteriously in his prison cell. If an excuse for the Tzar's conduct towards his first-born can be found, it lies in the fact that in sacrificing thus his son and heir he was honestly convinced he was acting for Russia's future weal. Alexis left an infant son, Peter, who was henceforth regarded as the heir.

Unfortunately the Emperor died (1725) when his grandson was only ten years old. The throne was left to the widowed Empress Catherine I, but the latter survived her husband only by two years, and Peter, a lad of twelve, was proclaimed Emperor of Russia. Spoiled by over-indulgence and flattery, he scarcely fulfilled the expectations of his grandfather as to what a Russian monarch ought to be. His reign, however, lasted only three years, for he died from smallpox at the age of fifteen.

After the death of Peter II a strange state of things ensued. There was no direct heir to the throne, and the boyars of different parties struggled to have a Sovereign after their own inclination. For some inexplicable reason the unmarried daughter of Peter the Great, the Grand Duchess Elisabeth, was overlooked, and the daughter of Peter the Great's brother Ivan, the widow of the Duke of Courland, was chosen to be Empress of Russia. She was known as the Empress Anna Joanovna, and her reign lasted a decade.

Coming from Courland, full of German ideas, she imported from Mitau her favourite, Biron, who subsequently became Duke of Courland, hence the family Biron de Courlande, that still exists abroad. A great many Germans from Courland invaded the country at the same time, and became a terror to the Russians. Biron was a brutal man. During the reign of Anna Joanovna he was practically the ruler of Russia. The Empress, on the whole, was not a bad woman, though her weakness made her an easy victim of her favourite Biron. She was subjugated by him, and many of his acts of cruelty and injustice were unknown to her. Biron was loathed by the Russians, and, knowing the general hatred he inspired, he surrounded himself by, and filled the Court and Government with, Germans.

Anna Joanovna was childless; therefore she adopted a niece of her late husband, Princess Anna Leopoldovna, who was pretty, pleasure-loving and frivolous. She was married to the Duke Anthony of Brunswick, and her new-born son was proclaimed heir to the throne of Russia. The unfortunate infant, whose birth had caused such rejoicing, celebrated by magnificent festivals, was only three months old when the Empress Anna Joanovna died and he became the Emperor Ivan VI. The Regency was left to his mother, Princess Anna Leopoldovna of Brunswick, and Biron was to be her adviser, but the Princess was too careless to take her duties seriously. She left everything to Biron, heedlessly giving her signature, thinking only of pleasure and dress, and taking no notice of the iniquities perpetuated by the German Duke. All the same, she detested him, for Biron was a bully, and treated the Regent with scant ceremony.

Things came to a climax, for such a position could not be tolerated. Peter the Great's daughter Elisabeth was now recalled to mind. So far the Grand Duchess's lot had been rather a hard one. For over ten years she had been kept in the background, rarely appeared at Court, and was on the point of entering a convent. In the interval Count Münich had taken the upper hand in the Government, and had prevailed upon Anna Leopoldovna to have Biron and his family arrested and exiled to Siberia.

About this time (1741) a conspiracy, partially led by the French Ambassador, Count Lestocq, brought on a Palace revolution. The officers of the Preobrejensky Regiment – Peter the Great's own regiment, which when still a boy he had formed from among his playmates – adored the daughter of their former chief and would do anything in her behalf. A night was chosen when the sentries at the Palace were supplied from the Preobrejenskys. The Duke of Brunswick, his wife and the infant Emperor were arrested in their beds and taken to the fortress of Schlüsselburg, where for many years they led a miserable existence. Count Münich was arrested simultaneously and sent to Siberia.

At that time Elisabeth was in the prime of womanhood. She

had attained the age of thirty-three, and was a handsome woman, with an imposing figure. Whatever her defects may have been, she was a true Russian, always sincerely concerned to ensure her country's welfare. Her reign was a prosperous one. Elisabeth hated the Germans and she took a prominent part in the Seven Years' War as the ally of the Empress Maria Theresa of Austria. The victory of the Russian army, led by Prince Soltykoff, at Kunnersdorff (1759) placed King Frederick of Prussia in a very precarious position. Some of the Russian regiments entered Berlin, and in remembrance of this occurrence silver trumpets were conferred on them.

On the occasion of one of Kaiser Wilhelm's visits to Russia he noticed the silver trumpets of the Viborg regiment, of which His Majesty had been appointed honorary Colonel. He inquired of one of the officers for what feat the silver trumpets had been granted to them. 'For entering Berlin, your Majesty.' 'Oh,' replied the Kaiser. 'Let us hope a similar event will not repeat itself.'

It was in Elisabeth's reign that, by the treaty of Äbo, Finland was joined to Russia. She endeavoured to further literature and art, and was as wise a Sovereign as her abilities permitted. She had a horror of bloodshed, and in her reign not a single execution took place.

Elisabeth's rule lasted twenty years, but in all her wisdom she had overlooked the necessity of giving an heir to the throne. Averse to matrimony, she had remained a maiden Empress. To supply this want Elisabeth thought of her elder sister Anna wedded to the Duke of Holstein-Gothorp, who had died many years before. The Empress sent for the latter's son Peter, who received the title of Grand Duke of Russia; but her endeavours to imbue him with Russian views and tastes were in vain. The choice of his future wife fell on the Princess of Anhalt-Zerbst, known as the Grand Duchess Catherine of Russia.

The Empress Elisabeth died on Christmas Day, 1761. Her nephew the Duke of Holstein-Gothorp was proclaimed Emperor of Russia under the name of Peter III.

The new Tzar was an uncouth, brutal German, underbred and with next to no education. Except from his aunt, of whom he was in awe, he never disguised the fact that he hated Russia. Frederick of Prussia was his ideal. To show his devotion to this monarch, Peter III commenced his reign by unexpectedly concluding a separate peace with Prussia, leaving Austria to her own devices.

Not satisfied with this, the Russian Emperor chose to manifest his generosity to Germany by bestowing the town of Dantzig upon Prussia as a gift.

Everything once more became Germanised at the Court of the new Tzar, who could hardly speak the language of his subjects. He scorned and shamefully insulted his wife, led the most shockingly dissolute life, spending most of his time in riotous feasting with his boon companions, and totally neglected his duties as ruler of such a vast Empire.

Such a terrible state of things had never yet oppressed the country. A crisis was inevitable.

Entirely different had been the conduct of Peter's Consort. From the first days of her arrival in Russia, Catherine had endeavoured not only to win the Empress Elisabeth's favour but to gain general affection and esteem. When her son the future Emperor Paul was born, the child was instantly taken away from her by the autocratic Elisabeth.

A wet-nurse was hired and the nursery of the baby prince established close to the Empress's private apartments, where the infant's mother was rarely admitted, for the Empress Elisabeth was a very jealous woman. Up to the age of seven Paul, systematically estranged from his parents, was pampered and spoiled by a doting great-aunt in the most pernicious way. No one dared oppose him or check his ungovernable fits of passion; no one ventured to contradict him or control his conduct.

The Grand Duchess Catherine, openly neglected by her husband and kept in the shade by the all-powerful Elisabeth, devoted her leisure to serious study. Several hours of the day were given up by the young Princess to lessons. She acquired a thorough knowledge of the Russian language and became cognisant of the nation's history, traditions and legends. She likewise improved her mind by going through a course of reading, showing a marked predilection for the works of French philosophers of the eighteenth century.

Whilst Peter was becoming an object of universal hatred and contempt, Catherine was gaining wisdom, moral strength and popularity. The crucial moment arrived when the Emperor's decision to disinherit his son and discard his wife became generally known.

The moment was too critical to admit of hesitation. A cleverly laid plot, led by two officers, Gregory and Alexis Orloff, succeeded.

SHADOWS OF THE PAST

Peter III was taken captive and forced to sign an act of abdication in favour of his wife. He was incarcerated in one of the summer palaces – 'Ropsha', but he died a week after his imprisonment. It is surmised, and not without reason, that he was assassinated by Alexis Orloff, the brother of the Empress's favourite.

The reign of the Empress Catherine II was in all respects glorious. In Russia she is called the 'Great Catherine'.

Although a German by birth, no Russian monarch could have been more devoted to the interests of the country than was Catherine II. Her Court was composed of Russians, and the Sovereign did everything to ensure the might and uphold the dignity of the Empire she ruled so wisely. She continued the reforms of Peter the Great in a more enlightened and less arbitrary way. She founded the Academy of Science in Petrograd, and furthered the education of women by establishing colleges for girls. The Council of the Empire came into being in her reign.

Her wars were victorious, the treaties she concluded were to the country's advantage. It was in her reign that the Crimea was joined to Russia and an opening made to the Black Sea, which greatly benefited trade. The Empress had a wonderful instinct for discovering clever and capable men, who justified her choice by distinguishing themselves as brilliant statesmen or valiant generals. She encouraged art and literature, and endeavoured to develop trade and agriculture, doing her best to ameliorate the conditions of life all over the country.

As a Sovereign the Northern Semiramis was indeed great, though her private life could not bear microscopic investigation. Foreign historians have dealt harshly with her memory, laying more stress on her failings and foibles than on her sterling qualities. The skeleton in the Empress's cupboard was her son. The Tzessarevitch Paul was a continual source of worry, and her feelings towards him were a combination of dislike and contempt, whilst his were a mixture of fear, hatred and sullen defiance. The breach between mother and son was never healed. The Grand Duke was married to a pretty and sympathetic Princess of Würtemberg, but she had little influence over her husband. They had a large family, and during the last years of the Empress Catherine's reign led a secluded life in Gatchina.

Their first-born son, Alexander, was adored by his grandmother, and indeed he was a grandson to be proud of. He spent the greater part of his life with the Empress, who had him well taught and most carefully brought up by a Swiss tutor, La Harpe. Catherine II, however, was not fortunate in the choice of his wife, a princess of Baden. The Tzessarevna Elisabeth was an angel of goodness, and she was sincerely devoted to her handsome young husband, but, according to the memoirs of that time, the feeling of Alexander towards his wife was akin to aversion.

When the Empress Catherine died, after a reign which lasted thirty-four years, her son Paul succeeded her. His first act of power was to have the body of his father disinterred and laid out in state beside the deceased Empress Catherine. Honours to the dead were simultaneously rendered to both the late Sovereigns, and a double funeral procession followed; Catherine II was buried together with Peter III.

In acting thus Paul committed a repulsive breach of good taste which revolted everyone. He wished to inflict a posthumous humiliation on his dead father, but succeeded only in arousing general indignation, for the late Empress was sincerely beloved and her death looked upon as a national calamity.

The Emperor Paul in his views, tastes and inclinations was the opposite of Catherine II. He endeavoured to undo all that his mother had done. Like his father, he was a staunch partisan of Germany. Changes were made in the army to make it more like that of Germany, and Germans were again in favour. The atmosphere reeked of harshness and severity. The Emperor's distrust and jealousy of his eldest son, the Tzessarevitch Alexander, kept the latter in the background and made him a continual object of suspicion. The Emperor Paul's character was a mixture of violence, overbearing arrogance, despotism and unexpected rays of kindness that occasionally broke out. His warped unbalanced nature utterly unfitted him for the heavy responsibilities of a monarch. Fortunately his reign lasted only five years. He was succeeded by his son Alexander.

Alexander I was a dreamer inclined to mysticism, chivalrous, noble-minded, but not always sincere. He ruled Russia wisely, but his foreign politics were prompted by a personal point of view. When Napoleon I, who considered an alliance with Prussia the best safeguard for maintaining the future equilibrium of Europe, wished to contract a matrimonial alliance with the Emperor Alexander's sister, the Grand Duchess Catherine, both the Dowager Empress Marie Feodorovna and the Tzar were infuriated at the 'upstart's' presuming to wed a scion of the Russian Imperial

Family. The Grand Duchess was hastily married to a Prince of Oldenburg, and Napoleon's offer was rather unceremoniously declined. The French Emperor never forgot this slight, and from that moment he commenced to plan the war with Russia.

Alexander I played a prominent part at the time of Napoleon's downfall, but pursuing a political course, inspired by chivalry and sentiment, under the influence of his infatuation for Queen Louise of Prussia, he took Prussia's future welfare more into consideration than the advantages of his own country. Prussia owed its very existence to Alexander I's noble disinterestedness. Russian historians and politicians consider the attitude of Alexander I during that period as a serious mistake from the national point of view.

The marriage of Alexander I was a childless one. The Heir-Presumptive was his brother Constantine, next to him in age, but the Grand Duke Constantine had contracted a morganatic alliance with a Polish lady, Princess Lovitch, besides which he was not ambitious of wielding power, feeling himself unfitted for the onerous burden of sovereignty. Constantine had inherited his father's violent temper, and his fits of rage were terrible. Princess Lovitch alone could control and calm him. When these mad fits were upon him, she had a very beneficial influence on her husband, and was sincerely liked and esteemed by her Imperial relations. A family arrangement was made in the lifetime of Alexander. Constantine signed an act of renouncement, voluntarily yielding his rights to the throne to his younger brother Nicholas. This gave rise to disturbances amongst the people at the time of Alexander's death, for they could not understand why the elder brother had been passed over, and surmised foul play. Some extreme liberals took the opportunity to bribe some of the fellows who were mobbing the Winter Palace to call for 'Constitution', which in Russia is pronounced 'Constitutzia'. Nothing loath, they lustily bellowed for 'Constitutzia', but, on being taken up before a police officer and questioned as to what they meant by claiming a Constitutzia, they answered that they had been told to cheer Constantine's wife.

The Emperor Nicholas's manly conduct and firmness soon put an end to the riots that disturbed the first days of his reign.

Nicholas I was very Russian, but his wife – a Princess of Prussia – was quite the reverse. The alliance had been a love-match, and the Empress Alexandra Feodorovna had great influence, especially in organising the Court and appointing Court dignitaries. She was a very imposing Empress of Russia, with gracious dignified manners, but in her heart she always remained a German. Her conversion to the Greek Orthodox religion had been accomplished prior to her nuptials with the Grand Duke Nicholas, but the general opinion was that the conversion had been only nominal, and that she secretly continued to worship God according to Luther's teaching. In the private chapel of the Winter Palace, where the Tzar and his family regularly attended religious service, a glass pavilion was erected for the Empress Alexandra Feodorovna on the plea that she could not stand the smell of incense. Screened all round by walls of glass, Her Majesty could follow the service without being inconvenienced by the incense. People asserted, however, that this seclusion was demanded by the Empress in order that her German Prayer Book might pass unnoticed.

Nicholas I was an autocrat, but his chivalry, loyalty and personal bravery were amongst the predominating qualities of his noble nature. He was true to the core, and his word could always be depended on.

It was his chivalry that led the Tzar, in 1849, to stand up for the rights of the young Austrian Sovereign, Franz Joseph, a youth of nineteen, and send his troops over to help the Austrians to quell the insurrection in Hungary and save the throne of the Hapsburgs. In acting thus, Nicholas's complete disinterestedness can be proved by historical documents, which, though committed to oblivion, still exist.

On the 1st of August, 1849 – an ever memorable date in the annals of Russian military history – the Hungarian insurgents gave themselves up to the Russian Tzar, because they knew the honour of his Apostolic Majesty was not to be trusted.

The Russian army had accomplished with glory the task entrusted to them of saving the dynasty of the Hapsburgs. Without any feeling of sympathy towards the Austrians, the Russian soldiers conquered the Hungarian army as they were bidden. One Hungarian fortification after another, though invincible to the Austrians, fell before the Russian armed forces. The last fort, 'Villagosha', had capitulated – 11 generals, 2,000 officers and 30,000 soldiers had just laid down their arms in surrender. The leader of the insurrection, the Hungarian Dictator Gergey, came over to the Headquarters of General Froloff, the Russian commander, to discuss the preliminaries of a general surrender. The Hungarian Chief came over by himself, too sure of Russian loyalty to feel any anxiety lest a trap had been laid for him. The Russians, actuated by feelings of delicacy, wished this surrender to be made to the Austrian Commander-in-Chief Heinan, but Gergey, who despised General Heinan for his brutal ferocity, flatly refused 'as before God'. 'The Austrians,' said the Hungarian patriot, 'from the moment of applying to Russia for aid, thus proclaiming their helplessness, lost the right to this honour.'

Before the final surrender Gergey, in his frantic struggle to shake off the Austrian yoke, made a last effort: in the name of his fellow-countrymen he offered the throne of Hungary to the Tzar's second son Constantine but Nicholas I, strict adherent of monarchical legitimacy, was too loyal even to contemplate the advantages to Russia of such an arrangement. The offer was courteously but firmly declined. Gergey's life and liberty were saved, thanks to the personal influence of the Russian Emperor. Before the final surrender of Hungary to the Austrians, His Majesty insisted on Gergey's safety being guaranteed, or else the Hungarian Dictator would be taken to Russia. Field-Marshal Prince Paskevitch returned to Gergey eight hundred half-sovereigns which had belonged to him but which the Austrians had confiscated.

This gave the Austrians the chance of revenging themselves on the hated Hungarian. The rumour was spread that Gergey had been bribed by the Russians. Slander is always believed by the masses, and Gergey lost the confidence of his former confederates and the popularity he had always enjoyed in Hungary.

The insurrection was over, the delighted Austrian Sovereign gave the most ardent assurances of his lifelong devotion and gratitude to the Tzar, and the Tzar believed him. A little more than five years later the Crimean war broke out. In his hour of need Nicholas bethought himself of His Apostolic Majesty's protestations, and confidently hoped to find assistance in that quarter. Instead of help the treacherous Austrian Sovereign sent his army to threaten the Russian frontier. The Emperor Nicholas had a sincere affection for Franz Joseph. A statuette of the latter, artistically made in terra-cotta, adorned the Russian monarch's writing-table. But when the Tzar lay on his death-bed he cursed the Austrian Sovereign and his reign and broke the statuette.

Nicholas was very proud: he hated usurpers and upstarts. Napoleon III was amongst the people he most disapproved of.

When Napoleon ascended the throne of France in 1852 he wrote letters to all the European monarchs, as the custom is amongst Royalty. The Emperor Nicholas answered the letter as courteously as the occasion required, but, instead of the usual formula 'Sire et cher cousin', the Tzar addressed the French Emperor only as 'Sire'. Napoleon noted the omission, deeply resented it, and ever afterwards his feelings towards Nicholas were unfriendly.

Alexander II succeeded his father, Nicholas I. The new Tzar had been carefully brought up and educated, but his German mother had instilled in him a veneration for his uncle, the King of Prussia, subsequently the Kaiser Wilhelm I, and a profound admiration of everything German. The Tzar frequently consulted his uncle, studied his wishes and mostly gave in to them. Had Russia helped France in 1870, if only by sending troops to the Prussian frontier, many future events would have had a different development. But Alexander was too loyal to his mother's brother to profit by the opportunity of putting a spoke in his wheel. The conduct of Germany, however, during the Berlin Congress after the Russo-Turkish war in 1878 was not in accordance with Russian anticipations. Bismarck called himself 'the honest broker', but his attitude was astute and well thought out. He let Lord Beaconsfield have a free hand, and pretended to give in to the inevitable, threatening Russia with hostile action on the part of Britain if a protest were forthcoming.

When the question of a future ruler for Bulgaria was discussed, the Tzar declared his indifference to the choice of a prince so long as no member of the Russian Imperial Family were chosen. In the Russian Sovereign's eyes a 'Prince of Bulgaria' savoured too much of the adventurer. His Majesty did not foresee that it would have simplified the continual complications arising in the Balkan peninsula to have a Russian ruler in Bulgaria. Alexander II's refusal to admit the candidature of any Russian prince to the throne of Bulgaria was the outcome of a personal objection to put any member of his family in a false position.

At that time, it must be remembered, when the terrible tragedy of the Archduke Maximilian was still fresh in everyone's memory, the position of newly hatched Sovereigns was regarded as risky. When Prince Karl Hohenzollern-Sigmaringen consulted Prince Bismarck in 1866 about the wisdom of accepting the crown of Roumania, the Iron Chancellor replied: 'Why not, it will always remain a pleasant memory', which proves that even Bismarck had grave doubts as to the lasting success of alien princes being sent to reign in a strange land.

Politicians reproach the former Russian monarchs for not sufficiently studying the country's weal in dealings with foreign Powers; for having stood up for the advantages of Germany and Austria at Russia's expense; for mixing politics with sentiment, and for having been actuated by chivalry in their relation with individuals who were the reverse of chivalrous.

The Tzar Alexander III is considered the only real national Sovereign. He was a true Russian in all respects. 'Russia for the Russians' was his motto. The Emperor directed the country's politics himself, showed firmness and resolution in no matter what crisis, and ignored Germany and the wishes of the German Government, taking into consideration what he thought best for Russia. During the all too short period of his reign there was a marked tendency toward Russification. It seems paradoxical to speak of 'Russificating' Russia, but so it was. The Emperor started wearing a beard, such as his forefathers, anterior to Peter the Great, had worn. The soldiers who had been obliged to shave were now encouraged to let their beards grow, the military uniform was modified to resemble the Russian caftan, high boots were introduced and the soldier's headgear was likewise changed.

The Emperor always spoke Russian during the audiences he gave, as well as in society – his predecessors had generally spoken French – and naturally everyone around him followed the Sovereign's example. During the preceding reigns French had been the universal language of Russian society; our grandmothers and great-grandmothers thought it vulgar to converse in Russian. The Russian language was only used to speak with inferiors or to give orders to servants. Many Russian ladies in the thirties of the last century who spoke French like Parisians hardly knew their own language, making egregious mistakes and being often guilty of the most appalling solecisms when they ventured to converse in their own tongue. A few years later the English language became the fashion, but French continued to be spoken in society. In Alexander III's reign this was changed. Russian became the established language in the most select drawing-rooms, with occasional lapses into French if a foreign diplomat were present.

When the Napoleonic wars were over in the early part of the nineteenth century it became the custom for rich landed proprietors and wealthy members of the aristocracy to absent themselves for years from Russia, living in foreign parts, mostly in Paris.

They foolishly left their vast estates in charge of land agents, whose principal duty was to send regular remittances. These land agents were usually chosen from amongst the Germans, who had the reputation of being the best agriculturists. They were endowed with unlimited powers by their employers, and filled all subordinate situations, such as foresters, cattle-breeders, gardeners, etc., with their own countrymen. In this way a regular net of Germans was spread all over the country. Instead of teaching the Russian peasants and developing their latent faculties (a well-taught Russian peasant is capable of any amount of good work), these Germans treated them not only with undisguised contempt but with actual cruelty. The proprietors suspected nothing, for a German land agent in his intercourse with his employer and in his dealings with defenceless peasants is two very different men.

In factories the German masters were detested by the Russian workmen, for indeed no more hard, overbearing and gruff taskmasters exist. English overseers, notwithstanding their strictness, get on much better with the workmen of this country; their firmness never borders on brutality, they are always just and they treat the workman as a fellow-creature of whom work is required. In return the workman does his level best to give satisfaction. A German, on the other hand, is never pleased with anything, but always full of contempt and abuse.

In looking back over the last two centuries one notices the growing hatred inspired by the Germans, which like a red thread can be traced through all these years. The German is looked upon by the Russian as the foe who has usurped all that is best in this country. The most important positions at Court have been given to Germans; Germans take a prominent part in trade, every profession or industry is filled with Germans. For years the Russians have silently resented this. These long years of regression have at last given vent to an outburst of the most violent antagonism against the hated Teutons. This explains the extreme popularity of the present war amongst the middle classes and the people, for the 'Niemetz'[1] is not only the country's enemy but the private foe of every Russian.

1 'Niemetz' = the Russian word for German.

Chapter VI

SHADES OF THE PRESENT

IT must not be supposed that the German influence in the development of Russia's affairs has suddenly ceased. The traditions of two centuries were too firmly implanted to be instantaneously and for ever uprooted. When the indignation caused by the Kaiser's declaration of war had calmed down, and the reaction after the first burst of patriotic enthusiasm had set in, people began to reflect. The Germanophile party was evidently shaken, but, by some inexplicable process of their psychological faculties, the adherents of this party came to the odd conclusion that the present conflagration must be looked upon as a 'temporary misunderstanding', and that, the war once over, Russia's future welfare and safety continued to lie in an alliance with Germany. They did not believe in the sincerity of Great Britain's friendship and doubted its duration.

This party, which fortunately forms the minority of Russian opinion, does not consist only of people bearing German names, but includes descendants of old boyar races: members of the aristocracy, who have lived abroad for a long time and boast of a personal acquaintance with the German potentate; former diplomatists who have spent many years in Berlin, as well as the followers of those diplomatic traditions inaugurated by Count Nesselrode and Prince Gortchakoff. The political programme of this party is that Russia must endeavour to renew the old terms of friendship with Germany. These opinions are naturally prudently reserved for political drawing-rooms, where such sentiments are received with warm applause. But the discussion of them is not a secret to anyone and it causes a great deal of heart-burning and trouble.

The majority, led by the Press, is infuriated to hear such sentiments professed. In their eyes the gulf which the Kaiser and his satellites have created between Russia and Germany will never be bridged over. Peace will eventually follow the war, but no true Russian will ever forget the Kaiser's treachery, nor forgive the Teuton his crimes. The animosity towards the Germans increases daily.

Unfortunately the mistrust inherent in every Slav gave rise to a most fatal suspicion of the sincerity and devotion to Russia of the Empress. Those who accept this view think that her sympathies are given to the German party, and they fear that Her Majesty, who has a great ascendancy over the Tzar, will infect him with her views. The monarch's unwillingness to make a change amongst the principal dignitaries of the Court and eliminate the entire German element is ascribed to the Empress's influence. In justice to the Empress it must be said that her attitude has always been correct in every particular, and the Emperor's stern and determined insistence upon the ideals of the Allies do not suggest that he is being influenced in favour of Germany. The displeasure which Count Fredericks's presence inspires generally has been rapidly increasing, and it has spread amongst the working people, and, worse still, amongst the soldiers. One hears continual criticisms because the Emperor tolerates a German Court Minister in his vicinity.

The general mental strain after two years of anxiety, suffering and all kinds of hardships is so intense that most people are really not quite in their normal state of mind. The most incredible stories are spread and, worse luck, believed by the majority.

After that very unsavoury person Colonel Miassoyedoff had been shown to be a spy, who for years had been in Germany's pay, followed closely by the discovery that Captain Benson, the Assistant of the Russian Military Agent in Paris, was also a traitor, this nervous tension became disquieting; spies and German intrigues were suspected in all directions.

The general opinion in Russia is not always quite just to the Empress. From the first moment Her Majesty endeavoured to help, to the best of her ability. She had herself trained as a sister of mercy, but the Russian mind does not admit a Sovereign in the lowly position of a hospital nurse, and, though it bows in deep and heartfelt admiration before the hospital labours of the other members of the Imperial Family, the Russian warriors want their

'Gossoudarina' to appear in all circumstances surrounded by a halo of grandeur. They would prefer that Her Majesty take upon herself the part of consoling angel, intent on bringing hope and comfort to the wounded, endeavouring to talk with them in Russian, showing the undoubted interest she takes in them and theirs. She would be worshipped; but speech has ever been the Empress's stumbling-block, her shyness, which is taken for coldness, prevents her from expressing what she feels. Her Majesty's deeds have always outweighed her words, but, for those who are not cognisant of the deeds, a few kind words from the Empress's lips would be so precious and far-reaching.

A few months after the war began there was a persistent rumour to the effect that the Empress was doing everything in her power to ensure a separate peace being speedily concluded between Russia and Germany. It was believed that the Sovereign's brother, the Grand Duke of Hesse, had come incognito to Petrograd to convince his sister that Russia's welfare, the safety of the dynasty, would be endangered by a protracted war. A little later it was said that Her Majesty's sister, Princess Irene of Prussia, had come over secretly for a couple of days in quest of peace. Useless to add that these arrivals of Her Majesty's relatives only took place in the excited imagination of gossiping busybodies. The Empress was accused of putting implicit faith in the prophecy made to her by one of the fanatics she specially favours, that her son would die if peace were not concluded in the autumn of 1914. If this prophecy was really made, it was an act of wanton cruelty, and gives one the impression that the prophet was inspired by a German bribe.

What really did happen in the early days of 1916 was the somewhat mysterious arrival in Petrograd from Austria of Mlle. Marie Wassiltchikoff, and her very strange behaviour. Mlle. Wassiltchikoff belongs to a good old family. Her late father had been an important personage and was the Director of the Imperial Hermitage. She is highly connected, and moved in the best society. When the Empress married, Mlle. Wassiltchikoff was appointed to attend the Sovereign as her personal maid of honour. This arrangement, however, did not last, for Her Majesty did not get on with Mlle. Wassiltchikoff, and the latter not only left the Court, but was not at all reticent in her ill-natured remarks about the Empress's treatment of her maids of honour. Subsequently she left Petrograd and established herself in Austria. The reason of her thus abandoning her country was a romantic one – she had fallen in love with Count S., a member of the Austrian Embassy in Russia, and when Count S. left Petrograd Mlle. Wassiltchikoff followed. She acquired from Prince Nichtenstein a small country seat in the neighbourhood of Vienna, and has lived there ever since. All this happened so many years ago that it was quite obliterated from people's memory. Suddenly, about the Russian Christmas time, Mlle. Wassiltchikoff arrived in Petrograd, took a luxurious apartment in the most expensive hotel, settling herself as if for a prolonged stay. Lavish in her expenditure, she sought out all her old friends and went a great deal into society, discussing politics in an authoritative manner, but always from the German point of view.

Mlle. Wassiltchikoff requested an audience of the Empress, which was refused. She had an important interview, however, with the President of the Duma, M. Rodzianko, who happens to be a connection of hers, and imparted to him the most alarming information, endeavouring to bring him round to her point of view.

Before coming to Russia Mlle. Wassiltchikoff had been invited to the house of the Grand Duke of Hesse at Darmstadt; here she met Prince Henry of Prussia, and both Princes, inspired by their attachment to their Russian relatives and their affection for Russia, begged the Russian lady to undertake this crusade of peace, and carry the warning to Russia that the country would be put in a precarious position if it hesitated to demand peace. England had already made secret pacific overtures to Germany; France would follow England's example, and Russia would be left isolated. The message was given with the Kaiser's full consent. 'The strength of Germany,' added Mlle. Wassiltchikoff, 'was inexhaustible, her resources kept increasing, all was flourishing in the interior; to struggle with such gigantic forces was impossible.'

This enterprising lady demanded an audience with the Minister of Foreign Affairs. M. Sazonoff received Mlle. Wassiltchikoff chiefly from a sense of courtesy, mixed with curiosity, to see this former 'society lady' turned peacemonger. Not for a single moment did M. Sazonoff believe in the importance of the German emissary's mission, and her opinions could have no value in the eyes of the Minister. It is therefore not to be wondered at that the interview proved unsatisfactory, M. Sazonoff keeping within the limits of courteous irony.

SHADES OF THE PRESENT

At that very time a feeling of general depression was to be noticed in all classes of Petrograd society. Strange and disquieting rumours were afloat to the effect that England's forces were exhausted, that in England everyone was clamouring for peace. These rumours coincided with the appearance of Mlle. Wassiltchikoff in Petrograd. But the police had an eye on this emissary from Germany – her movements were watched, and a visit made to her apartment produced some startling results. All was kept very quiet, and no one knows precisely what happened, but Mlle. Wassiltchikoff was arrested and her papers and documents confiscated. Some of the papers were of a compromising nature, a list of names was found amongst them of those who were considered in Germany to be trustworthy, as being well disposed to that country and desirous of the re-establishment of peaceful intercourse with her. An important official in the Foreign Office was mentioned as the man to whom Germany would like the preliminary peace transactions to be entrusted. Could insolence and self-satisfaction go further . . . even in the land of the Teutons?

Mlle. Wassiltchikoff was not severely dealt with; she was examined, sent out of Petrograd to her sister's estate near Kharkoff, where she is to remain under the police's surveillance and on her sister's responsibility till the end of the war.

That was all, but tongues kept on wagging in the most senseless and venomous way. The circumstance that once upon a time Mlle. Wassiltchikoff had been a maid of honour to the Empress, her visit to Her Majesty's brother prior to her starting for Russia, were points against the Empress. The fact that the Sovereign had disliked this former attendant of hers and had lost no time in getting rid of her was passed over, and Her Majesty's refusal to receive her relative's emissary was not taken into account. People were determined to believe that Mlle. Wassiltchikoff's peace crusade had been sanctioned by the Empress, the absurdity of which must be obvious to all. Surely the dullest person can see that the attitude of the Empress was correct in every detail.

At the same time the Grand Duchess Elisabeth, who up to then had been so popular in Moscow, became also the object of mistrust and suspicion. 'Ona Nemka'[1] was said of her, and that alone was an accusation. A coolness is said to have arisen between the Empress and her elder sister Elisabeth. The Grand Duchess came

---

1 'She is a German' in Russian.

to Tzarskoe Selo intent on opening the Empress's eyes to the doings of some of her favourite clericals, and of the harm that would ensue if this were tolerated. Her Majesty took offence at her sister's outspokenness. The Grand Duchess Elisabeth, having failed to convince her sister, returned to Moscow to look after her many organisations on behalf of the wounded. A certain intriguing member of the priesthood, who is patronised by the Empress's circle, wished to associate himself with these organisations, but the Grand Duchess flatly refused to have any dealings with him. Soon the most ridiculous stories were spread about regarding the marked predilection the Grand Duchess Elisabeth shows for the German captives, in preference to the Russian wounded soldiers. One of these reports produced a perfect scandal. It was launched just before the riots and anti-German manifestations took place in May, 1915, in Moscow – and spread not only in the two capitals, but all over Russia. It was said that the Grand Duchess visited a hospital just after the arrival of a fresh contingent of wounded soldiers and German prisoners. There had not been time to sort them, and the hospital was over-full. Some of the prisoners were lying on the floor. Her Imperial Highness inquired the reason of this. She was told that there were no spare beds. The Grand Duchess is reported to have turned to the matron and told her to have the Russian wounded soldiers put on the floor and the German prisoners lifted into their beds. 'The Germans are used to culture and comfort, and the Russians won't feel the difference,' added the Grand Duchess.

A friend and well-wisher of the latter repeated some of these reports to her. The Grand Duchess looked very much surprised, and absolutely denied the least foundation for such calumnies. She had *not even seen* a German prisoner. 'God is punishing me,' added the Grand Duchess, 'for it would have been my duty to visit them, and yet I could not bring myself to see them.'

Such are the methods of 'Kultur'. Nothing is too mean or debasing for the Germans to turn to in order to achieve their ends.

Thinking to give pleasure to the Empress, several German wounded prisoners were sent to the Palace hospital in Tzarskoe Selo. When the Empress heard about this she became indignant, saying: 'I think I might have been spared this.' No one ever mentions this incident, which is known only to a very few, but a great hue and cry arose when Her Majesty, in speaking to some high official of the Red Cross, expressed the hope that the prisoners were well cared for, as she would not like it to be said abroad that they had been neglected in Russia. This very natural observation from the lips of a Sovereign was twisted into a proof of the great interest and compassion shown by the Empress to the German captives.

Even the members of the Emperor's family, so it was said, were divided in their sympathies, the Tzar, the Tzessarevitch and his eldest daughter Olga being very Russian – the Empress and her second daughter Tatiana inclining to Germany. In reality the Imperial Family is as united as ever. Indeed, the home life of the Imperial Family is a model one. Mornings and afternoons are given up to work, study and sport. At present they are mostly devoted to hospital work and the care of the wounded and the bereaved. In the evenings the family circle assembles together. The Empress is very musical. The Tzar also loves music, and when in a cheerful mood is not averse to singing a song himself. The Grand Duchess Tatiana has a lovely voice, and there are sometimes the most charming family concerts.

A year ago the Emperor founded a new order of 'Saint Olga' for women who distinguished themselves during the war. According to the Statutes of the Order of St. Olga, the two Empresses were to sign each paper, conferring the order. A whole year has passed, many women have been wonderful in their heroism, self-abnegation and generosity, but none has received the order! It is said that the lists of suggested recipients of the two Empresses never agree. The only lady who has been honoured by the Order of St. Olga is Madame Panaeff, and in her case it was the Emperor who conferred it. Madame Panaeff is a widow, who had four sons, three of them in the army and one in the navy. The three officers in the army distinguished themselves in many battles by the greatest valour, and all three were killed. The Emperor heard of this, and, deeply moved by the mother's bereavement, sent her the Order of St. Olga 'for bringing up her sons to be such brave men and such devoted servitors of their Tzar and their country. Such exemplary sons,' he added, 'must have had a beautiful-minded mother.' At the same time the Sovereign ordered the fourth son, Lieutenant Panaeff, to be sent back to Petrograd and given a post in the Admiralty, where he could work without risking the life of his mother's last son. After a few months spent in Petrograd with his mother, Lieutenant Panaeff, with his parent's full sanction, sent in a petition to return to the fleet, for he felt that this was the time when each individual counts, and healthy, strong men must act and not sit still.

Some of the bereaved mothers inspire the deepest respect and admiration for the courage they show in bearing up under the loss of their beloved ones.

One of the most moving stories is that of Baroness de Witt. Two of her sons were killed in battle; the third returned to her a cripple. Instead of giving way to grief, this brave woman kept back the cry of agony that was tearing her soul in twain and reducing her despair to active energy; this lady – the widow of a general, surrounded by every luxury – became a voluntary worker in a munitions factory. Early every morning, dressed in plain black, Baroness de Witt is the first at her stand and the last to leave it – the more ammunition and projectiles she gets ready the better pleased she is, for the only solace she finds is in the thought that she is helping her country to conquer the Germans, who are the cause of her blighted life.

The workpeople are used to this silent, sad-eyed, hard-working 'Generalsha',[1] they know her story, and they treat her with the greatest respect and consideration.

The increasing hatred of the Germans created the Baltic question, which has become a very sore and complicated one, owing to the continual baying of the newspapers. They seem to think it their mission to start a press crusade against the Germans of the Baltic provinces. Injustice and tactlessness on both sides have embittered the situation.

The Baltic Germans have always been loyal subjects, that is, they have never been actively mixed up in any revolt; they profess devotion to the Russian Sovereigns and the Imperial Family.

It would be useless to deny the fact that the Baltic Germans led a narrow-minded, separate life in their German provinces, enjoying the privileges granted to them by the Empress Elisabeth, with only local occurrences to interest them, and intermarrying mostly amongst themselves. Berlin was their Eldorado, and a journey to Germany constituted their greatest felicity. It is only quite lately that the men commenced to learn the Russian language, but the women will not speak Russian on principle. In bygone days, though not very long ago, the Governor of Vitebsk was a Baron Gerschau-Flotow; his wife, by birth a Baroness

1 In Russian the wife of a general.

SHADES OF THE PRESENT

Kloppmann (from Courland), flatly refused to speak Russian, although she was the wife of a high Russian official. Her mother-in-law, the Dowager Madame de Flotow, who for over forty years had been lady-in-waiting to the Dowager Empress Marie, a charming old lady, not at all narrow-minded, endeavoured to shake this foolish resolution, explaining to her son's wife that it was her duty to converse in Russian with the ladies with whom she came in contact; but all persuasions failed, and nothing would induce the wife of a Russian Governor to speak the language of her own country. Before the war such matters were good-naturedly tolerated, if somewhat ridiculed, but no serious attention was paid to the vagaries of these stiff-necked Barons and their obstinate women-folk.

Occasional spasmodic efforts were made by the Government to Russificate the Baltic provinces, but little was gained, for the Government was not energetic or persevering enough, and the Germans, though showing no open resistance, were stubborn in their resolve that the old order of things should remain unchanged. They used the influence of their highly connected fellow-countrymen in Petrograd. When it became obligatory for the Russian language to be spoken in all Baltic schools, the Barons retaliated by closing the institutions subsidised by the local nobility, and sending their sons to study in Germany.

When war broke out there was a wave of patriotism amongst the Baltic Barons, and many of them hastened to the front to fight for Russia. There were, however, several fiery Germans, as, for instance, one Baron who has three sons fighting in the ranks of the Germans against Russia.

There always have been cases of the Baltic Barons sending their sons to be officers in some of the crack German regiments, where they were received with open arms. In some families one son served in Germany and the other in Russia. But what used to be tolerated prior to the war has now become an unpardonable crime. When the Press began to persecute the Baltic Germans, they ferreted out all such cases, unjustly picking out the exceptions to be held up before the public as samples of Baltic loyalty to Russia.

Instead of sending in a violent protest against this wholesale condemnation, the leaders of the Baltic nobility remained silent, forgetting the great truth of the French proverb: '*Calomniez, calomniez – il restera toujours quelquechose.*' Count Reutern-

Nolcken, the Marshal of the Courland nobility, it is true, sent a letter of refutation to the *Novoe Vremia*, but it ought to have been sent directly after the appearance of the first aggressive articles; besides, the letter was not skilfully indited, and was by no means convincing. The Marshal of the Livonian nobility, Baron Pilar von Pylchau, appealed to the Emperor. In the name of the nobility of which he was the leader, he assured the monarch of their feelings of loyalty and submission, observing that under the circumstances, while hundreds of young Baltic Germans were shedding their blood for Russia, and showing their devotion to their country and their Tzar, this unwarranted persecution seemed as unjust as it was unmerited. Baron Pilar himself was amongst the bereaved fathers, for one of his sons, an officer in the Chevalier Guards Regiment, had been killed in one of the first battles.

The newspapers, nevertheless, continued their attacks; they collected all kinds of gossip, and every day some sensational disclosure appeared about the Baltic Germans.

The peasants and simple inhabitants of Livonia and Courland are mostly Letts, who hate the Germans for years of oppression. They were glad of the opportunity to revenge their wrongs, and were none too scrupulous in the methods they adopted.

The Letts are at present most ardent in their protestations of devotion to Russia, but in reality in their hearts they like neither Germans nor Russians. Their dream is to acquire the land belonging to the German proprietors, and form a small Lettish republic, ruled by their own people. The Russians have implicit faith in the loyalty of the Letts, and public opinion is inclined to make heroes of them. People have forgotten their behaviour in 1905–6, when, hidden in ambush, they shot Russian officials, and ostentatiously filed out of church when the pastor began the usual prayers for the Tzar and the Imperial Family.

In consequence of all this, the relations between the Russians and the Baltic Germans are very strained, and this has had a harmful effect upon the patriotism they manifested prior to this outburst of antagonism. The fear of being molested in Russia has driven many of the well-intentioned Baltic Germans to Sweden, where they will remain till the war is over.

At one time there was a great tendency for Russian Germans to change their names. The Imperial Chancery for Requests was overwhelmed with such petitions. This was the opportunity of a lifetime for the Hebrews; they hastened to get rid of their Jewish-

SHADES OF THE PRESENT

sounding patronymics and to blossom into descendants of boyar races.

A wicked but amusing story was related about this changing of names. An important official in the Foreign Office, boasting of a high-sounding, historical German name, was asked if he had the intention of changing it? 'I did think of it,' was the prompt answer. 'I wanted to take the name of Romanoff, but I was forestalled by the Holstein-Gothorps.'

Chapter VII

THE TZAR AND HIS GENERALS

NOT the slightest responsibility can be attached to the Russian Sovereign for having provoked this devastating war, entailing such terrible bloodshed, disaster and misery. The Tzar's love of peace is universally acknowledged, he did all in his power to avert the calamity of a European conflagration. Till the last the monarch, as well as his subjects, believed in the sincerity of Kaiser Wilhelm's mediation. It has since been proved that Austria wished to give way to Russia, but that Germany prevented her. It can also be proved that all German male subjects in Russia liable to military service were urgently recalled back to Germany *seven days before the declaration of war*. Germany and the German Kaiser have been the instigators of this war, let the curse of its many victims lie on their head!

Once the die was cast the Tzar became a transformed man. He revealed an energy, an activity and a firmness of purpose that no one expected. During the first months his activity was limited to occasional visits to the different fronts and frequent journeys all over the country to visit the various war hospitals. Only those who have seen the Emperor at the bedside of the wounded soldier have had a glimpse into the real self of Nicholas II. His expressive mobile features betray the strong feeling that moves him when he approaches a desperate case or a hopeless cripple. The sympathy and understanding shown by His Majesty at such times are womanly in their depth of tenderness and pity.

It is in a hospital ward that his beautiful nature reveals itself fully. Upon entering the Tzar's first question to the chief doctor invariably is: 'How many hopeless cases have you here?' Then according to the doctor's answer the Sovereign takes the required number of St. George's crosses, going up to each dying soldier with words of consolation and gratitude, pinning the cross on to the wounded man's shirt. In doing this it must not be thought that the Tzar acts merely from motives of sentiment just to gratify a dying soldier. He is actuated by the thought that the cross means an increased pension for the hero's bereaved family, and that many a man's dying moments are eased by knowing that his dear ones will not be destitute.

In Vilna the Emperor was told of two hundred desperate cases. His Majesty entered the ward of the dying and visited each of the two hundred men, bringing them their last reward. One of the wounded men was sinking fast, the death agony had set in, and the doctor wished to prevent the Emperor from witnessing this painful sight. The Emperor remained firm, however, and approached the pallet of the dying soldier. Pale to the lips, with sorrowful eyes, heavy with unshed tears, the Tzar gazed upon the dying soldier. Stooping, he made the sign of the cross, blessed the man hovering on the verge of eternity and pinned the St. George's cross on to his coverlet. This war has taught the soldiers to love their Sovereign – the wounded worship him.

In Kiev three sisters of mercy, hearing of the monarch's presence, ran out to catch a glimpse of him. The Emperor noticed them, and, approaching, spoke to them in his kind, courteous way, questioning them about their work, their experiences and impressions. One of the sisters, Mlle. G., told him that she had worked in Livoff and only left the town when it was evacuated. The Emperor listened with interest to the details she gave him. He then remarked: 'But how is it you have not got the St. George medal?' And turning to General Ivanoff: 'We must amend this omission.' General Ivanoff was personally acquainted with Mlle. G. and was aware of her brave conduct and self-abnegation. He told His Majesty that 'Sister G.' indeed merited this recompense. The medal was instantly produced and pinned on by the Emperor himself to the overjoyed sister's apron. When she attempted to thank the Tzar, she was quickly interrupted by His Majesty: 'It is I who owe you thanks for nursing my brave, wounded soldiers with such devotion.'

In relating this episode to her mother, Mlle. G. said that the Emperor was so simple in his manner and looked at her so kindly that she quite forgot she was speaking to the Sovereign, and felt no embarrassment or restraint. It was only when the incident was over that she felt frightened at her own temerity in having spoken so unceremoniously with the Tzar.

The change in the chief command of the Russian army was effected in the course of August, 1915, and was followed by the appointment of the Grand Duke Nicholas to the Vice-Royalty of the Caucasus. The removal of the Grand Duke from the principal front was received with mixed feelings. In military and political circles it was welcomed with relief, but the public at large, who had pinned its faith on the Grand Duke's valour and strength of mind, were dismayed and ascribed the change to the ascendancy of the German party. His Imperial Highness had always been a popular man in Russia.

His late father, the field-marshal, Grand Duke Nicholas senior, had been an adored chief of the Russian army, as well beloved by the superior officers as by the rank and file. Some of his popularity had descended to his son, but during the first months of the war Nicholas junior was regarded as a sort of demigod. The people were intoxicated by the first successes achieved.

No more popular and admired member of the Imperial Family existed than the Grand Duke Nicholas.

His position as Commander-in-Chief of the Russian army, his noble, energetic attitude and the successes he achieved made him the cynosure of all eyes. Every Russian eye anxiously turned to him, and in the early days of the war all Russia's hopes were centred in him.

Very tall and imposing in figure, he was always considered 'a chip off the old block'. In Russia a stalwart stature has a great deal to do in calling forth enthusiasm and admiration. The national ideal of manhood, heroism and valour is represented by the 'bogatyr' (the hero of all the old Russian ballads and legends). It seems paradoxical to say such a thing in the twentieth century, but in this country a tall man with a commanding air has many more chances of appealing to people's hearts and gaining popularity than a short one. Napoleon would never have achieved his brilliant career in Russia. The Grand Duke Nicholas is a typical soldier, a great sportsman and shines more in the hunting field than in a ballroom. His wife, the Grand Duchess Anastasia Nicolaïevna, is the eldest daughter of the King of Montenegro. They lead a secluded life and seldom appear in society. Their intercourse with the Emperor and Empress has always been very cordial and friendly. At one time the Grand Duke Nicholas used

THE TZAR AND HIS GENERALS

to be very much interested in spiritualism, and it was rumoured that several times a week an intimate circle of believers, including the Emperor and his Consort, assembled at the Grand Duke's town palace, and spent hours in table rapping and in consulting the spirits of the dead. The best mediums were invited to the Palace, and it was reported that the spirit of the late Emperor Alexander III appeared at these sittings, and when any serious change in the Government was impending this spirit was always consulted by the Emperor. The Dowager Empress did not approve of these spiritualistic meetings, and at one time there was a decided coolness between her and the Grand Duchess Anastasia.

The great merit of the Grand Duke Nicholas is his care for the soldier's welfare. In this he is superior to his father, who put too much trust in the commissariat officers. No rogues are tolerated by the present Grand Duke, who made it perfectly clear that any abuses in the provisioning of the army would be regarded as high treason and as such severely punished. The soldiers were, and continue to be, well fed and admirably clothed. At one time there was a scarcity of boots, but the want has been supplied. There never yet was a war during which the soldiers were so well cared for as the present one. The inhabitants of the towns may have lacked meat, and at times there was a scarcity of sugar, wheatmeal, groats, etc., but the army has continued to be well supplied with the best of everything. It is therefore only natural that the Grand Duke should be popular with the soldiers. His generals, however, were not so enthusiastic. They were not given the free hand they desired, and they thought the Grand Duke not sufficiently discriminating in his appreciation of merit. He was never considered intellectual. He has a passionate nature, and he was always known to be somewhat gruff in his manner. His firmness of purpose, his detractors aver, borders on stubbornness and prevents him from acknowledging a mistake. But in the character of Commander-in-Chief his strength of will was a quality, and his straightforwardness was also in his favour.

When General Joffre came to Russia a few years ago, a plan of a possible war resulting from Germany's aggression was worked out between him and the Grand Duke, and France wanted the Grand Duke to be at the head of the Russian army to ensure the carrying out of this plan. Indeed his nomination was generally approved of, and his prestige as a member of the Imperial Family had a great significance for the soldiers.

The tendency on the part of all to regard the Stavka (Headquarters) as the hub round which Russia revolved soon began to attract attention. Ministers were for ever going back and forth to consult the Grand Duke on affairs not by any means coming within the scope of the duties of a Commander-in-Chief. The Grand Duke must sometimes have wondered whether he were a soldier or a politician.

The Grand Duke is reproached with having attempted the campaign of Galicia in 1914-15 without being sure of his ability to remain there. The great mistake, it is argued, was the attempt to cross the Carpathians when, as Commander-in-Chief, he ought to have been aware that the Russian army was lacking in ammunition. He should have stopped after taking Przemysl.

It is said there was a moment, after the surrender of Przemysl to the Russians, when Roumania wished to join the fray and send her army to help the Russians against Austria, stipulating that Bukhovina should be given to Roumania. At that time no important decision was taken by the Government without consulting the Grand Duke, so M. Sazonoff journeyed to the Stavka and laid Roumania's proposition before the Commander-in-Chief; but the Grand Duke is said to have been opposed to the project as the Russian army would attain its object unaided. M. Sazonoff is reproached that he failed in his Balkan politics, but the only accusation that can be brought against him is that he was not steadfast enough in carrying out his own points of view.

When war began and Turkey was obviously playing a fast and loose game, Russia wanted to send a naval squadron to the Bosphorus as a threat, but one among Russia's allies advised M. Sazonoff not to have recourse to such violent measures, which would certainly produce a most unfavourable impression on the neutral countries. M. Sazonoff's great mistake was to consult anybody but his Emperor.

One of the reproaches directed against those responsible for the conduct of the war in the early days is that many of our fortresses were not in a proper condition to resist the German avalanche, and that their commanders were not the right men; but whatever the truth of this none can question the glorious heroism of the Russian army, officers and men.

A series of reverses followed one after the other; Warsaw and Vilna were evacuated, our troops retreated from Galicia, and though from a military point of view this retreat is considered a

THE TZAR AND HIS GENERALS

remarkable feat of strategy and valour, yet people must be excused if they did not appreciate the brilliant fulfilment of the plan, but rather deplored the need for the sudden withdrawal of the conquering Russian army. These reverses, coming after the successes we had achieved, were bitterly felt. A change was inevitable. The Tzar wrote a beautiful letter to his uncle expressing his gratitude for the services which His Imperial Highness had rendered, but observing that the recent reverses proved that all was not as it should be. The Tzar was responsible before his people for the development and final issue of the war, and, this being the case, he considered it his duty to be in close touch with his army in order that he might hear every report and, in crucial moments, take decisions for which he alone was responsible. For this reason the Tzar deemed it advisable to take the Chief Command into his own hands. In conclusion the post of Viceroy of the Caucasus was offered to the Grand Duke.

This letter was delivered to His Imperial Highness by General Polivanoff, who at that time was Minister of War. At Headquarters the letter produced the effect of a shell exploding. The Grand Duke showed himself to be a true Russian by accepting the Tzar's decision without question and proceeding to the Caucasus, where later he made himself felt.

The Emperor fills the post of Commander-in-Chief with marvellous wisdom and tact. He enters personally into every detail, everything is reported and explained to him; he carefully examines plans and studies all hypothetical movements; but His Majesty never obtrudes, he only discusses, leaving the initiative to more skilled and experienced strategists. The active, open-air life suits the Tzar, and lately he has wonderfully improved in health and personal appearance. The atmosphere of the Headquarters is magnificent. Everyone is devoted to the Emperor and determined to win the war.

In urgent cases, if a general receives an order that he does not deem adaptable to his position at the moment, he can safely venture upon a remonstrance without fear of being treated as a defaulter. The following incident happened a few months ago. General B. received a telegram from the Commander-in-Chief containing orders which astounded him. He hesitated, knowing the fatal consequences of acquiescence, and the danger to himself of disobeying such a peremptory command. He resolved, however, to take the risk, and instead of carrying out the prescribed movement he hastened to Headquarters and asked for an audience. When he was in the Sovereign's presence the General, after excusing himself for not having obeyed the order, went on to say:

'But has your Majesty reflected upon the danger if I had executed the flank movement Your Majesty ordered? It would have uncovered part of the northern front and given an opening to the enemy.'

The Emperor stared in surprise, so did General Alexeieff, the Chief of the Imperial Staff.

'What order do you mean?' queried the astonished Tzar. 'We have sent you no wire.'

It turned out that the incriminating telegram was an ingenious German forgery, sent for the purpose of facilitating their attempt to break through the Russian front. General B., owing to his wisdom and courage, saved the Russian army from a dreadful disaster. General Alexeieff was aghast. The Emperor, deeply moved, repeatedly thanked the astute General for not having acted rashly.

The result of the present system is that military plans are worked out with care, forethought and talent. General Broussiloff, the hero of the recent movement, owes the wonderful success his army achieved on the western front to the wisdom of a deeply thought-out plan, brilliantly executed by this valiant commander.

Nearly two years of war have produced in Russia several distinguished generals and many brave officers. Heroic deeds have been numerous. Some of our army leaders have shown brilliant talent and remarkable courage, but unfortunately Russia was not prepared for war, and we had no Lord Kitchener, or anybody equal to him in genius to organise. Experience and adversity have taught us many bitter lessons, but, owing to the wonderful spirit and endurance of the Russian soldier, the former mistakes have proved a blessing in disguise, for they are leading the way to success.

When the war commenced, the Russian War Minister was General Soukhomlinoff. Under his guidance the mobilisation plan was carried out in a masterly way, and all went smoothly and swiftly, without a single disturbing incident. After this feat, the general confidence in the War Minister increased. During the mobilisation days the sale of alcoholic drinks was strictly prohibited. This measure proved so efficacious that it has been continued, with the result that cases of intoxication are at present exceptional.

When the Minister was consulted about the quantity of munitions on hand, he not only replied that there was more than enough, but refused Japan's offer to supply Russia with more. The problem of solving General Soukhomlinoff's case, from a private point of view, is as difficult as it is complicated, for very little has been given out officially. I shall therefore endeavour to give an unbiassed narrative of all particulars relating to this unfortunate General, and leave any English readers to form their own impression.

General Soukhomlinoff belongs to a good middle-class family, moderately endowed with wealth, who succeeded in attaining the summit of a military career. For several years prior to his appointment as War Minister he was the Governor-General of Kiev. Here he made the acquaintance of his future wife, and, subsequently, at the age of sixty-one, contracted a marriage which gave rise to a great deal of gossip.

Madame Soukhomlinoff is a good-looking, sympathetic, clever woman of Hebrew origin. She is one of those small, slight, well-proportioned women, who have more womanly grace than actual beauty. At a first glance, she seems insignificant, not even pretty, but her attractions seem to grow upon one; she does not dazzle but she fascinates, and knows how to keep a strong hand over men.

Mlle. Gashkevitch (that was Madame Soukhomlinoff's maiden name) commenced her career as a copyist in a notary's office in Kiev, where she had the opportunity of coming in contact with her first husband M. Boutovitch, a wealthy landowner from the south of Russia. The marriage turned out a failure, and Mme. Boutovitch obtained a divorce from her unwilling husband. The General's marriage with Mme. Boutovitch took place seven years ago, when he had just been appointed Minister of War. Society began by holding aloof and looking askance at the Minister's wife, but her tactful attitude, her graceful ways, her elegance and, above all, her perfectly ordered dinner-parties overcame all obstacles.

A year or two before the war a startling article appeared in the *Vetchernoe Vremia*, accusing Colonel Miassoyedoff of suspicious transactions on the Prussian frontier. This accusation was supported by so serious a person as M. Gretchkoff, an influential member of the Duma. A great hue and cry was raised, but General

Soukhomlinoff silenced everyone by his staunch defence of Miassoyedoff's rectitude, vouching for his innocence and integrity. The whole affair ended in a scandal at a race meeting. Colonel Miassoyedoff knocked Boris Souvorine's (the editor of the *Vetchernoe Vremia*) hat off and a duel ensued. Subsequent events proved, however, that the accusation was unfounded and that the Colonel had been for years in the Kaiser's pay.

Madame Soukhomlinoff attained the pinnacle of her ambition during the first months of the war. A born organiser she soon became the centre of practical activity on behalf of the wounded. For a time she was the dispenser of work in the Winter Palace; later on she started her own depot, and daily work was carried on at her apartments. Madame Soukhomlinoff organised hospital trains and went to the station at all hours to meet the wounded and superintend their assignment to different hospitals. She quite entered into the role of a War Minister's wife, and displayed an amazing energy and extraordinary organising capabilities, which were universally acknowledged and admired. The papers were full of Madame Soukhomlinoff's activity; her kindness to the soldiers, her solicitude for the wounded.

The first blow fell when Colonel Miassoyedoff was arrested for high treason. Strange to say his treachery was not discovered in this country. It was General Pau who brought the proofs of the Colonel's dealings with the enemy. His guilt had transpired through some compromising documents that had been found on dead German officers, and amongst the belongings of the prisoners of war in France. Six hundred thousand roubles were found in Miassoyedoff's private safe in German gold; the trial proved his guilt. The whole country shuddered with shame and indignation on hearing that a respected member of society, a soldier bearing a Russian name, had transgressed in such a dastardly manner and had been convicted of treason to the Tzar and the country. It was discovered, during the trial, that the Colonel's wife was a German Jewess, and she was indirectly involved in her husband's disgusting affairs. Miassoyedoff was hanged and his wife exiled, but the burden of shame fell on their innocent children, a son and a daughter. The boy was a cadet in a military college, but his comrades refused to have a traitor's son in their midst. He had to be removed to another military college, and, to avoid persecution from the other cadets, he was permitted to use another name. The daughter was engaged to be married, but her fiancé would not wed a traitor's daughter, so the match was broken off. Bereft of love, honour, family, shunned and looked down upon by her former friends and acquaintances, the poor girl leads a miserable and solitary life, trying to hide from everyone. Whilst loathing the father's crime, one cannot help being sorry for these unhappy children, who, I have been told, feel their disgrace terribly.

Miassoyedoff's conviction and condemnation was bound to react fatally on the position of General Soukhomlinoff. The Colonel had been on intimate terms with him and his wife; he had enjoyed General Soukhomlinoff's support and patronage. People recalled to memory the old story of the newspaper article, and how the Minister had put himself forward as Miassoyedoff's guarantor. There was an atmosphere of suspicion. When it was known that our progress in Galicia had to be suspended through want of munitions and that the war, so auspiciously commenced by brilliant feats and important conquests, was turning into a series of reverses, because our soldiers could not parry the enemy's attacks for want of arms and munitions, then suspicion increased. General Soukhomlinoff was dismissed from office, but remained in the Emperor's suite and retained his seat in the Upper Chamber. A few months later he received his total dismissal, and an enquiry was instituted into his work as Minister of War.

When General Soukhomlinoff relinquished his portfolio as War Minister, his wife ceased her work on behalf of the wounded. The valuable stores in her depot were given over, in perfect order, to the Dowager Empress, as well as 700,000 roubles that remained in the cash-box.

The result of the enquiry, which was entrusted to the Senate, was a perquisition at General Soukhomlinoff's domicile, carried out in the presence of the Senator who presided over the enquiry. It lasted several hours and was followed by an interrogation of General and Madame Soukhomlinoff, at the end of which the former War Minister was arrested and incarcerated in the fortress of St. Peter and St. Paul. All the General's papers, letters and documents were confiscated and carried away in four huge chests. Madame Soukhomlinoff made frantic efforts to have her husband liberated on bail, but this was firmly declined. This is all that is known at present. The enquiry is being continued in haste, but no one knows when the trial will take place. The General, meanwhile, is busily preparing his defence. He says that his only fault was an error of judgement in not foreseeing the gigantic dimensions of the coming war, a fault, adds the General, shared by our allies, who likewise did not think the war would attain to such formidable developments. In justice to him it must be remembered that even the Germans themselves underestimated the expenditure of ammunition. The Grand Duke Serge Mikhailovitch, who was the Chief Commander of the Artillery department, at the time of the declaration of war, had been dangerously ill for many weeks and was not expected to live. This was an unfortunate circumstance, as his help and advice would have been invaluable. The Grand Duke Serge has since done a great deal to improve our artillery; all the new innovations were introduced into the Russian army owing to his intervention, and under his able command the artillery has distinguished itself by its skill and great courage, which at present is astonishing the world.

The assistant War Minister, General Polivanoff, was appointed successor to General Soukhomlinoff. During the few months of General Polivanoff's work at the War Office, he did a great deal towards establishing the munition factories on a proper footing. All the available manufactories were put in motion to produce rifles, munitions, etc.; work went on unceasingly day and night, with three shifts of workers receiving very high wages.

General Polivanoff was certainly energetic, but he was not a popular man, and the Emperor was not prepossessed in his favour. Then came the time of the reopening of the Duma, in the early winter of 1915, when M. Goremykine was still Prime Minister. The War Minister's attitude towards the Duma provoked displeasure, for he visibly sought its good graces, conforming his speeches and some of his plans in accordance with its wishes. This was resented in high quarters. The General's doom was sealed, though he lingered on for a few months longer, quite unsuspicious of his coming fate. He received his dismissal in the following manner. The Emperor was at Headquarters, and General Polivanoff had sent in the usual weekly report, and some papers to which the Commander-in-Chief's sanction had to be obtained. When the papers came back the Minister found among them a note written in the Tzar's own hand.

'Two ukases to be prepared and sent to Headquarters:

'No. 1. Appointing General Schouvaieff Minister of War.

THE TZAR AND HIS GENERALS

'No. 2. Relieving General Polivanoff from the duties of War Minister and thanking him for his faultless fulfilment of them and for his untiring zeal.'

Up to this moment General Schouvaieff had been at the head of the war-intendantships. He is renowned for his honesty and trustworthiness. Under his wise administration the intendancy was perfectly managed and revealed none of the hateful abuse of former wars. General Schouvaieff has done his best to impress his subordinates with the same principles of integrity, though it seems questionable if the worthy general's endeavours have met with entire success.

The new Minister of War is elderly. He was never a brilliant man, but as the administration of the War Office is at present reduced to the management of economic matters, General Schouvaieff is sure to fill the post to everyone's satisfaction.

Amongst the Russian commanders, General Ivanoff must be regarded as one of the best. A clever strategist, an able leader, himself as brave as a lion, he knows how to arouse heroism in the troops under his command. Last year's campaign in Galicia was mostly carried out according to the General's plans. He was in command of the South-Western Army, and wherever he led his men success followed. The soldiers adore their chief and believe implicitly in him. A subtle bond of sympathy unites them, for by birth he belongs to the ranks.

Many years ago, during a review in the presence of Alexander II, a soldier met with an accident. The injured man was carried to the nearest hospital, and the Emperor followed. The case was hopeless, and the Tzar approached the dying man, inquiring if he had any dispositions to make, or any wish to formulate. The soldier said he was leaving a motherless son of about eleven years old, who would henceforth be destitute, and with his dying breath he confided his son to the Tzar. The Sovereign solemnly promised to take care of the boy, and with a sigh of relief the soldier expired. The Emperor kept his word. He sent for the lad and had him placed in one of the numerous cadet corps, where he was educated at His Majesty's expense. This boy was the future General Ivanoff. Talent and capacity helped to pave his way to a remarkably distinguished career.

The Grand Duke Nicholas did not appreciate General Ivanoff at his full value, and did not get on with him at all, indeed many breezy passages passed between the former Commander-in-Chief and his General. But the Emperor had a sincere liking for General Ivanoff, which, since the war, has deepened into profound regard and admiration. During recent months General Ivanoff has given up the command of the South-Western Army and is attached to the Tzar's person. He resides now at Headquarters, and is one of the Sovereign's chief advisers, and most of the plans of campaign are the work of his brain.

Some time has elapsed since General Kouropatkine re-entered active service. I am aware that the English have a very favourable opinion of this ill-fated General. His reverses in Manchuria are ascribed to the fact of his being handicapped by orders and counter-orders from Petrograd.

Many years ago, when our favourite modern hero, 'the White General' (Skobeleff), was still alive, and Kouropatkine – then a quite young man – was his orderly officer, General Skobeleff gave him the following piece of advice: 'Misha,' said the General, 'you are brave, you are clever and practical; you are entitled to a distinguished military career, but beware of ever taking upon yourself the leadership of troops, for you do not possess a single quality that makes a successful commander. You lack initiative, you are not gifted with unhesitating firmness of resolve and you never know "the right moment". Bear my advice in mind, you will never succeed as a commander.'

These words were spoken in 1878, at the time of the war between Russia and Turkey . . . and they have proved prophetic. General Kouropatkine is a gifted strategist, a wise administrator, but he is not an inspired leader of an army.

At present the General is one of the Staff at Headquarters. Specialists acknowledge his distinguished strategic gifts.

The hero of the present moment is General Broussiloff. His portraits are everywhere, in shop windows, in illustrated magazines, on the tables of hero-worshippers and the newspapers are full of his prowess. But he has honestly merited this widespread fame. General Broussiloff possesses most of the qualities of a great commander. He is a born leader. He has unbounded ascendancy over the soldiers under his command, who look up to him with adoration, mingled with awe, and unlimited confidence. The General has the rare power of electrifying his men and inciting them to feats of the greatest daring.

General Broussiloff was brought up in the Pages' Cadet Corps (Corps des Pages) in Petrograd, and afterwards entered a dragoon regiment quartered at Iver. As a young officer he attracted the notice of the late Inspector-General of Cavalry, Toutolmine, who gave him an influential helping hand. Nearly the whole of his career was spent in the officers' cavalry school in Petrograd, and subsequently he succeeded General Soukhomlinoff (the former War Minister, now incarcerated in the fortress) as director of this school. Before the war he commanded an army corps in the district of Odessa.

General Broussiloff has lately been promoted to the highest military position in the Emperor's suite, that of Adjutant-General.

He has been married twice. His first wife, née Hagemeister, died leaving a son, an officer of the Horse Grenadiers of the Guards, at present on one of the fronts. His second wife, née Telecheff, is of a good old Russian family.

The following episode is an instance of the magical influence he wields. Some time ago, prior to our recent successes, the Austrians attacked a position occupied by the Russians. Our forces were insignificant in comparison to the enemy's. The officer in command, deciding that the Russians could not hold out much longer, sent an orderly to General Broussiloff to explain matters and demand instructions. The General listened attentively. 'I will answer directly, but I have suddenly remembered some important business that I cannot put off. I shall soon be back; wait for me here.' With these words the General left the room, called for his horse and, without saying a word to anyone, rode off to the threatened position. The General's unexpected arrival stimulated the soldiers wonderfully and encouraged them to hold out. He remained the whole night and convinced them that their position was not at all desperate. The Austrians, seeing this firm attitude, felt sure the Russians had received reinforcements and beat a hasty retreat. In the morning General Broussiloff returned to his staff, where the messenger was impatiently waiting for the answer that was no more required.

After months of defensive warfare General Broussiloff led his army on to attack the enemy, and achieved a brilliant victory. The Russians broke through the Austrian front and put the enemy to flight, taking tens of thousands of prisoners. The Austrian fortifications, on which they had worked for over three months and which they believed impregnable, were swept away before the devastating fire of the Russian artillery. Tchernovitzy, Kolomya, the Tchartorysky fortifications, and several minor forts surrendered, and the Russian army successfully crossed the river Styr.

Many Russian generals are covering their names with glory during this war. General Russky – the hero of Livoff in the autumn of 1914 – has at present left active service. His health and nerves gave way under the continual strain; he was obliged to undergo a serious cure in the Caucasus, and is now enjoying complete calm and repose in the country. He is considered one of the best and ablest commanders, and it is hoped that his restored health will soon permit him to rejoin the army. General Evert and General Letchitsky have gained laurels on the Austrian frontier. General Selivanoff, to whom Przemysl surrendered in the spring of 1915; General Rodkevitch, the hero of some remarkable feats of courage; besides many others, will have their names immortalised in the future annals of this war.

One of our most valiant army leaders is a Bulgarian. General Radko-Dmitrieff was the Bulgarian Minister-Resident in Petrograd, who gave up his diplomatic career when the war began, and hastened to buckle on his sword in the service of Russia. The General is not the only Bulgarian fighting in the Russian ranks. The son of the former Bulgarian Minister of the Interior, Captain Lutzkanoff-Tzankoff, hurried over to Russia, where he had received a first-class military education, as soon as the first battles were fought. A little while ago Captain Lutzkanoff-Tzankoff married Mlle. Marie Ermoloff, a maid of honour, daughter of the former Minister of Agriculture and Secretary of State. After a short honeymoon the bridegroom returned to his regiment, and his bride followed him as a sister of mercy to work in one of the nearest war hospitals. Captain Lutzkanoff-Tzankoff's brother-in-law, M. Patoff, had spent several years in Petrograd as the Secretary of the Bulgarian Legation, but when King Ferdinand struck out a personal line of politics, which threatened to become treacherous, M. Patoff gave up his diplomatic career, installed himself and his family permanently in Petrograd, and obtained a lucrative post in one of the leading banks. This proves how averse many of the Bulgarians are to their King's fatal subjection to Germany.

Meanwhile the Grand Duke Nicholas's activity in the Caucasus has been very productive of success. He has with him General Youdenitch. The attacks on the Turkish army have resulted in the taking of Erzerum and Trebizond, and in the progress of the

THE TZAR AND HIS GENERALS

Russian army towards Mesopotamia, where the Russian vanguards have succeeded in getting into touch with the forces of our brave British ally.

Twelve years ago General Youdenitch distinguished himself during the war with Japan. He is an experienced soldier, and it is for the second time that he is successfully fighting in his present locality. As a promising subaltern, thirty-eight years ago, the present army leader took part in the assault of Erzerum in 1878. The full powers of the General are somewhat extended: he has a free hand to act as he thinks best.

The working out of plans and decisions in the Stavka continues in the most active and amicable way, the Emperor judiciously maintaining the equilibrium between the generals. The august presence is extremely beneficial. The Tzar finds relaxation from labour in daily walks. One of the generals usually accompanies His Majesty, but these excursions on foot are not appreciated by the worthy generals, for the Sovereign is a remarkable pedestrian, and few of the generals care for this exercise. One day the Emperor wished personally to ascertain the weight of the soldier's equipment during a military march. He got a soldier's uniform, plain, high boots, a knapsack filled with the usual things a soldier must carry, took a rifle and started on a walk of ten versts. Thus disguised no one recognised the Tzar, who duly saluted every officer he met.

The Emperor often takes his son with him to Headquarters. The Tzessarevitch is delighted to be with his father, he takes a keen and intelligent interest in all that is going on, and accompanies the Tzar on visits to hospitals, and on such occasions it is the little Grand Duke who hands the medals of St. George to the wounded soldiers. This life at Headquarters has a salutary influence on the Imperial boy, for it teaches him discipline and brings him into contact with real life. His studies do not suffer in the least, for his French tutor and a Russian master accompany him. The boy's health is wonderfully improved; he has lost the old wan look, and seems a sturdy little fellow dressed in khaki, with the most intelligent and winning face. He finds great pleasure in talking to soldiers who have been in battle, and eagerly listens to their tales. He has endeared himself to all at the Headquarters, and has lost most of his overbearing ways. There is not a single man among the most serious and crotchety of the generals who considers the boy's presence a nuisance.

Chapter VIII

THE TZAR'S DAUGHTERS AND SOME OTHER MEMBERS OF THE IMPERIAL FAMILY

THE Tzar's daughters are bright, intelligent girls who learn quickly, and acquired the average amount of knowledge a well-bred young lady of the twentieth century should possess. They are good linguists and have many accomplishments. They have been carefully taught to sew, and are efficient in all kinds of embroidery and artwork. They draw and paint and are musical. The Empress had them well instructed in all branches of science, literature and art. They generally speak Russian, which is due to their mother's influence. In Alexander III's reign, notwithstanding his true Russian feelings, the language mostly spoken in his family was English, for the Dowager Empress spoke the language of the nation with difficulty. Her daughter-in-law, on the contrary, learnt Russian easily, and made it a rule for the Imperial children to speak their own tongue. Mlle. Sophie Tutchev – a maid of honour – was appointed governess to the two elder Grand Duchesses, but after a few years' service she suddenly threw up her appointment, because she did not get on with one of the Empress's new favourites, who made too free of the schoolroom, and, as remonstrances were unheeded, she preferred to quit the Court. It was a great pity, for Mlle. Tutchev was eminently suited to the position, and her influence upon her young charges was a good one. Since then the Grand Duchesses have had no personal attendant, and when they go out and about they are accompanied by one of their mother's maids of honour.

THE TZAR'S DAUGHTERS

Among her own family the Empress stands on a pedestal; love, homage and admiration are lavishly bestowed upon her by husband and children. The daughters are very attentive to their mother, and when the Empress is ill their care and anxiety are unbounded.

The Empress is subject to cardiac cramps, caused by a nervous affection in the region of the heart. The Sovereign once asked a lady if she knew the feeling of cramp in the leg. 'Well,' continued the Empress, 'that is precisely what I am continually feeling in my heart.' For this reason all exercise is forbidden, and at times the Empress is not even allowed to walk.

One day a high functionary from the provinces was accorded an audience by the monarch. At the appointed time he made his entrance into the Palace of Tzarskoe Selo and was ushered into the waiting-room, adjacent to the Tzar's study. One of the Court officials informed him that His Majesty was in the park and he would have to wait a few moments. The sound of voices and laughter reached the ears of the gentleman, and he stepped to the window, which opened on to the park, to see where the voices came from. Suddenly this picture disclosed itself to his eyes: the Empress sitting in a huge swan on wheels – a plaything probably of the Grand Duke Alexis – the Emperor pulling the swan in front, the Tzessarevitch pushing it from behind, and the girls running on in front, throwing flowers and leaves before them. They were all laughing merrily, looking so gay and full of fun, unsuspicious that they were being observed. In describing this little family idyll, the gentleman declared that he felt quite moved and had seldom seen a prettier sight.

The Empress has endeavoured to suppress all feeling of self-consciousness in her children, which in nine cases out of ten causes the painful shyness that assails bashful people, and at times makes life a misery to them. From their infancy the Grand Duchesses were used to free intercourse with all the people who surrounded their parents. They talk pleasantly to everyone, and take a lively interest in all that is going on. No holding aloof entered into the scheme of their education. It is therefore not to be wondered at that the two Grand Duchesses, who are now grown up, converse without any embarrassment, and are charming and simple in their manner. Both take an ardent interest in their own institutions, organised to meet the requirements of the present moment.

The Grand Duchess Olga is the patroness of a committee to give help to the families of reservists who were called back to active service when the war broke out. Every Wednesday the Grand Duchess Olga, accompanied by her sister Tatiana (the two sisters are always seen together), adjourn to the Winter Palace; here in one of the ancestral halls Her Imperial Highness receives the gifts brought to her, consisting of money or clothes. She takes the offerings, graciously thanks the donor, and in the most businesslike way hands a written acknowledgement for the articles received. She would not be her mother's child if she did not take her duties seriously. It is therefore natural that the Grand Duchess should reveal great energy and eagerness to help deserving cases, so plentiful at present. Children are clothed and placed in schools, mothers receive assistance, and all is done to lighten their burdens. This organisation spreads all over the country, but the Central Committee sits in Petrograd. The Grand Duchess Tatiana's Committee gives help to the unfortunate people who have had to leave the provinces where the war is waging. Enormous sums have been collected to relieve the misery of those unhappy people, many of whom have lost everything. Homes have been founded to shelter them; soup kitchens established to give them food; infant asylums and refuges instituted for boys and girls, where they can be taught a trade, etc., all of which are maintained by the 'Tatiana Committee', as it is called. The Grand Duchess presides personally at the meetings of the committee, and everything is referred to her. A member of the Upper House, M. A. B. Neidhardt, is the chief administrator of this organisation.

The Grand Duchess Olga is more stately and reposeful in manner than her sister, and is more dignified in her graciousness; but the Grand Duchess Tatiana is most winning with her vivacity, and the mischievous sparkle in her eyes is irresistible. As a child Tatiana was full of pranks and mischief. A few years ago, when the Imperial Family was visiting Moscow, the children were sent home from a review, which they had been taken to see, whilst the Emperor and his Consort went on somewhere else.

The carriage was an open one and it was very windy. The little girls had to hold on their hats to prevent them being blown off. The Imperial equipage was recognised by the crowd, and the Grand Duchesses, holding on their hats with both hands, bowed right and left, as they had been taught to, in answer to the flourishing salutes they received. At first the Grand Duchess Tatiana was amused, and she bowed and laughed and looked delighted, but after a while she grew tired and looked cross, bobbing her head like a Chinese Mandarin, until at last she gave it up, dropped her hands and put out her tongue at the bowing crowd. This childish outbreak was received with a delighted roar of laughter and the exclamation: 'Just like our own children!' The Grand Duchess Olga cast a reproachful glance at her naughty sister, who blushed scarlet, looking half mutinous, half ashamed. An eye-witness declared it was a most amusing scene, vastly appreciated by the crowd.

From their childhood the Grand Duchesses were accustomed to shake hands with ladies and give their hand to be kissed by gentlemen. This chivalrous tribute appealed especially to the Grand Duchess Tatiana, who as a child never lost an opportunity of bringing herself under general notice. In the course of one of the Sovereign's journeys through the country, the little girls were left in the train at the station whilst the Sovereigns attended some function in town. People, curious to see the Imperial children, assembled in front of the carriage allotted to the nursery. Little Tatiana came to the window, but she could not reach high enough to look out, so she climbed on to a footstool and calmly surveyed the people. At first she smiled and looked coyly at them, then she diffidently put out her hand, giving it to the lady standing nearest. The delighted lady kissed the chubby little paw, so confidingly held out; this was the signal for all others to come forward, and the seven-year-old Tatiana gave her hand to every individual of the assembled group. It was a most amusing incident, and the Emperor, when he heard of it, considered it a great joke that the Grand Duchess Tatiana had held her first reception.

The Grand Duchess Olga will be the richest of the Tzar's daughters. Nicholas II was born in 1868, in the reign of his grandfather; he was Alexander II's first grandchild, and to commemorate the event the Emperor deposited a large sum in the State bank, which was to be handed over to his grandson's eldest child, on his or her marriage day. Until then the interest is to accumulate. Consequently, when the Grand Duchess Olga marries, she will be endowed with enormous wealth, for, besides the usual marriage portion of a Russian Sovereign's daughter, she will be dowered with the fortune left to her by her great-grandfather. The Tzar's eldest daughter is very Russian in all her views and tastes; the idea of marrying a foreign prince and leaving the country is extremely distasteful to her.

When in January, 1914, the question of an alliance was mooted between the Crown Prince Carol of Roumania (at that time he was only Prince Carol) and the elder daughter of the Emperor of Russia, the Grand Duchess Olga was miserable and wept bitterly, until her father told her she was at liberty to decide as she liked, for no one would coerce her into a marriage against her inclination. It was a great disappointment to the present King of Roumania, and more so still to his wife and his mother-in-law, the Dowager Duchess Marie of Saxe-Coburg-Gotha (by birth a Grand Duchess of Russia). Subsequently it was decided that Prince Carol was to pay his court to the Grand Duchess Tatiana, and, to give them the opportunity of getting to know each other, Prince Carol was to come over to Livadia (in the Crimea) in August, and stay for some time as the guest of the Russian Sovereigns, but the war put an effectual stop to all these plans.

It is generally supposed that the Grand Duchess Olga will wed a Russian prince, which will enable her to spend the rest of her life in this country.

The two younger Grand Duchesses, Marie and Anastasia, are not often seen in Petrograd, for up to now they have been kept in the schoolroom. The Grand Duchess Marie, just turned seventeen, is developing into a lovely girl, and decidedly the beauty of the family. She daily visits the Court hospitals in Tzarskoe Selo, reads to the wounded, writes their letters for them, and endeavours to make herself generally useful. The youngest Grand Duchess, Anastasia, takes after her paternal grandfather; she will be tall and broad-shouldered. The two youngest sisters pair off together and are inseparable; but Anastasia is likewise the playmate, confidante and adviser of her little brother, though it does not prevent them from quarrelling occasionally, and, when they were younger, from fighting many a pitched battle.

The Grand Duchess Anastasia Nicolaïevna, wife of the Grand Duke Nicholas, and the Grand Duchess Militza (the younger sister of the Grand Duchess Anastasia), married to the Grand Duke Nicholas's younger brother Peter, are both princesses of Montenegro.

From the first days of the war the sisters have been very assiduous in their care for our wounded. The Grand Duchess Anastasia and her daughter, Princess Helen Romanovsky, have become hospital nurses. The two daughters of the Grand Duchess Militza, Princess Marina and Princess Nadega, are also sisters of mercy. The two Grand Duchesses Anastasia and Militza have recently founded a large hospital in Kiev, where at present two hundred wounded men can be nursed, but which will soon be enlarged to admit a thousand or more.

The niece of these Grand Duchesses, Princess Helen of Servia, is married to Prince Johann Constantinovitch, the eldest son of the late Grand Duke Constantine Constantinovitch and his widow, the Grand Duchess Elisabeth Madrikievna (by birth a princess of Saxe-Altenburg).

The Grand Duchess Elisabeth Madrikievna has suffered more than any other member of the Imperial Family from the war. At the time Kaiser Wilhelm declared war on Russia the Grand Duke Constantine was alive. He and his wife were in Wildungen, where His Imperial Highness was undergoing a cure. On hearing of the war, the Grand Duke wanted to start instantly for Russia, but the German authorities objected to this, saying he was a prisoner of war. The Grand Duchess Elisabeth volunteered to send a telegram to the German Empress, with whom, before her marriage, she had been on intimate terms; but was curtly informed by the German officials that private telegrams could not be despatched. The Grand Duchess quietly observed that her wire would not be a 'private' one but an 'Imperial message'. The German officials used scant ceremony in their intercourse with the Russian Imperials, not even giving them their title, but addressing the Grand Duke as 'Mein Herr' and the Grand Duchess as 'Gnädige Frau'. After much parley the Grand Duke, his wife and his suite were allowed to depart. Several miles before Eydkuhnen, the station on the Prussian frontier, the train stopped and the Grand Duke was bidden to get out and proceed to Wirballen, the first Russian station, on foot.

The party found themselves in the midst of fields; not a house or a human being to be seen, and no conveyance to be had for love or money. The Grand Duke and his wife were compelled to walk all the way to Wirballen. Considering the state of health of His Imperial Highness, it is not surprising that the physical fatigue he endured had a fatal effect on the development of his malady, and he was quite ill when he arrived in Petrograd. A couple of months later, the Grand Duke's son Oleg died in the hospital of Vilna from the effects of terrible wounds received in battle.

Regardless of his health, the father hastened to Vilna to be at the bedside of his dying son. The Grand Duke brought Prince Oleg's body to Petrograd, and thence he took it to his favourite country seat 'Ostashovo', between Petrograd and Moscow, where the young hero was buried.

The grief, excitement and fatigue were too much for his shattered health, and he died a few months later; but, before death claimed him, he had to witness the sorrow of his daughter, Princess Tatiana, wife of Prince Constantine Bagration-Moukhransky, who was killed on the Caucasian front in March, 1915. Hers had been a love match. Prince Bagration-Moukhransky was as handsome as a Greek god, and had been an officer in the Chevalier Guards Regiment, and Princess Tatiana had to overcome many obstacles before she obtained her parents' consent to this marriage. They had been married only three and a half years when the Prince was killed, but the union had been an ideal one, and they adored each other. Princess Tatiana, accompanied by one of her brothers, went to Tiflis to be present at her husband's funeral, but before leaving that town she was apprised of her father's death, and had to hurry home to be in time for his obsequies.

The late Grand Duke Constantine – the brother of the Dowager Queen of Greece – was a dreamer. He was no politician, but a man of cultured intellect, and his ambitions were limited to his artistic studies. A poet himself, the Grand Duke always preferred literature to all other branches of art. His continual aim was to create literary interests in the circles in which he moved. For instance, during the years of his military service in the Ismailov Regiment of Guards, the officers, owing to the initiative of the Prince, founded a literary and dramatic society, under the name of 'Ismailovskie Dossugui' (the leisure hours of the Ismailovsky Corps). Not long ago this society celebrated its twenty-fifth anniversary, and during these years it gained a high and well-earned reputation for the useful and sympathetic results of its activity, justifying its motto: 'Valour, Goodness, Beauty', and the emblem: a sword and a lyre entwined in flowers.

The members of this society assembled once a week in the messroom of the regiment to read the works of Russian authors and poets, and to act detached scenes from native dramas and comedies. They had the privilege of being the first to listen to any new works from the Grand Duke's pen. At these evening gatherings the best music and singing were heard, as well as recitals by any musical or dramatic celebrities who may have been passing through Petrograd.

When the members of the 'Ismailovskie Dossugui' had gained power and experience, the Grand Duke decided to organise representations of classical pieces. Actresses from the Imperial Dramatic Company were invited to take the female parts, and the regimental messroom not being large enough these performances were given in the Hermitage Theatre of the Winter Palace with the flower of Petrograd society for audience. Everyone who was anybody felt eager to be present, and invitations were eagerly sought. The intense interest shown in these representations can well be appreciated when we realise that on one of these occasions Shakespeare's *Hamlet* was given, translated into beautiful Russian verse by the Grand Duke Constantine himself. It had taken him seven years to accomplish this work, which is considered the best of all translations of *Hamlet* extant in the language. He began it in 1889 and finished it in 1896. The Grand Duke played the part of Hamlet, and gave a beautiful and vivid interpretation of the character. Salvini attended the last rehearsal, and his presence caused a great sensation. The celebrated tragedian paid a tribute of astonishment and admiration to the acting of his august colleague, praising very highly his conception of Hamlet – the best part in Salvini's repertory.

Referring to the 'Ismailovskie Dossugui', one must not forget to mention Schiller's tragedy *The Bride of Messina*, given in the Chinese Theatre at Tzarskoe Selo, as well as the representation of *The King of the Jews* by the Grand Duke Constantine, produced with immense success in the autumn of 1913 at the Hermitage Theatre. The part of Joseph of Arimathea was taken by the author himself. *The King of the Jews* was the last public performance organised by the Grand Duke outside the walls of the regimental messroom.

The late Grand Duke Constantine was one of the simplest men, and, although of imposing presence, was unassuming in his manner. Always amiable, he had the gift of placing those he conversed with completely at their ease. At one time he was the Chief of all the Military Colleges in Russia. He was pleasant to deal with, for he made himself accessible to the boys' parents, and was adored by the cadets. It was a red letter day to them when he visited their college.

Life in the Marble Palace, the residence of the Grand Duke Constantine in Petrograd, was of the simplest description. In summer the family lived in one of their beautiful country palaces, Pavlovsk or Strelna. Their favourite resort, however, was their property called 'Ostashovo'. Here all etiquette was abolished, and the Grand Duke and his family led the life of any wealthy landowner. All the children of the Grand Ducal couple are imbued with the same simple ideas. The eldest daughter, Princess Tatiana, proved it to such an extent that she insisted on disregarding the privileges of her birth and making a love marriage; for, although Prince Constantine Bagration-Moukhransky was of Caucasian royal descent, the family is only considered as belonging to the local aristocracy. Poor Princess Tatiana Constantinovna! She was only twenty-five when she became a widow – in the space of six months she lost brother, husband and father. She is heartbroken, and time has done little to assuage her grief. Surrounded by her husband's portraits, she lives only for her two fatherless boys, going periodically to Tiflis to visit the grave of her dead love.

The late Grand Duke Constantine Constantinovitch was a very religious man in the true orthodox spirit, and he has inculcated the same strict religious precepts in his children. It had always been a grief to him that his wife professed a different faith to the rest of her family; but he was too delicate-minded ever to interfere with her religious beliefs.

The present war has upset many preconceived opinions and appreciations and singled out people, showing them up in a quite different light. Before the war people did not set a high value on most of the Grand Dukes belonging to the younger generation. They were generally supposed to be pleasure seeking, selfish, utterly spoiled by circumstances and surroundings. But when the hour of danger struck, they all rose up in defence of Holy Russia, putting aside all superficiality, and they proved that their lives belonged to their country, and that they would fight to the last drop of their blood to save Russia and their Tzar from the hands of the invader.

The Emperor's brother, the Grand Duke Michael Alexandrovitch, hastened home from England, where he and his family were established at Knebworth. Both brothers were glad of the occasion which bridged over their misunderstanding and called forth a reconciliation. The Grand Duke Michael is the Emperor's junior by ten years. They were always fond of each other, and it was remembered in the family that the younger son had been his father's favourite. Stern to others, Alexander III was as wax in little 'Misha's' hands, and never could deny him anything. Undoubtedly the boy was spoilt, but, like all the children of Alexander III, he has a good and honest disposition, and this over-indulgence did not diminish his natural sterling qualities. The misunderstanding which estranged the Grand Duke Michael from his family was caused by a marriage which the Dowager Empress and the Tzar were bound to resent. If anything were to happen to the Tzessarevitch the Grand Duke Michael would be the Heir Presumptive to the throne of Russia, and his marriage, contracted at a time when the state of his nephew's health was very precarious, would in the future be a source of trouble and complication.

The Grand Duke Michael went to the front directly after his return. His Imperial Highness has shown great courage, and the men under his command are devoted to him and will follow him anywhere. At present he commands an army corps in Galicia. When the Grand Duke is on leave in Petrograd, he is continually seen together with the Emperor. It is therefore evident that the old affectionate terms have been resumed.

On the ominous day of the reopening of the Duma, February 9th/22nd, 1916, the Tzar surprised everyone by being present at the religious ceremony. It was a spontaneous resolve, and the Duma's President, M. Rodzianko, was informed by Count Fredericks of the Sovereign's intention only an hour before the opening. There was no time to prepare a fitting reception, but all went off beautifully, and the very unexpectedness of the occurrence enhanced the impression of its sincerity. When the Tzar entered the hall of the Duma, accompanied by his brother, the members, regardless of party or faction, were all delighted at the high favour shown them (it was the first time the monarch had been inside the Duma), and, clustering around him, they gave him a warm welcome. The Tzar remained for the *Te Deum*, and was then shown over the building and asked to sign his name in a book kept for distinguished visitors. Pleased by the welcome received, the Emperor was very gracious, addressing some of the members in his pleasant way and asking various questions. The Duma *in corpore* escorted the Tzar to his carriage. An outburst of enthusiastic cheering (the Left shouting as lustily as the Right) conveyed to the departing Sovereign the acknowledgement of the honour conferred upon the Duma. The Grand Duke Michael stayed on, he entered the Imperial gallery and remained during part of the sitting.

The Grand Duchess Marie Pavlovna is very energetic in her endeavours to help her adopted country in its hour of trial. She has organised various war hospitals, hospital trains, ambulances; has started a depot and a workshop in her palace, and has been several times to the front to visit her field-hospitals and take gifts to the soldiers. Marie Pavlovna is one of the most important members of the Imperial Family. By birth a Princess of Mecklenburg-Schwerin, she is the widow of the Emperor's uncle, the Grand Duke Vladimir Alexandrovitch, and is the only one who gives life and brilliancy to society, keeping it in continual movement.

At first the Grand Duchess attended only parties in her immediate set, but gradually it has become the fashion for her to be present at all the smartest receptions of the season. This has become so usual that when a party is being talked of the question is generally asked, 'Will Marie Pavlovna be there?' Her presence adds lustre to the festival and gives it the requisite 'style'. None but a very foolish hostess would think of neglecting to invite the Grand Duchess, whose presence would ensure the success of her party. Dinner-parties graced by Her Imperial Highness are always extremely luxurious. Only people of ample means can afford the pleasure of inviting her to their hospitable board.

The Grand Duchess was always a handsome woman, and, in spite of the fact that she is no longer slim, her figure is still most imposing, and her presence bears the stamp of her high position. She is always most charming and gracious to everyone.

The death of her husband, the Grand Duke Vladimir, was a great grief to his widow. She sorrowed for him sincerely, and since his death has never gone out of mourning. She adores her sons, but her daughter, the lovely Princess Helen of Greece, was her father's favourite; and on the day of her marriage to Prince Nicholas of Greece the Grand Duke Vladimir – strong man as he was – broke down and wept like a child.

The Grand Duchess Marie Pavlovna loathes solitude. She never dines alone, and always has people to spend the evening with her. At one time she and her guests played lotto, and the winner received a gift, which the Grand Duchess fetched from a special cupboard where such prizes were kept. At present lotto has given way to bridge. She is an ardent adept of this game, and all her privileged friends arrange bridge parties in her honour.

The popularity of the Grand Duchess Marie Pavlovna has been steadily increasing during recent years. About seven years ago she – who had been considered so faithfully attached to her German antecedent – surprised the world by suddenly changing her religion and becoming a member of the Orthodox Church. No one knew of her intention, which had been maturing for years, except her husband and her children.

Early in the morning of the day fixed for the religious ceremony, her intimate friend, Madame de Peters, a countrywoman of Her Imperial Highness, received a bulky letter by special messenger. Madame de Peters was still in bed when the letter was brought to her. The envelope contained a short note apprising her of her august friend's change of religion. Another letter was enclosed in it, addressed to the German pastor who up to that day had been the spiritual adviser of the Grand Duchess. Madame de Peters was requested to deliver this letter personally to the clergyman as quickly as possible, before he should hear of Marie Pavlovna's change of faith through some official channel. The letter was a long one, and contained all the reasons which had strengthened her irrevocable decision to be converted to the Orthodox Church.

Great was the grief and astonishment of the venerable pastor. His first impulse was to rush off to the Palace, try to stop the ceremony, and dissuade the Grand Duchess from taking what he considered a fatal step. But Her Imperial Highness had laid her plans warily, and everything had been foreseen. When the letter reached the pastor the religious ceremony was over and nothing could be done to prevent it.

I think it will interest the English reader to know the principal reasons given by the Grand Duchess which led her to abandon the cult of her youth. The Russian faith admits prayers for the dead, which give the bereaved the consolation of remaining in touch with the beloved departed even after their disappearance from this vale of sorrow. The faith of the Russians in the Blessed Virgin had always appealed to Her Imperial Highness; even as a Lutheran she had an ikon of the Holy Virgin in her sanctuary. During the Russo-Japanese war she fervently prayed to the Virgin Mary for the safety of her son Cyril. His miraculous escape after the wreck of the *Petropavlovsk* was attributed by his mother to the Virgin's protection in answer to her daily prayers.

Out of the gladness of her heart she promised to become a member of the Church that believes in the Divinity of the Holy Virgin. Still it took several years to break entirely with her religious past. So long as religious freedom did not exist in Russia she hesitated to make the change. Her resolve, however, remained firm, and as soon as all religions were tolerated in this country she considered herself a free agent, at liberty to be openly converted to enter the bosom of the Greek Orthodox Church, which had always attracted her.

On the eventful day the usual Court circle assembled in the Grand Duke Vladimir's palace for lunch, including Madame de Peters, who had come to relate the result of her mission. The Grand Duke and his wife gave no outward sign of any extraordinary occurrence. Madame de Peters turned to her neighbour, one of the Grand Duke's adjutants, Count Fersen – a rich landowner of the Baltic provinces – remarkable for his rather obvious efforts to imitate the mannerisms of the Prussian officers.

'The Grand Duchess has changed her faith and become Orthodox,' whispered the lady in a low voice.

Count Fersen stared at Madame de Peters in a startled way, and during the rest of luncheon avoided holding any conversation with her. When the repast was over he furtively approached one of the other courtiers and whispered to him that 'Poor Madame de Peters had suddenly gone mad.'

This anecdote proves what an intense surprise the conversion of Her Imperial Highness was to everybody, including her own entourage and her intimate friends.

The Court of the Grand Duchess Marie Pavlovna is incontestably the most animated and interesting one in Petrograd. Her Mistress of the Robes is Countess Marie Schouvaloff, widow of a former Russian Ambassador in Berlin. The zenith of the Countess's successful career was attained at the time of her husband's appointment as Ambassador to Berlin. Young and pretty, with pleasing manners, she soon made a conquest of the leaders of German society. Her brilliant receptions were crowded, and attracted the most exclusive circles. Even the Kaiser was under the spell of Countess Schouvaloff's charm. He was a frequent guest at the Embassy, and lost no opportunity of accentuating the goodwill he bore Count and Countess Schouvaloff. When they left

Berlin he presented the Countess with a life-size portrait of himself, which in bygone times was given a conspicuous place in her drawing-room. Lately the portrait has disappeared, but the ultimate fate of the Kaiser's picture is unknown to me. Has it been relegated to the lumber-room? Has it been burnt? Or does it adorn the walls of the servants' hall (though I hardly believe any respectable Russian servant would tolerate it)? It remains an unfathomable mystery.

The long companionship of such a highly cultured man as the late Count Paul Schouvaloff and an innate charming disposition make Countess Marie Schouvaloff eminently suitable for the position of Mistress of the Robes. Her unfailing tact and charm of manner render her invaluable at the Grand Ducal Court. Unfortunately the Countess is getting infirm, and her increasing deafness is a sore trial to her.

The Emperor's brother-in-law, the Grand Duke Alexander Mikhailovitch, is one of the handsomest and most elegant men in Russia. When he enters a room he attracts notice by his superior height and shapely figure, and he rivets attention by his peculiar charm of manner and great affability. He is a 'grand seigneur' to his finger-tips and is very popular in society. He is a great diner-out, a very good bridge-player and is considered something of a ladies' man. He used to be regarded as a very ambitious man, but for the last ten years has taken no part whatever in the Government. His wife, the Grand Duchess Xenia (the Emperor's sister), is very shy with strangers, which makes her at times appear stiff. She feels completely at her ease only in her own intimate set. She has inherited her mother's lovely eyes and beautiful skin, but her manner lacks the latter's assurance. She dresses well and is very elegant in all her appointments. When she comes into a ballroom or a theatre, she tries to slip in without attracting too much attention.

The Grand Duke Nicholas's youngest brother, Peter Nicolaïevitch, is also married to a Princess of Montenegro. They and their family are rarely seen in society; they spend a great part of the year in the Riviera, or on their estate in the Crimea.

The youngest brother of the Emperor Alexander III, the Grand Duke Paul, has for several years lived in Paris. After the morganatic marriage he contracted with Madame Pistohlcorse, born Karnovitch, against the wish of the Emperor and still unacknowledged at Court, he was forbidden to return to Russia. The reconciliation between nephew and uncle took place at the time of the Grand Duke Serge's assassination. Since then the Grand Duke Paul and his wife, the Countess Hohenfelsen, have spent a few weeks every year in Petrograd during the season. Parties have been given in their honour, and in society the Countess Hohenfelsen holds a brilliant position. In the spring of 1915 the Grand Duke Paul and his family came to live in their new palace in Tzarskoe Selo.

It is still an unsolved question what position the Countess will take in society, since she and her husband have settled down in Tzarskoe Selo. Evidently it will be a very distinguished one. The Countess has two powerful auxiliaries: the wonderful luck which has never failed her yet, and has successfully carried her through the most distressing situations, helping her to overcome all seemingly invincible obstacles, and her admirable tact. Her grandeur has not turned her head; she is simple in her manner and charmingly amiable with everyone. In her intercourse with her husband's relatives she keeps a safe reserve, never putting herself forward. This has been duly noticed and very much appreciated.

The newly constructed palace of the Grand Duke Paul in Tzarskoe Selo is a magnificent dwelling. Decorators from Paris have been busily at work and the result is marvellous. The palace is full of curios and art collections, beautiful pictures, old china, rare carvings, etc.

The Countess Hohenfelsen is a very pretty woman still, with radiant brown eyes that have the power of being caressing, or full of mirth, at will.

The couple is a well-assorted one, for the Grand Duke is a very handsome man, with a tall, commanding figure, and resembles his mother the Empress Maria Alexandrovna, who was a lovely woman; he has inherited her chiselled nose and deep melancholy eyes.

Their son, Vladimir Hohenfelsen, is a delightful youth just turned nineteen, with his mother's glorious eyes; he has the soul and gift of a poet united to a noble disposition. He has just passed his exams and will soon be going to the front.

The two daughters are pretty little girls.

It is reported that since the war the Grand Duke Paul objects to his wife and children bearing a German name, and that the Emperor has consented to give Countess Hohenfelsen the name of Princess Jaroslawsky, which is an historical one, belonging to the Romanoff family. Nothing is officially known, but rumour says the matter is settled.

The Countess Hohenfelsen is on very friendly terms with her stepdaughter, the Grand Duchess Maria Pavlovna junior, and with her stepson, the Grand Duke Dmitry Pavlovitch.

The Grand Duke Cyril (the Emperor's first cousin) is a very handsome man in an elegant style. He has a very good figure and his whole personality bears the stamp of birth and breeding. Since the injuries received at the time of the disaster to the *Petropavlovsk*, he has always been rather delicate. His marriage with the late Duke of Edinburgh's second daughter, the Grand Duchess Victoria Feodorovna, is a very happy one, although for a long time it was not acknowledged, on account of the contracting parties being first cousins, such marriages being prohibited in Russia.

It is said that the Empress does not like her cousin Victoria, who for a short time as the wife of the Grand Duke of Hesse was her sister-in-law. The Emperor's stern refusal to countenance his cousin Cyril's marriage was attributed to the Empress's influence. Whether this is true or not, the relations between the two cousins have remained very cool.

The Grand Duchess Victoria helps a great deal to animate society. She leads an active life and takes a prominent part in all important society events. She particularly encourages motoring, and, under her auspices, several motor races have been organised. The last of them took place in the first days of July, just before war was declared by Germany. The race was called 'Victoria Fahrt'. Seventeen automobiles, headed by the Grand Duke Cyril and the Grand Duchess Victoria, took part in this race, which lasted eight days. The motorists started from Pskov, went through Courland and Livonia, finishing up in Riga. The race was interrupted at stated intervals by halts at several old baronial castles, where sumptuous receptions awaited Their Imperial Highnesses.

The Grand Duke Cyril's younger brother, the Grand Duke Boris, also a handsome man, was rather wild in his early youth, and many are the stories that have been told of him. He is much steadier now, and since he has the command of one of the Cossack Regiments of the Guard, he takes his duties very seriously.

No one ever credited the Grand Duke Boris Vladimirovitch with the valour and military capacities he has shown in leading the Ottoman-Cossack Regiment of the Imperial Guards into battle. His personal courage and power of endurance set a worthy example to his officers. At the present time the Grand Duke Boris is attached to Headquarters.

It is difficult to enumerate each member of the Imperial Family, but it is the general opinion that all have done their duty under the most trying circumstances. The Grand Duke Dmitry Pavlovitch has distinguished himself by many acts of amazing heroism. After a fierce fight with the Germans in the first months of the war, the Grand Duke saw a soldier belonging to his own company who was incapable of moving. Taking the wounded man on his back, he carried him out of the battlefield to the nearest ambulance station, and thereby saved his life.

The relations between officers and soldiers are perfect. Many officers have rendered similar services to the private soldiers, while the latter are devoted to their superiors and never leave a battlefield without a thorough search for any of their own officers. They will go any distance to bring hot food to their 'barin'[1] in the trenches, sometimes having to crawl all the way in order to pass unnoticed by the enemy.

Every regiment has one or more dogs. The following simple story is an eloquent illustration of the Russian soldier, his naïve mentality and his devotion to animals.

In Lessnoy, at a short distance from Petrograd, in one of the best private hospitals, organised and maintained by the Maid of Honour Countess Vera Borissovna Perovsky, a badly wounded soldier was being nursed back to health. His name was Fedor Netchaïeff, and he was a bombardier in one of the artillery batteries. A German shrapnel burst within a few inches of where he stood, covering him with fragments and splinters that entered into all parts of his body. From pain and loss of blood Netchaïeff fainted; when he regained consciousness his wounds were bandaged and he was about to be carried to the nearest ambulance. 'Where is Mushka? Has she been killed?' was the first question uttered by the wounded soldier. A small white dog with tan spots was springing round him trying to lick his sound hand.

'As soon as I saw her,' relates Netchaïeff, 'I felt better, and a load seemed to be taken off my shoulders. I don't remember how and where I was transported, I only know that the pain was awful. When I came to myself I was in a hospital train, which was taking me to Petrograd.

1   Barin = Master.

THE TZAR'S DAUGHTERS

'Poor Mushka, she is certainly lost to me for ever now . . . but no sooner had this thought flashed through my brain than lo and behold! there was Mushka herself creeping from under my cot. The rascal had hidden there all the time, and only ventured to come out of her hiding-place when the train was moving. She jumped on to my bed, curled herself up at my feet, and dropped off into deep slumber.

'Thanks to the kind forbearance of our senior sister of mercy, Mushka was allowed to remain with me. The sister told me that Mushka had followed me to the train, running all the way to the station, about fifteen versts. No one saw how she got into the train, but there she was – and the sister had not the heart to turn her out.

'Four years ago,' continues Netchaïeff, 'when I became a soldier, I found Mushka in the barracks of our battery. Nobody knew where she came from, or to whom she belonged. We became greatly attached to each other, Mushka and I, and she followed me like my shadow.

'When we received marching orders, Mushka seemed to understand everything, and was greatly excited. She was so afraid of being left behind in barracks that she ran on before we started, and only joined us after an hour's march. Well, we safely accomplished the campaign, Mushka and I. I fed her with the remains of our rations. We took part in eight battles, and thanks to God's mercy all went well with us; Mushka got quite accustomed to the firing, and when the battery went into action she would run backwards and forwards barking fearlessly. The ninth battle was to be our last, for a time at least.

'So we arrived in Petrograd, Mushka and I, but the thought of what was to become of the dog, all by itself in a large city, was a dreadful anxiety to me, for of course she could not be admitted into the hospital.

'I was carried out of the carriage, Mushka jumping and barking round me. A lady dressed in the garb of a sister of mercy approached to inquire how I felt. "Oh! I am all right, but what is to be done with the dog?" – "Would you like the dog to be taken care of in the house of the War Minister?" – "What next will you suggest? How is the dog to get to the Minister?" – "I am his wife," replied the lady, "and I shall ask him to allow your dog to be taken care of till you recover."

'Tears filled my eyes . . . for very joy I felt no pain, but still I demurred: "The dog will give you trouble." – "Never mind, I shall like to take care of her, and I will bring her to see you."

'I was taken to the hospital, my wounds were examined and bandaged, the pain was very great, but the hope that I should soon get well enough to go to the front again with Mushka sustained me through all the suffering.

'On the first Sunday after I was in the hospital – we had just had our dinner – when the door of our ward opened to give admittance to a General accompanied by the lady who had met us at the station. "That must be the Minister of War," said I to myself, trying as well as my bandages permitted to get into position and salute His Excellency. Hardly had I time to do so when I heard a joyous bark, and Mushka, a strap attached to the leather collar I had bought her, was led into the ward. A sign from the lady, and Mushka was let loose, she sniffed for a second or two, then, straight as an arrow, she ran up to my bed. Oh, how happy we were to meet again, Mushka and I!

'His Excellency came up to me, asked me how I was getting on, questioned me about the battles in which I had taken part, and how I got wounded.

' "Don't trouble about me, Your Excellency, I am much better, and shall soon be able to do my duty. But let me thank Your Excellency for your kindness to Mushka, I shall never forget it as long as I live." Mushka looked flourishing, she had put on flesh, and I am afraid she will be spoiled for a soldier's life, and will not care to go back to the front with me.

'The General's wife told me the particulars of Mushka's installation in the Minister's house: "At first she was quite unmanageable, would not go near anyone, barked at the General, growled at the servants, would not touch food, and sat in a corner glowering and whining. I did not know what to do, until the idea struck me to send for a soldier. As soon as Mushka saw a soldier she was mollified, consented to be fed by him, and after a good meal contentedly dropped off to sleep." '

Another story will show how the German prisoners are treated in Russia. It is one of the many thousands of similar incidents, but it proves that there is no occasion to repine at their discomforts. I am quoting an extract from a private letter, written by the Empress's Maid of Honour Mlle. Eudoxie Djunkovsky, the Lady Patroness of the Eugenia Community of Sisters of Mercy in Petrograd. Mlle. Djunkovsky has spent nearly the whole time of the war in one of the field hospitals at the front. In the name of truth, I hope she will forgive the liberty I am taking with her letter:

'A German sergeant was brought to our hospital, badly wounded in the leg. Morose and surly he would answer no questions, nor would he touch food. But when his neighbours commenced eating "Borstch"[1] with meat and a plateful of the soup was offered to the wounded man, he took it and ate it with evident relish. He told me that in Germany they would not have mixed such a quantity of provisions, but would have used the meat separately, and, as for the vegetables, they would have been made to last for several days.

'The surgeon attentively examined the German prisoner's wound. His verdict was that an amputation of the injured limb was imperative, for the wound was complicated by a compound fracture of the bone. The doctor looked at the man with kindly pity in his eyes: "If I were you," he said, "I should consent to have the operation done; at your age you are sure to get over it. Otherwise serious complications might set in." The wounded man listened to the surgeon with growing astonishment in his wide-open eyes. The next moment he broke down, bursting into a storm of tears. When he grew quieter, he caught the surgeon's hand impetuously and kissed it, saying: "Oh, God Almighty! If I had only known that the Russians were so kind to their enemies and took the same care of them as of their own people, asking their consent even before performing a necessary operation, I would not have been so cruel during the war. Why! I finished off many wounded soldiers on the battlefield, regardless of their outstretched hands and their prayers for mercy! Many a wounded man, who could have been saved, did I put away with the bodies of the dead. Oh, Lord, forgive me my iniquities . . . Of course, I consent to everything, and may Heaven bless you for your goodness. I am certain you will heal my body as quickly as you have healed my soul."'

---

1 A Russian soup made of red beetroot.

Chapter IX

CHARACTERISTICS AND IMPRESSIONS

THE touch of Western civilisation has comparatively lately reached Russia. The peasants form the overwhelming majority of the Russian population. Mystical fatalists by nature, they believe completely in predestination. Two sacred sentiments, enshrined in the depths of their hearts, give the keynote to the Russian character: their adoration of God and their veneration for the Tzar. Both these sentiments are so closely connected in the simple mind of the Russian peasant that they partake of one religious principle – God is the Almighty Sovereign of the universe, the Tzar is the 'anointed' emissary of the Lord. Woe betide those philosophers and learned men who try to shake this belief. The peasant's mentality would not be able to grasp new doctrines, and it would result in the upheaval of their spiritual and moral convictions . . . leaving them nothingness.

It is quite a usual sight to see the Tzar's portrait in the sacred corner of the peasant's 'ishba'[1] hanging next to the ikons.

The ikons play a great part in the peasant's existence; the reverence bordering on worship with which they regard them has a strong influence on their life, though it seldom prevents them from committing evil deeds. For instance, it is quite within the range of possibility for a peasant contemplating a theft to prostrate himself before the ikons, devoutly kiss them and fervently implore the Almighty's help; but a man who is not a Galahad can

---

1 Ishba = cottage.

only kneel before the ikons – he is considered unfit to touch them. A man may come home in a state of intoxication, but before going to rest he will not forget to pray before the ikons, imploring God's blessing. After brutalising his wife he will go down on his knees and crave the Lord's pardon. An oath taken or a promise given before the ikons is binding on every right-minded peasant.

In Russia everything begins with a religious ceremony. The opening of every session of the Duma is preceded by a *Te Deum*. After the summer vacation the new school year is commenced by prayers held in each college or school. An engagement is only given out to the world after the priest has said prayers and blessed the betrothed couple with ikons. The opening of a new bank, factory or shop is inevitably inaugurated by a religious ceremony. The mobilisation was accompanied all over Russia by religious services. Prayers were said, blessings given before the men started with faith and hope in their hearts. Each regiment was accompanied by its own chaplain and a portable chapel, where divine service is held. This war has brought out the military chaplains in quite a new light. They have shown wonderful courage, self-abnegation and endurance. There have been cases in which a priest, the holy cross glittering in his uplifted hand, with a prayer on his lips, has led the soldiers to the attack. Many priests, at the risk of their lives, have succoured the wounded and the dying on the battlefield or, braving the enemy's fire, have performed the burial service over the dead and given absolution to the dying. Several priests were killed in fulfilling their duty in this noble manner.

The Russian peasant's blind faith and absolute devotion to the Tzar is often carried almost to the point of worship. The very simplicity of their outlook gives greatness to their feelings. The following episode proves my meaning better than any words could do.

I was spending a few weeks with friends in a charming old country place full of relics of olden times. Not far from the manor-house, in a squalid cottage, lived an old woman, 'Agafia' (in English Agatha). Her third and last son was to be sent to the war. Her first-born was killed during the Russo-Japanese war; her youngest had succumbed to a German bullet on the Prussian frontier in the first weeks of the war. The village elder had come that morning with instructions for the third son to prepare for enlistment. We were sitting on the large veranda overlooking the beautiful park when the servant entered saying: 'Barynia [mistress], Agafia has come to you.' We know already what had happened, but, as many people came to consult the squire's wife in cases of difficulties, we supposed Agafia had come to ask her to plead with the authorities to let off her only remaining son. Agafia entered pale to the lips, but quiet and self-possessed. 'They are taking Andrew?' asked the lady of the manor. 'Yes, they are taking him,' answered Agafia laconically; 'they have put his name down.' A silence ensued – what could be said to comfort the unhappy woman?

Suddenly the old peasant looked at the corner where the ikon hung, and, making the sign of the cross, she dropped on her knees. 'I sacrifice my last! I sacrifice him to God and to the Tzar for our faith.' With these words the old woman bent her head low and remained motionless for a few moments. When she rose we were astounded and awed by the inspired air of calm resolve that seemed to emanate from the old wife's hard-worked and weather-beaten face.

People in England have formed a high estimate of Count Leo Tolstoy and are great admirers of his writings; but they do not realise the amount of harm Tolstoy has done to the Russian people in tampering with their faith and depriving them of their sacred beliefs. Tolstoy was one of the most gifted men of the last century. As a novelist and a dramatic author he stands forth like a giant of strength who will always have a pre-eminent place in Russian literature, just as *War and Peace*, *Anna Karenina* and some of his earlier works will ever remain literary masterpieces. His religious philosophy, however, is full of paradoxes; it is only fit for ripe and unwavering minds, and was never entirely fathomed or understood by the people at large. Notwithstanding all his assumed simplicity, Count Tolstoy courted popularity, and he succeeded in being one of the most talked of, important and harmful of men; but his disciples and numerous converts were even more harmful than their master, for they shared his errors without possessing his greatness of mind or his genuine kindness of heart. In the name of Tolstoy untold evil has been done by these followers of his, who degenerated into a sect called 'Tolstoyïsts'. They shielded themselves behind Tolstoy's fame and widespread popularity, and used and misused his name. It had become the fashion at one time to affect the simple life and turn Tolstoyïst. Brilliant Guardsmen such as Vladimir Grigorievitch Tchertkov, aristocrats such as

CHARACTERISTICS AND IMPRESSIONS

Prince Hilkoff[1] gave up everything to lead the life recommended by Tolstoy. Colonies were established where the 'Tolstoyïsts' lived according to the precepts of their master. No Church was acknowledged, no servants of God recognised, no rites required. Children remained unbaptised, their parents lived together without their union having been hallowed by the Church, the dead were buried without any funeral service. Nature was the sole religion of the Tolstoyïsts, their solace and the source of all inspiration.

The Holy Synod blundered when it insisted on Count Tolstoy's excommunication. It would have been far wiser to ignore the Count's vagaries and leave him unmolested. This excommunication caused an uproarious sensation, and Tolstoy posed a persecuted martyr, thus heightening his influence and increasing his adherents.

The peasants looked on with mild irony at the 'barin',[2] who assumed the exterior and guise of a 'mujik',[3] made bad stoves and tinkered at ill-fitting boots instead of writing immortal books.

They looked upon these vagaries as 'barskie'[4] whims which must be humoured. Tolstoy's popularity amongst the peasantry was caused by the encouragement he gave to their belief that the land ought to belong to them.

Count Tolstoy was full of contradictions, and did not live up to the maxims he so eloquently professed. For instance he did not admit any kind of personal property or possession either in land or in literary work; nevertheless he retained his land to the day of his death, and though he did not profit personally from the gains of his writings his wife did, and the Countess was known to be a good businesswoman in her dealings with publishers. Tolstoy was against wedlock, but he had a wife, and for over forty years led an apparently happy family life. Tolstoy's idea was to let this sinful world gradually die out, and advocated the expediency of not giving birth to children, whereas he himself had five sons and three daughters. It was generally believed that he was a model husband, warmly attached to his wife, who shared his literary labours; but he left his home. The memory of the last days spent in the room of the stationmaster in Astapovo, into which his wife was not admitted by her own daughter, and the undignified

1 Prince Hilkoff has since settled in Canada.
2 Barin = master.
3 Mujik = peasant.
4 Barskie = appropriate to the barin.

wrangle that followed between his widow and her children over the testamentary dispositions of the deceased were very unfortunate.

Tolstoy was a great man, but he would have been greater still had he not overreached himself.

The most brilliant epoch of Russian literature was in the first part and in the early sixties of the last century. Pushkine, Lermontoff, Count Alexis Tolstoy, Tutcheff, Fet, Joukovsky, Kryloff, Kozloff, Nekrassoff, Gnéditch (the translator of Homer's *Iliad*), Apoukhtine, form a group of poets of which Russia may well be proud. Turgenieff, Gortcharoff and Markevitch wrote their lovely books at the same epoch, which was also the time when Count Leo Tolstoy's first writings appeared.

Our modern literature is quite different; it is not that we lack talent, it is the minds of the authors that have deteriorated. Most of the writers of the present day belong to Bohemia. Tolstoy's influence can even now be traced in their writings. Kuprin, Leonide Andréeff, Kamensky, Maxim Gorky, Artzibasheff are all men of talent and education, but their good taste seems rather doubtful. The scum of the earth has a particular attraction for the modern Russian author. Their everlasting pursuit of realism leads them to describe revolting cynical scenes. Their favourite subjects are chosen from amongst the lowest depths of humanity, or among those who are outside the pale of society, depicting facts and circumstances that are usually not mentioned in decent society. The idea of the modern author is to simplify the outlook of life, discarding not only convention but morality. Everything centres upon sexuality. Ideals, conscience, sacred sentiments are empty words to the heroes and heroines of modern Russian fiction. If a man and a woman feel a mutual attraction they must belong to each other, no matter what obstacles in the shape of husbands, wives, duty, or principles may happen to stand in the way. Any other solution seems stilted and unnatural to the modern writer. A gulf divides the heroines of today from Turgenieff's Lisa, who, returning the love of a married man, but unable to overcome her scruples, and convinced of the hopelessness of her passion, entered a convent to avoid the temptation to lead a life of sin; or Pushkine's Tatiana, who, married to an elderly man whom she respects, sends away the man she loved as a girl because she is too honest to bring shame upon the husband who trusts her.

CHARACTERISTICS AND IMPRESSIONS

The modern heroine begins as a girl of sixteen to have student friendships of a very questionable nature with whom she permits all manner of liberties. If she becomes disappointed in one she turns to another. At twenty she knows by experience what many women of fifty only know by hearsay. Satiated and *blasée*, she marries, because one must get settled in the world; but she has no feeling for her husband, and finding her married life dull and unprofitable, she continues her adventures with more fearlessness than before. She is invited to parties *où l'on s'amuse* and becomes a *soupeuse* until she is suddenly attacked by a fit of moral nausea at the life she leads, turns on some man whom she knew as a girl and abuses him in the crudest language for having spoiled her life and made her into the woman she is.[1] Here the novel comes to its last page, therefore the reader remains in ignorance of what this heroine will do for the rest of her days, but it is to be supposed that she will continue to flutter from one supper to another, leaving her little daughter to become as depraved as herself. Some of these books are so full of cynicism and unclean details that they make a pure-minded woman shudder.

Girls in the middle classes are brought up with great freedom; they gloat over these books, draw their views and opinions from them and endeavour to imitate their favourite heroines. What is to be expected of a girl whose mind whilst it was still unformed was fed on Artzibasheff, Verbitzky, Kuprin, etc.? What kind of wife or mother will she be when her turn comes to enter the holy estate of matrimony? Women novelists are just as bad – they idealise the free woman.

Fortunately the Russian peasant is untainted by these literary attempts at realism. The war has had the most beneficial influence on his well-being. Every soldier's wife or mother is well provided for by the Government, the money is delivered into her own hands, and the poor down-trodden peasant women have never known such affluence nor such felicity. No 'vodka' is to be had, the public houses are closed, therefore all the money is either saved or spent on home necessities. The cottages are much improved; a brass samovar – the pride of the Russian peasant woman who possesses one and the ambition of those who do not – shines on the shelf, and other household utensils are no longer missing;

---

[1] Ella, the heroine of Artzibasheff's last novelette, *The Woman in their Midst*.

the inmates are properly clothed, eat nourishing food, and no drunken brute of a husband ill treats them. Not long ago a peasant woman from Tamboff declared that these two years were the only happy ones she had known, and she hoped the war would last many years. Scientists affirm that this well-being of the peasantry will have the most favourable influence on the generation which is now being born into the world. In this Russia scores a point on Germany, for in that country the conditions of life are terrible and the emaciated peasant women suffer all kinds of privations, which does not promise a strong and healthy future progeny.

It is in the Russian nature to be genial, generous, kind-hearted and rather exuberant. This exuberance is sometimes taken by foreigners for vulgar gush, but that is very rarely the case and is explained rather by the intense wish most Russians have to please and to show the kindness they feel. A good definition of this is given by the national saying, 'An open soul.' Russians are very sincere in their sympathies and affections, whilst they last, and they are faithful and devoted in their friendships, but they are apt to show their dislikes a little too frankly. They are too confiding, easily seeing friendship where none is meant. They have a dash of frivolity in their disposition, are inclined to mysticism and are easily influenced. But this seeming shallowness is only on the surface, for when the Russian soul is seriously touched it shows depths unfathomable.

The great fault of the masses is education without breeding, but in the higher circles of society this is not the case, and the breeding of the Russian aristocracy and of the higher middle classes is perfect. In bringing up the latter generations great care has been given to manners, especially at table, and a Russian lady or gentleman will pass muster in any London or Paris drawing-room. Man's attitude towards woman in Russia is a quaint mixture of chivalry and despotism, the echo of the original submission in which the boyars held their womenfolk, modified by culture and civilisation.

Morals in Russian society are getting very loose; the sanctity of marriage is being challenged by too great a facility for obtaining divorce. Many girls marry in haste to get their independence, and look upon their first matrimonial venture as a step to better themselves in the future. It seems paradoxical, but it is nevertheless a fact that it is far easier for a married woman than for a spinster to find a husband. The breaking off of an engagement creates a scandal, but the severing of matrimonial bonds is becoming quite the usual thing. The most insignificant misunderstanding causes husband and wife to break their marriage vows and go their different ways. Gossips chatter about impending divorces as much as of budding engagements. In Russia a divorced woman does not lose a tithe of her reputation, if no outrageous scandal attaches to her divorce. Should she marry again she returns to society with her new husband and enjoys all the prerogatives of her new position. The victims of the state of things are the unfortunate children.

Not very long ago there was a divorce between a Guardsman and his very pretty wife. They had one child, a little girl of about four or five years.

When the conditions of the divorce were discussed, there was no dispute between the parents as to which of them should keep the child; on the contrary an altercation ensued on account of both parents declining to have her. The mother was looking forward to a new marriage, and knew that her baby would be an unwelcome inmate in her new family. The father put forward as an excuse his military career and his inability to look after an infant. The solution finally arrived at was that the poor little girl was to be brought up by her paternal grandmother.

Contemporary parents do not give much thought to their children; they state quite openly that they do not consider it their duty to sacrifice their whole life to them. What can be expected in the future from children belonging to living parents brought up with neither a father's firm hand nor a mother's tender care, without a real home, without what the French call *le respect de la famille*?

This is a very grave question and ought to be seriously taken into consideration in influential quarters, for this lightly throwing over of family ties, this laxity of principle and morals is bound to have the most evil consequences in the future.

There are likewise cases of elderly men discarding their wives, who for over thirty years have been their devoted helpmates, because they still 'feel young and wish to mate with a young woman'. The more devoted the wife, the more easily the husband obtains her consent to this self-immolation in the name of her unbounded love for the choice of her youth. The husband marries, forgets all about his first wife and flaunts her successor in the eyes of society. Society begins by being mildly shocked, but if the lady plays her game cleverly she does not find invincible obstacles, and his wife, notwithstanding the martyrdom she has endured, has forgiven everything and continues to worship him.

This open laxity of morals did not exist in the reign of Alexander III. The Emperor had a high standard of honour for himself and for his subjects. Besides it was well known that the Empress Marie Feodorovna loathed people who led immoral lives. In those days the new-fangled wives of divorced generals, courtiers and politicians would not have been admitted to Court receptions; society would naturally have followed the Sovereign's lead, and this ostracism would have effectually quenched the eagerness of enterprising women to unsettle amorous donkeys, who are old enough to know better, and induce them to fresh matrimonial ventures. But unfortunately we now have no Court life in Russia. The present Sovereigns lead a secluded and isolated existence; they never stay in Petrograd, and do not know what happens in society, except a few incidents that occur in the highest aristocratic circle, with which they are in touch. The Dowager Empress has retired from the world and takes no part in the doings of society, and the Empress, who could have influence on the moral standard of society, keeps completely aloof. The consequence is that Petrograd is becoming a veritable Babylon.

The English reader must not, however, carry away the impression that Russians are immoral. There are families which lead the most patriarchal existence, where principles and traditions are respected, where love and harmony reign, where the parents teach their children to hold high the standard of honour and set them an example of faithfulness and duty fulfilled. But alas! such families are becoming the minority, and if some potent influence is not speedily exercised to stop this moral decadence they will die out and vanish completely.

Chapter X

THE RUSSIAN FOREIGN OFFICE

SINCE I commenced writing this book, an immense change has taken place in our Government. The Minister of Foreign Affairs, M. Sazonoff, has resigned his post, and the Prime Minister, M. Stürmer, has taken the portfolio of the Foreign Office.

This change, which one is bound to consider important, may have been expected in spheres closely connected with high quarters, but to the general public it was a surprise, and not a pleasant one.

In the light of events, a change of political leadership appears undesirable at the present moment, and must have produced a doubtful impression on the Allies. The Allies' ambassadors applied to the Minister of the Imperial Court for information as to whether this change of ministers meant a change of policy. Would M. Stürmer[1] continue to conduct affairs in the same spirit in which M. Sazonoff had conducted them since the commencement of the war? On receiving Count Fredericks's report, the Emperor measured the ministers with a glance, saying: 'The matter is settled, I beg you, Count, never more to refer to this question.'

M. Sazonoff, far from infallible, may have committed mistakes. Mistakes have been made by all the Allies, and not only by them, but first and foremost by the Germans themselves. Still, the minister had the indubitable merit of having held high the dignity of the Russian nation during these trying years. M. Sazonoff was

---

1 Stürmer was Prime Minister for a very short time.

a staunch advocate of an alliance between Russia and Great Britain. Years ago, when he was a member of the Russian Embassy in London, he formed his political opinions in this respect, and in conversing with Lord Kimberley he touched on this subject, declaring his firm conviction that only an alliance between Russia and England could maintain the equilibrium of Europe, and effectually stem Germany's growing aggression. If this alliance had been concluded ten or fifteen years ago, who knows but that this devastating war might have been avoided.

Before the war, M. Sazonoff's political attitude was as conciliatory as possible. No reproach can attach to the Russian Foreign Office for having called forth Germany's antagonism; on the contrary the minister's endeavours were continually directed to smooth away any difficulty as it arose, and gently to stem the torrent of German arrogance. But once the gauntlet was flung down, he accepted the challenge with the dignity compatible with the representative of Russia. During these last two years, when Germany was ever on the alert to sow dissension amongst the Allies, M. Sazonoff strained every nerve to avoid complications and succeeded in maintaining harmony. This alone ought to be considered a victory over Germany. It is likewise due to M. Sazonoff's efforts that our relations with Japan have consolidated into a firm and seemingly lasting friendship, which has lately been confirmed by the Russo-Japanese Agreement.

M. Sazonoff is reproached with having mis-managed affairs in the Balkans, and for having taken up a tactless attitude towards Bulgaria during the Balkan war. His diplomatic notes are said to have paralysed the effect of Russia's generosity in providing Bulgaria with millions and with ammunition. I have had occasion to mention in one of the preceding chapters that, since the beginning of the war, the Minister was not always free to act as he thought right. But his chief error was – at such an important crisis – in keeping the wrong men in Bucharest, Athens and Sofia, as the representatives of Russia; men who were not qualified to wrestle with the web of intrigues ingeniously spread by the Kaiser Wilhelm and his agents. In analysing the Balkan complications, one must take into consideration that M. Sazonoff had to expiate the faults of his predecessors. Why was a German prince tolerated and recognised as the Sovereign of Bulgaria? The character of Ferdinand of Coburg was universally known, and no one laid any great stress on his professions of devotion towards Russia.

THE RUSSIAN FOREIGN OFFICE

It would likewise have been wiser if our diplomacy had opposed the German wiles in their endeavours to bring about a matrimonial alliance between the then Crown Prince of Greece and the Kaiser's sister. Russia always kept aloof, preventing the members of the Imperial Family from accepting sovereignty in the Balkan Peninsula, and avoiding matrimonial alliances with the Balkan monarchs. The Kaiser, on the contrary, foresaw the utility of such close connections, and, thirsting for war from the first day of ascending the throne of the Hohenzollerns, he left no detail neglected which might help him to reach the coveted goal.

Russia, on the other hand, implicitly believed in the traditional friendship of Germany, and, if some pessimists indulged in discussing the possibilities of a future war with Germany, no one seriously believed them. We continued to live peacefully, *en grands seigneurs*, without a thought of future complications and strife. M. Sazonoff can scarcely be made responsible for a whole series of political errors, committed for several generations. He and his predecessor, M. Iswolsky, were the only two Ministers of Foreign Affairs who strove to abandon the old grooves and take a new political course.

This sudden and unexpected change in the Foreign Office caused great perturbation in political circles. The strangest rumours spread with the rapidity of lightning, and people's tongues wagged unceasingly for many days. Various explanations were given; possibly none of them had any serious foundation. I take upon myself the part of a phonograph and, without entering into any endeavour to weigh or analyse recent events, will confine myself to the exact repetition of what I have heard in different influential drawing-rooms.

The official reason for M. Sazonoff's resignation was attributed to his wish to bring forward the question of the immediate bestowal of an autonomous government on Poland. In high spheres the present moment was not considered suitable for raising such a burning question, so in order to avoid fresh complications, M. Sazonoff's fate was sealed. No one, however, believes this story, and people are convinced that the Polish question is only a pretext. The Imperial rescript to M. Sazonoff was a very cold one, but a private letter of the Tzar, which accompanied it, was written in the most amiable tone.

A little more than a year ago, whilst the State Duma had not been convoked, the President and the principal leaders of the

Duma assembled to give vent to the displeasure they felt at the protracted inaction of the Duma, and to discuss privately the position of affairs in this country. They worked out a sort of memorandum, which was laid before the Government and reported to the Sovereign. This memorandum consisted of three points:

No. 1. The convocation of the Duma at a precise date.
No. 2. The change of most of the ministers.
No. 3. The establishment of a responsible Ministry.

The Emperor and all the ministers adjourned to Headquarters, where the Grand Duke Nicholas was omnipotent at the time. A council was held, at which the monarch presided. The Grand Duke, owing to the high tributes paid to him by the leaders of the Duma, had suddenly become very liberal; he gave his decision in favour of a full consent to the three demands of the Duma. Most of the ministers had prepared a written definition of their opinions. M. Sazonoff's political views are considered liberal (he is suspected of being at heart a 'cadet', that is of being in sympathy with the programme of the constitutional-democratic party). He also was inclined to satisfy the requests of the Duma. But the Emperor, supported by the Prime Minister, M. Goremykine, opposed this plan of surrender with great spirit. His Majesty contended that the Government ought to take the Duma's wishes into consideration by meeting them half-way, but not giving in completely. The convocation of the Duma was fixed for the autumn of 1915. Some of the ministers, to whom the Duma objected as being too retrogressive, would be changed, but a responsible Cabinet would not be established. Conforming to this plan of action, the Minister of the Interior, M. Maklakoff, the Minister of Justice, M. Stcheglovitoff and the Procurator of the Holy Synod, M. Sabler, were replaced by Prince Stcherbatoff, M. Alexis Khwostoff and M. Samarine. This was likewise the turning-point of the Grand Duke Nicholas's career as Commander-in-Chief of the Russian army. His sharp opposition to the Tzar's opinions caused the first breath of coolness between nephew and uncle.

A few months later, after a stormy sitting of the Council of Ministers, under the leadership of M. Goremykine, eight ministers – M. Sazonoff amongst the number – signed a declaration to the Sovereign, setting forth the impossibility of working under the leadership of M. Goremykine, and containing also a few

THE RUSSIAN FOREIGN OFFICE

suggestions as to the Emperor's attitude towards his ministers. This declaration was very unfavourably received and excited the Tzar's serious displeasure. It is not in His Majesty's nature to apply harsh measures, still he never forgets an offence, and gradually the eight ministers who signed the paper received their dismissal. That is said to be the real reason of the war Minister General Polivanoff's removal and also the cause of M. Sazonoff's resignation.

Another rumour attributes the recent change in the Foreign Office to the Empress's influence. M. Sazonoff safely removed, Her Majesty hoped to gain her own ends and bring about a speedy conclusion of peace. She is credited with an ardent wish for peace and does not desire to see her former fatherland crushed or humbled. She wants a peace to be concluded that would be dignified for Germany, as well as for Russia. If England is displeased, it will put all idea of an alliance with Russia out of the question and facilitate the furthering of Her Majesty's plan of bringing Russia and Germany back to the old understanding. If France gains nothing – 'tant pis'. At least Germany will be saved! . . .

This rumour had better be dismissed. It savours rather of German methods to sow dissension among us Allies. Germany has never scrupled to attribute to royal personages views that are in direct opposition to their actual conviction.

M. Sazonoff cannot be accused of being bloodthirsty, but he is too clear-sighted to support the idea of peace before a decisive victory has been gained over Germany. The Russian nation would never forgive the Tzar for a rashly patched-up peace, which could not be a guarantee of our future welfare. Things have gone too far; blood has flowed in torrents, misery and suffering have been endured, such as will not be forgotten! Russia cannot be content to let the war end in a draw.

The curious feature of the affair is that a few months before it actually took place the Germans were aware of the impending change in the Foreign Office. About Easter, when no one in Petrograd had the slightest premonition that M. Sazonoff's days as a minister were numbered, a German lady informed her friends that in two months' time M. Sazonoff would retire and M. Stürmer would succeed him. This seemed so unlikely – especially M. Stürmer's accepting the portfolio of Foreign Affairs – that no one believed her. As things turned out, however, the lady was right

{133}

in her prognostication: she only mistook the time – three months instead of two having passed since her words were spoken.

M. Sazonoff's intention was to send in his resignation as soon as the war was over; the continual strain for more than two years has naturally somewhat impaired his health; but he considered it his duty to hold out until the end, deeming it inexpedient for a new man to take the reins at a time when everything was in a tangle. He may not possess all the qualities required in a brilliant statesman, but he had his great merits and his straightforwardness and loyalty were intensely appreciated by the representatives of the Allied Powers.

By birth M. Sazonoff belongs to a good old family of the untitled nobility; he is a man of wealth and of culture, an excellent linguist, he has read deeply and is greatly interested in all art questions. As a host the ex-minister was perfect, and as a guest at other people's hospitable boards he had the art of making himself extremely agreeable. He is a clever conversationalist and a good orator. Madame Sazonoff is a well-bred woman of the world, her dinner-parties are always beautifully ordered as regards fare, floral decorations, old silver and rare china. Both M. and Mme. Sazonoff are a very popular couple in society, sincerely liked by the officials of the Foreign Office.

His successor, M. Stürmer, has only recently turned into a statesman. He is a man of sixty-eight, and has hitherto never been considered an eagle. For several years he was the Governor of Jaroslav, was subsequently appointed director of the Section of General Affairs in the Ministry of the Interior, and after a few years became a member of the Upper Chamber. He always belonged to the Right, and when M. Goremykine resigned the post of Prime Minister he recommended M. Stürmer to the Emperor as a suitable successor. M. Stürmer's great fault, in the eyes of the public at large, is his German origin. He has, however, received a thoroughly Russian education and belongs to the Greek Orthodox Church. His wife is a Russian; she was a Mlle. Strukoff. M. Stürmer regards himself as a true Russian, and his friends declare that his sentiments and convictions are sincere when he speaks of his devotion to the Tzar and the country. His family consists of two sons.

The Nationalist Press in Petrograd accused M. Sazonoff of filling the Foreign Office with Baltic Germans. A tactless campaign was led against Baron Schilling, who up to this occupied the post of Director of the Foreign Office's Chancery. Baron Rosen was obliged to quit the Russian Legation in Stockholm. M. Klemm, occupying the place of Chief of the Department for Oriental Affairs, is continually attacked because of his German name. In the face of these circumstances, it seems strange to confide the leadership of Foreign Affairs to a gentleman who bears the name of Stürmer. As soon as M. Sazonoff's resignation became official, Baron Schilling sent in his resignation. He is credited with the following witty observation: 'Sazonoff and Schilling could pass muster, but Stürmer and Schilling is an impossible combination.' Baron Schilling has been made a Senator, which gives him an excellent position.

The new Minister of Foreign Affairs is a man of intellect, but up to the present he has only been interested in the administration of the internal affairs of the country. It seems difficult to change one's calling at the age of sixty-eight, but to become at a moment's notice, not only an efficient diplomatist, but the initiator of the most important political moves, seems very hard indeed. To be a successful Minister of Foreign Affairs at such an historical moment it is scarcely sufficient to be clever. A man is needed possessed of a wide intellectual outlook, the gift of foresight, skill to decipher the complex changes of political positions, fearlessness in facing what is inevitable, and an iron will to take timely decisions, however harsh they may appear, if they can save the situation.

Far from the thought of endowing M. Sazonoff with all these qualities – though he certainly has some of them – I only wish to point out that M. Sazonoff, in addition to his mental powers, had the diplomatic experience of years, whereas M. Stürmer to all intents and purposes is untried. The Goddess Chance and favourable circumstances may help him to attain the summit of political glory.

It would be desirable to have some reforms introduced into the Russian Foreign Office, for our diplomats, as a body, leave much room for improvement. To be attached to the Ministry of Foreign Affairs is considered nearly as 'chic' as entering the regiments of the Chevalier Guards (Horse Guards). Young men whose principal aim in life is to be smart, after passing their last examinations in the Imperial Alexander Lyceum, the School of Jurisprudence or the University, hasten to fulfil the necessary formalities in order to be attached to this Ministry. But that is by no means all.

The sanctuary of the Foreign Office is its Chancery, and the ambition of every budding diplomat is to be admitted into this 'Holy of Holies'. It gives him at the outset a patent of smartness, turning him suddenly from an ordinary young man into a person of the first rank. From that moment the young man feels convinced he has his foot firmly in the stirrup and that his diplomatic career is secure; for, strange to say, the nominations of secretaries of Embassies and Legations in foreign parts are mostly made from members of the Chancery, without any reference to their suitability.

It happens thus that, having passed up the necessary steps, the budding diplomat, at the age of forty, blossoms into a minister resident in one of the smaller countries, or into a councillor of an Embassy.

The budding Russian diplomat lays great stress on his appearance – his principal aim is to be perfectly groomed, the parting of his hair must be irreproachable, his clothes have a faultless fit, his boots the necessary shine, his hands be carefully manicured; a monocle is considered an elegant appendage, but the important thing is to look as foreign as possible. The members of our Embassies abroad endeavour to appear Parisians in Paris, Englishmen in London, and refined cosmopolitans in other parts of the world. Not one of them remains Russian. The members of our Embassies in foreign capitals keep aloof from their fellow countrymen, and avoid them as if they were pestiferous; woe betide the unfortunate Russian traveller who has to be extricated from some difficulty. Everyone who has had occasion to apply to a Russian Embassy or Consulate abroad is always full of complaints at the way they were neglected or ill-treated by the representatives of the Russian Government.

One of the features of the Russian nature is the facility we display in adapting ourselves to foreign countries and habits. That is one of the reasons why Russians make such good wives to foreigners, because they merge their nationality into that of their husbands, and in a few years' time forget that they ever belonged to another country. I have known cases where such ladies with difficulty remembered their own language. But what may be commendable in a wife is decidedly blameworthy in an official representative of Great Russia, who above all things must remain a true Russian and strive to hold the Russian standard high.

I think the following story will interest the English reader, although it happened over a quarter of a century ago. It is an eloquent example of how a statesman of bygone days firmly stood his ground on the occasion of an incident between the representative of a foreign Power and the Russian Press. The episode was described to me at length by a friend, who was an eye-witness of the whole scene.

It happened in the reign of Alexander III, during the time when Count Dmitry Tolstoy was Minister of the Interior. General Williôme was the German military plenipotentiary personally attached to the Russian Sovereign. A startling article appeared in the *Novoe Vremia* (at that time the *Novoe Vremia* was considered the best-informed and best-intentioned daily paper in Russia), accusing the German general of abusing the privileges which his high position gave him to act the spy for his Government. The article produced a sensation – but it caused dismay at the Embassy. The Foreign Office could do nothing, reprisals upon newspapers were not in its province, and the Minister of the Interior refused to interfere. The German Ambassador, General von Schweinitz, decided to apply to Count Tolstoy personally. The Minister was working in his study when the German Ambassador was announced. The Count pleaded urgent business as an excuse for not being able to receive the Ambassador. The representative of Germany, however, was persistent: he insisted on admittance 'just for five minutes on the most important business'. An official carried the Ambassador's message, but the Count was obdurate and repeated his refusal to receive the German Ambassador, on the plea of being engaged. The Ambassador made a third attempt to penetrate to the Count's study. He begged the Director of the Chancery to go and explain to the Minister that the Ambassador's business was very important and would not detain His Excellency for more than a few moments. 'Tell the Ambassador that I have left the Chancery,' was Count Tolstoy's answer, and he forthwith proceeded to his private apartment adjoining the Chancery. General von Schweinitz took his defeat quietly and did not renew his proceedings.

In conclusion – returning again to the present time – I must add that the reconstructed Cabinet of M. Stürmer was favourably greeted by the Liberals, notwithstanding that all the ministers who form the new Cabinet are staunch Conservatives. The reason for this can be found in the following observation, made by an experienced politician, that the Tzar has confided to this Conservative Cabinet the problem of carrying out some of the expected Liberal reforms. If such a problem were confided to a Liberal Cabinet, too many demands would be made, which the Cabinet could not possibly fulfil. If, on the other hand, a Conservative Cabinet achieves even part of these reforms, the public will trust the Cabinet, and its leaders will inspire confidence in high spheres. This system is adopted in England, where Liberal reforms are generally carried out by a Conservative Cabinet. It may be that our Government wishes to make a similar experiment, and certainly it will be intensely interesting to observe its results.

Chapter XI

THE WAR

NO conscientious annalist describing the conditions of the country during the epoch of the great war can pass over in silence the shameful way the merchants of the Russian Empire (with very few exceptions) behaved towards their fellow-countrymen. They disclosed a grasping, sordid greed that was contemptible. How is the fact to be explained that men belonging to the same class of the population as those who in 1608, led by their fellow-citizen Minine, were the first to carry into the market-place of Nijni-Novgorod their strong-boxes of money and valuables, the jewels of their women, and all they possessed, adopting as their motto the words: 'We will give our lives, our all, we will mortgage our wives and children, but we will never let Russia be insulted.' . . . How was it their descendants found no other impulse in their minds and hearts except the impulse to abominable speculations and sinful peculations in all the domains of trade and industry! Reproaches are parried by the calm and cold-blooded response: 'We waited two hundred years for such a war. If we do not make use of this opportunity, when are we likely to gain riches?'

It is a painful task for a Russian to have to confess the disgraceful motives of his own countrymen, but unfortunately it is quite true that the Russian tradesman has proved the staunchest ally of the German Kaiser, raising obstacles and impediments at a time when the whole nation should have united in the one aim – to annihilate the enemy.

It is true the merchants were lavish in their donations to the Red Cross and other organisations established to alleviate the sufferings of the wounded, but their money gifts cost them little, their gains covering such expenses a hundredfold, and they had the satisfaction of patting themselves on the back, exclaiming: 'What patriotic fellows we are!' Soon after the war commenced the Butchers' Corporation gave a large sum of several thousand roubles, which was to defray the cost of a hospital ward. However, about a year ago, when the meat crisis began, this money was returned to them by the order of the Empress, the august patroness of the Red Cross Society in Russia, with the intimation that 'money for such a sacred cause was not wanted from unclean hands'.

Simultaneously with the outbreak of war with Germany, the Russian merchants declared war upon their fellow-citizens, and the strife has been kept up with the utmost obduracy, and occasional violent attacks on people's pockets. Their plan of campaign is perfectly organised and skilfully carried out. Their headquarters cannot be discovered, and no one knows where the front is on which they operate, nor the whereabouts of their rear. Up to the present the merchant army has been victorious all along the line. Enormous fortunes have been made in the space of a few days. What conclusions can be drawn from this appalling difference between the modern merchant and his forefathers of the seventeenth century? Is it mental decadence, or is existence more complicated in the twentieth century, and the struggle for life more imperative in its exigencies? The fact remains that the heroic conduct of the Russian merchants in 1608 has been immortalised on the pages of history, whereas the part allotted to the same class of men in the annals of the present war will be one of opprobrium and shame.

The victims of this unsatisfactory state of things are the middle classes and people living on a limited income. The workpeople flourish and live in affluence, for their wages have been raised to an unheard-of sum. An efficient workman nowadays can easily earn from twelve shillings to a pound a day (6–10 roubles), which is higher pay than the average official receives. Considering that the former has hardly any expensive requirements and that the latter is used to a certain amount of comfort, the comparative difference of their exchequer is evident. Whilst the former can indulge in small luxuries and hoard his money in a savings bank, the latter can hardly keep himself and his family in food and clothes.

The question of food is becoming a serious one in Petrograd. If one examines the reports of the quantities of different products arriving daily by rail and by water, one is clearly convinced that the capital is amply provided with all kinds of foodstuffs except meat. Yet if one goes into a shop to make a purchase, either the product one demands is not to be had, or its price is exorbitant to a degree, which cannot be explained either by the increased expense of labour, the difficulties of transport, or in the fall of the rouble. At the same time in co-operative stores and shops organised by societies of consumers, one can find nearly all the requisite goods at a slightly higher price than the normal. This proves that the speculators are acting in full force and are either hiding the goods received in some dark corner until the prices shall mount higher, or have taken them to the neighbourhood of Petrograd, where it is so difficult to establish regulation prices that they have attained to monstrous dimensions.

The shortage of foodstuffs has at last awakened the anxiety of the Petrograd municipality; a plan has been formulated to establish public dining-rooms, organised by the town, for all classes of inhabitants, but people in general feel rather sceptical about this system of feeding.

The gift of organisation is not in the Russian nature, and the want of clever, practical and trustworthy organisers is painfully felt at the present time all over the country. Money is lavishly spent, bringing in no result whatever. The municipality of Petrograd started the plan of acquiring cattle in Mongolia. Sparing no expense, three members of the Town Council made the long journey there, but it finally turned out that the cattle could not be transported. The Food Committee interceded with the Railway Transport Committee to have the cattle transported immediately from Siberia to Petrograd. While deliberating this question, the representatives of the municipality were apprised that the outlets of Siberia were congested with more important loads in need of transportation, consequently the bringing of cattle from Mongolia became practically an impossibility. As an exception, however, to general rule, the Transport Committee promised to let the Municipality have one hundred and fifty wagons, but not before the month of July, 1916. This was the official report, and testifies to the acquisition of cattle before ascertaining the feasibility of transport. It would seem just as satisfactory to purchase cattle in Australia, where the oxen are finer than in Siberia, for the ultimate result would have been the same – the Australian cattle could never have reached Petrograd.

The butchers' shops established by the town are nearly always closed – a label on the entrance door informs the inhabitants that 'the shop is shut'. The reason why there is no traffic remains a mystery. The shop is shut and there is an end of it. To make good the shortage, one of the members of the Town Council proposed spending a million roubles on the acquisition of vegetables, which would be sold to the population at normal prices. This scheme was much talked of and discussed by the Press, but it ended in nothing. The other day one of the members inquired of the Mayor of Petrograd how the vegetable scheme was progressing. The reply was that 'Negotiations had been entered upon with kitchen gardeners, but without being able to come to terms; the Commission, however, was taking great trouble to bring the transaction to a satisfactory conclusion.'

Meantime this same self-ruling municipality, after failing in providing the town with either meat or vegetables, not only establishes shops to sell products at regulation prices, but suddenly plans to found dining-rooms for the middle, as well as for the poorer, classes. The result of this new scheme can be anticipated, for this enterprise will require an abundance of meat, vegetables, flour, meal, dairy products and various other items of which the worthy members of the Town Council have probably no notion. The Mayor of Petrograd is probably convinced of the futility of the attempt . . . but something must be done!

Things are certain to go from bad to worse, until the authorities step in and take charge of the food supply of the capital. They will do wisely to investigate from whence the numerous loads arrive at the different stations of Petrograd, take them from untrustworthy private hands and give them to the co-operative stores for sale.

It must be confessed that the municipality received but inadequate support from the police in Petrograd. Occasional fines of two or three hundred roubles are imposed, but to merchants daily gaining their thousands these fines are paltry.

At this very moment, whilst writing these lines, wheaten flour is not to be had in any but the best-provided co-operative shops, and sugar is fast disappearing, although the storehouses are filled with sacks of wheaten flour and thousands of kilos of sugar, the reason for this being that the merchants, in expectation of the prices being shortly raised, have withdrawn these products from the market.

The Ministry of the Interior has collected the figures of the rise in prices during the two war years:

Wheaten flour rose suddenly 83.3 per cent, oats 83, millet 100, butter 240, soap 221.4, coarse calico 130, wood 244.5, meat 86.1. The price of wood has risen higher than anything else, although it would seem that this product did not depend either on the harvest or on importation from abroad.

The banks are just as bad – a recent perquisition in a Russian Bank revealed 175,500 *puds* of secreted sugar, and the storehouses of two other banks revealed 33,000 *puds* of sunflower oil.

A certain rise of prices was to be expected in the present conditions of difficult transit and increased price of labour, but the actual exorbitant demands can only be the result of criminal speculation.

The question of the food supplies for the army and the provinces is under the jurisdiction of the Minister of Agriculture. About a year ago M. Naoumoff was appointed Minister. Until that time M. Naoumoff had occupied the position of an elected member of the Upper Chamber. He is a man of integrity, loyal to the backbone, well intentioned and full of energy. A man of great wealth, he belongs to the landed gentry. He was loath to accept this appointment, however flattering it might be; but the Prime Minister, M. Goremykine, wrote him a letter insisting on his acceptance as the fulfilment of his duty to the country. M. Naoumoff took his task seriously; he worked unceasingly, but the result was *nil*, for he was not supported by his assistants, who saw in him an outsider, and unfortunately M. Naoumoff lacked experience and technical knowledge. Above all, he was not possessed of the power of organisation. He worked himself into a nervous state of prostration, and, as in many points he disagreed with the Prime Minister, M. Stürmer, he preferred to resign. His successor is Count Alexis Bobrinsky.

The new Minister of Agriculture is sixty-four years old; he is a man of great wealth, the owner of a magnificent mansion in Petrograd, a beautiful country seat and vast sugar plantations near Kiev. Thirty-five years ago the Count was Marshal of the Petrograd nobility; subsequently he became a member, and later on the President, of the Town Council. He is a member of the State Duma and of the Upper Chamber, and assistant to the Minister of the Interior. He is a man of intellect and culture; his sincerity and good intentions cannot be doubted.

I cannot refrain from adding a few words in connection with the reform of the principal basis of Russia's exchequer and the sudden cessation of the sale of alcohol all over the Empire. Show me the country possessing a parliamentary regime where a measure of similar importance and of equal beneficial consequences to the people could have been carried out with the same rapidity and completeness. This law is a brilliant proof of the great significance of a monarch's unlimited power, when the latter truly understands the welfare of his people.

In England, in France, as well as in other countries the temperance propaganda commenced several years ago. Gifted writers, eminent scientists, as well as the members of numerous temperance societies have strenuously worked to further the interests of sobriety . . . and what have they attained? Is the day near when they will have convinced their Parliaments of the urgency of dealing a blow to the influential group of distillers and brewers for the ultimate good of the rest of mankind? If I am not mistaken, some feeble efforts have been made in that direction, but they met with scant success and very soon ceased.

In Russia this question was not brought before the Chambers. The Tzar gave out the ukase: 'The sale of alcohol is prohibited during the time of the war. The Minister of Finances is recommended to find other resources for supplying the Crown's income.' These few words sufficed to make the Russian people temperate, to strengthen their capacity for labour, to increase the well-being of every family, and augment the deposits in the savings banks of the Empire.

It has indeed proved a blessing and brought untold happiness!

Chapter XII

CAN RUSSIA FORGET?

THOSE who aspire to bring about a reconciliation with Germany must indeed be shallow-minded if they do not realise that they are the worst enemies of the country and the dynasty, and that their pacific proclivities are an insult to our long-suffering and glorious army.

It is true that one of the chief features of the generous Russian nature is to forget evil and to bear no grudge; a characteristic Russian proverb says: 'Who remembers old scores must lose an eye.' But the present war caused an upheaval of all the most fundamental Russian beliefs and convictions. The roots of bitter animosity towards the Germans, saturated in torrents of blood, have struck too deeply ever to be entirely eradicated. The Teutons have been shown up in their true colours. The slight veneer of superficial culture was soon brushed off, revealing the odious coarseness and the cruel instincts of the ferocious savage. A similar war to the one raging at present cannot be remembered. Such dastardly acts of wanton iniquity as are being daily committed by the Germans can only be found in the records of fifteen centuries ago. People were prepared for a devastating and murderous conflict owing to deadly new inventions, which carry war from land and sea, into the air and underwater. Actual fighting could not be different from what it is, but living in the twentieth century we had a right to expect that off the battlefield the proceedings between the hostile armies might be established according to the rules of civilised humanity. Instead of which no previous war can be compared to this one for cold-blooded cruelty. From the very first day the Germans revealed themselves.

Can Russia ever forget the opprobrium she was made to suffer, the insults that were heaped on her, the oceans of blood that were shed and the heartrending misery that was endured? It is an insult to Holy Russia to think it possible that the old terms of friendship with Germany and the Hohenzollerns – the principal authors of all this wretchedness and desolation – can ever be resumed. Peace will be concluded in due course, but the Germans must be shunned for ever by every self-respecting Russian.

Thousands of unsuspicious Russian travellers were caught in Germany and in Austria at the moment when the war broke out. How were they treated by the chivalrous Germans? The Dowager Empress Marie Feodorovna's train was mobbed in Berlin, although the Kaiser had sanctioned Her Majesty's passage through German territory, and no window could be let down for fear of more humiliating insults. Prince Youssoupoff, his wife and son, with the latter's bride, arrived in Berlin at about the same time. They were declared prisoners, and were only offered their freedom and permission to return to Russia on condition that the Princess Youssoupoff signed a document to the effect that all her possessions were given up to Germany. The Princess refused her signature to such an absurd transaction. Her daughter-in-law, Princess Irene, seeing her mother-in-law on the verge of a breakdown, volunteered to speak to the Crown Princess Cecilia on the telephone. The Crown Princess is Princess Irene's first cousin, and had frequently visited Russia, staying there with her Russian relations. Her Imperial Highness asked for an hour's time, but her answer was disheartening. She had spoken to her father-in-law, but he had requested her not to interfere; all that had happened was done by the Kaiser's own orders, and the Crown Princess could do nothing to alleviate her cousin's position and that of her parents-in-law. If it had not been for an English valet there is no knowing what might have happened. He was the only one who did not lose his presence of mind, and he appealed to the Spanish Ambassador for help. Prince Youssoupoff and family with their respective attendants were taken to the Spanish Embassy and from there to the Dowager Empress's train. They succeeded in leaving Berlin with only one mishap: in the hurry of leaving the hotel a small bag containing fifty thousand marks to defray travelling expenses was forgotten, but the family were so relieved to have escaped the German clutches that they willingly left that money as their ransom.

The wife of the late Viceroy of the Caucasus, Countess Worontzov-Dashkoff, was taking her annual course of baths and waters at Marienbad; the war cut short her cure, and she hastened to Berlin on her homeward journey. Regardless of her position and of her venerable age, the Countess was treated in the most ignominious way. She was hustled about and subjected to a personal search, extending even to her 'transformation', which was pulled off 'in case dangerous documents might be hidden inside'. But it seems that this brutal treatment left little impression on the Countess's mind, for a few months later, when Turkey had declared war on Russia and the Tzar visited Tiflis, the following incident occurred.

At an official banquet held in the palace at Tiflis the Countess, who was seated at the right hand of the monarch, turned to him saying: 'Oh! how impatiently I am waiting for this dreadful war to be over.' The Emperor responded by asking the reason of her anxiety.

'Why, as soon as the war ceases, I shall hurry to Marienbad.'

The Sovereign stared incredulously. 'Is it possible, Countess, that after all the indignities you were obliged to submit to on your return from Germany last autumn you can contemplate the idea of going there again?'

The Countess, seeing her blunder, murmured something about the wonderful efficacy of the Marienbad waters.

'Search well in the Caucasus, madam, you are sure to find waters there as wonderfully efficient as in Marienbad,' coldly replied the Emperor, turning his shoulder to the Countess.

I think a slight sketch of the Countess Worontzov-Dashkoff's personality will be of interest to my English readers, for she has played a prominent part in her husband's long career, especially during the time of his viceroyalty in the Caucasus, where in reality his wife was the vicereine. For many years the Count was a doomed man, suffering from a painful and incurable malady. He reigned, but his wife ruled. This state of things was even brought before the State Duma and caused one of the Caucasian members to speak out from the Duma tribune, accusing the Government of leaving such an important country as the Caucasus to the mercies of a fanciful old lady of eighty.

Countess Worontzov-Dashkoff, by birth a Countess Schouvalov, has never been noted for either tact or condescension. She queened it over society in Tiflis, and surrounded herself and her 'Court' with elaborate rules of etiquette, which gave rise to many funny stories, and were the joy of anyone newly arrived from Petrograd. The Countess's receptions on Tuesday afternoons were full of elaborate ceremony. As if on a throne the Countess sat in a huge armchair. Each newcomer approached her between two rows of chairs, placed on both sides of the mistress of the house. If it were a lady she respectfully shook two reluctantly extended fingers; if it were a man he bent and reverently pressed a kiss on the outstretched digits. This ceremony over, the visitor backed between the row of chairs, dropping into the first vacant one. A profound silence reigned, interrupted by a few questions languidly addressed to those who sat nearest. No tea was handed round, no general conversation was carried on, and if by any chance some bold visitor ventured to make a remark on his own account, he was instantly withered into silence by an irate glance from the Countess and the affrighted looks of those about her. The Armenians, known for their astuteness, speedily found out the weak point in the Countess's armour; they bowed low before her, treated her as a genuine Sovereign and got all they wanted. In Tiflis the Countess was called 'the Queen of the Armenians'.

Princess Susan Belosselsky-Belosersky, an American by birth and one of the smartest women in society, was likewise in Berlin when war was declared by Germany. She was to return to Petrograd in the train prepared for the Russian Ambassador, M. Sverbéeff. But the departure of the Russian diplomats from the land of pseudo-culture was not surrounded with the dignified courtesy which the 'Russian barbarians' manifested towards the German Ambassador and all those who left Russia under his protection. The Russian Ambassador was insulted on the way to the station and his hat was knocked off. As to Princess Belosselsky-Belosersky, she was knocked about and spat upon, and arrived quite ill at Stockholm, and had to stay there for a few days before being able to continue her homeward journey.

If illustrious and important travellers met with such ill-treatment, what could ordinary tourists expect? The German officials lost all sense of moderation and decency. Women were publicly divested of their garments on the plea that plans and documents might be concealed on them. Young women and girls were submitted to the outrage of being searched at the hands of men. A rich landed proprietor was travelling with his daughter, a remarkably pretty girl of nineteen. Mlle. K. was undressed and shamed by a German official under the eyes of her distracted parent, who was struck down by an apoplectic fit and the unfortunate daughter lost her reason. The wife of General Istomine was travelling with a small child; she and many other travellers were locked up and kept for hours in a railway carriage without any food. When Madame Istomine begged for some milk for her baby, she was given water which had been used to soak pigs' intestines. A draught of that water made the child sick; the little girl could not stand such treatment and by the time the Russian frontier was reached she was dying.

M. Sheremeteff was returning to Russia with his wife and children. They were stopped at one of the German towns and M. Sheremeteff was taken away to be examined. No one knows exactly what happened, but a few hours later the wife was informed that her husband had died suddenly from heart failure. The unhappy widow was denied permission to see her dead husband, and she and her children were hurried off to continue their homeward journey. It is supposed that M. Sheremeteff, a somewhat choleric gentleman, had not been guarded in his language and had been shot. Else why this strange refusal to let his wife see his body and have him properly buried!

I could fill many pages with similar instances of German brutality to helpless travellers, but I will confine myself to one more heart-rending story, which makes one shudder with indignation and horror. Madame Tougan-Baranovsky, the daughter of a well-known Russian professor and the wife of a high official in the Ministry of Ways and Communications, had met with an accident: her maid upset the spirit-lamp whilst curling her mistress's hair and the lady's face had somewhat suffered. Being young and handsome it was natural Madame Tougan-Baranovsky did not wish to remain disfigured for life by a scarred face. Wonders were related of a celebrated skin specialist in Vienna and of his marvellous cures. The afflicted lady placed herself in the hands of the well-known doctor. The operation had been skilfully performed, the skin was rapidly changing, but the scars had still to be bandaged, and Madame Tougan-Baranovsky was to remain for a few weeks longer under the doctor's care in his sanatorium. When the war broke out the doctor (who had been paid in full directly after the operation) not only refused to continue the treatment of his Russian patient, but turned her out of his establishment. Weakened by her recent operation, feeling wretched and ill, Madame Tougan-Baranovsky found herself alone and friendless in a strange town. She fell into the hands of the Austrian police, was subjected to an examination, searched, and the bandages of her scarred face pulled off to see if they did not conceal plans of some Austrian fortress. After innumerable hardships the unfortunate young woman reached Petrograd, where she was met by her husband. But blood poisoning had set in, and she was only sustained by her nerves and her indomitable will. She had the strength to ascend the stairs leading to her flat and to embrace her little seven-year-old son, after that she collapsed and passed away the next morning, adding to the endless list of the victims of German cruelty; but at least she had the consolation of dying at home surrounded by her nearest and dearest.

After a time this persecution of Russian travellers subsided, and a fortnight later Russian tourists returning home met with different treatment in Berlin and other German towns. The Kaiser's subjects had come to their senses and were frightened at the results entailed by the harshness shown to the 'Bade-Gäste', for naturally most of the travellers belonged to that category. What would be the ultimate fate of all the German health resorts if the Russians were to boycott them? All these places are kept going by Russian and British gold, spent lavishly at Marienbad, Carlsbad, Homburg, Nauheim, Teplitz and *tutti quanti*.

Two Russian Dowagers, the Princess Olga Petrovna Dolgorouky and her sister-in-law Princess Saltykoff, were fortunate enough to pass through Berlin when the reaction had set in. They were detained for several weeks in the German capital, but they were supplied by an obsequious hotel-keeper, and they were civilly attended to by the hotel servants. The two Dowagers seized the opportunity of their enforced stay in Berlin to improve their mind; they visited all the museums and picture-galleries of Berlin. They frequently dined at the house of the former German Ambassador in Petrograd, and most of their evenings were spent with Count and Countess Pourtales. When this became known in Petrograd it caused general indignation. People wondered at the Princesses consenting, under the circumstances, to accept the hospitality of Count and Countess Pourtales. The Dowagers' conduct in Berlin was severely criticised by public opinion in Petrograd, and both venerable Princesses were found wanting in the dignity which ought to belong to Russian great ladies.

The inhumanity and cruelty manifested by the Germans towards the Russian prisoners have been appalling. They showed leniency only in the Baltic provinces; here their watchword was 'Schonet die Balten.'[1] The Germans have a particular grudge against the Cossacks, and several of them were cruelly mutilated. A wounded sergeant, Filimonoff, had been overlooked by the Russian Red Cross Brigade and was taken prisoner. Before taking him to an ambulance to have his wounds attended to he was brought into the presence of several officers who questioned him as to the Russian forces and positions. When Filimonoff refused to answer these questions salt was rubbed into his raw wounds.

When the Germans were obliged to beat a hasty retreat from the village 'Zabudje' near Minsk they not only robbed the peasants of all they could get hold of in the shape of cattle, crops, etc., but before leaving the place they beat and ill-treated the villagers, a great number of whom were barricaded in a huge barn. The last thing the Germans did was to set fire to most of the cottages, as well as the barn, in which three hundred men and women were locked up. Fortunately the peasants succeeded in breaking open the door, and thus they escaped the awful death intended for them.

On one occasion when the Tzar and his Consort were visiting a military hospital in Moscow, the Emperor approached the bedside of quite a young soldier and noticed that both his eye-sockets were empty. On His Majesty's inquiring how such a dreadful accident had occurred he was told that the wounded soldier was lying on the battlefield unable to move. A German sister of mercy came up to him, but instead of giving him help she took out of her pocket a sharp stiletto, put both his eyes out and then left him to die if he had not been found by some members of the Russian Red Cross Brigade. On hearing this harrowing account of merciless cruelty the Emperor turned pale with suppressed emotion; horror and dismay were depicted on his mobile features. For a few moments he could not utter a word, then, stooping, the Tzar pressed his lips to the unhappy man's forehead and in a low but clear voice promised to have him provided for until the end of his life.

By way of contrast I will narrate another incident which brings into strong relief the unsophisticated good nature of the Russian soldier. The story was told by the famous dancer of the Imperial

1 Spare the Baltics.

ballet, the lovely Mlle. Schollar, as one of her experiences during the two years when she worked in Galicia as a sister of mercy. This is her story:

'It was about Christmas time in the first year of the war. Evening had set in, when the sound of knocking reached my ears. Hastening to the door of the dressing-station, I opened it into the cold dark night, and dimly discerned the figure of a soldier. "If you are wounded you can come in."

'"But we are two," was the reply, and to my amazement I saw a Russian soldier carrying an Austrian on his shoulders. The two had fought bravely a few hours before and they had wounded each other, but when the fray was over the Russian soldier, who was only slightly hurt, took up the Austrian, who had a serious wound in his leg, and carried him to the nearest ambulance to have medically attended the wound he himself had inflicted.'

One of the sisters of mercy of the Russian Red Cross who visited the concentration camps of our prisoners in Germany is a personal friend of mine. Some of her impressions were intensely painful. She says she will never forget the moment when she first came in contact with the sufferings of these wretched creatures – the slaves of the twentieth century. 'Sister, we have not enough to eat.' . . . 'Sister, they beat us unmercifully.' . . . 'Sister, look at this wound; the sentinel gave it to me with his bayonet.' . . . 'Sister, for mercy's sake get bread for us; at the rate we are fed we shall not live to return to our country', etc., etc. Groans, complaints and sobs filled the air . . .

The camp at Stargardt made a particularly depressing impression on the Russian sister: the exhausted look of the prisoners, the report of their continual punishments, filled her heart with sorrow. The commandant – a fat German with a red face and bloodshot eyes – listened with undisguised cynicism to the complaints the Russian sister of mercy considered herself entitled to make. It was in this camp that the sister heard the shocking account of pornographic photographs having been taken of the Russian soldiers. The latter did not want to lend themselves to these infamous devices, even the local photographer objected to take the groups, but the commandant sent for another photographer from the neighbouring town, and the soldiers were forced to submit. When the sister mentioned this disgusting fact to a German officer he denied it and endeavoured to convince her that it was all a mistake, for only gymnastic groups of the prisoners had been taken. But it is hardly to be supposed that the Russian doctors as well as the soldiers could have mistaken the one for the other.

The mud huts were shown to the sister in which after the battle of Soldau many of our soldiers had their nether limbs frozen; where they were devoured by vermin and contracted typhoid fever and cholera... but the huts were empty when the sister inspected them. In the camps of Hustrow and Parhim the prisoners suffered agonies. Nine of them belonging to the Koporsky and Poltava regiments were beaten to death for refusing to dig trenches. A Russian general told the sister that when he with his officers and soldiers were surrounded by superior forces of the Germans and taken prisoners, they had to sleep three nights in the fields. 'Subsequently we were divided into hundreds, with an officer at the head of each. In this order we were marched into the nearest town, where we were given brooms to sweep the streets.

'When I and the officers declined to take the brooms, saying that our soldiers would sweep the streets under our supervision, our epaulettes were torn off and we were struck with them across the face. The German Kaiser's son, Prince Joachim, was present, and it was by his orders that these things were done. Half dead with hunger, fatigue and misery we gave in and took the brooms. Prince Joachim then snap-shotted us, and after that we were permitted to let the soldiers sweep.'

It seems incredible that an Emperor's son, the great-grandson of Queen Victoria, should be such an unmitigated cad!... It only proves the coarseness and vulgarity of the Teutonic race. They did not lower the Russian army by this unprecedented act of clownishness, but they stigmatised the vaunted German culture with the brand of ever-lasting shame. The same general related the pathetic tragedy of a Russian colonel, a fellow-prisoner of his. Two of his officers were to be tried by a German court-martial for an act committed before their captivity. If I am not mistaken, the officers were accused of having fired shots in passing a small German town. The colonel was summoned before the court as chief witness against his officers. On the morning of the trial the colonel was found dead with his throat cut. He left a letter to the German military authorities, in which he claimed acquittal for the two officers. He (the colonel) was alone responsible for what had happened, the officers were innocent, they had acted under his orders.

In Mislovitzy our soldiers were forced to work day and night – the injured and sick likewise – in the coal mines; but not being familiar with the perils of the shafts, which had not been explained to them, they were the victims of constant accidents, and the local infirmaries were full of Russian soldiers who had been crippled in the mines.

In Neuhammer my friend the sister noticed that many of the soldiers had a band round their left sleeve with the cypher XV. When she inquired into the reason of this, the soldiers answered that they were being ordered to dig trenches against the French in the vicinity of Strassbourg. 'We don't want to, but we are forced.' The penal camp for Russian soldiers left the sister in a very dejected frame of mind. The prisoners are condemned to hard labour, underfed and pitilessly beaten for the slightest misdemeanour. Most of the prisoners were at work; but the sister saw their mud huts, without windows, stoves, or the possibility of any light. It was terrible! In one of the camps a girl of eighteen was amongst the prisoners. She came from the Don and had enlisted as a private soldier. The Germans called her 'Das Kosaken Mädchen'.[1] Her pluck and adoration for the Tzar and her country had even inspired the Germans with some respect, but at first she had been ill-treated. After Mlle. Konnevsky had been taken prisoner in one of the Polish towns, she exchanged her soldier's kit for the garb of a sister of mercy and nursed the wounded soldiers. She was taken to Germany for having tried to escape. When Mlle. Konnevsky arrived in Haffelberg, a German officer of the concentration camp hit her across the face for declining to take the Red Cross bandage from her sleeve. Several Russian officers were incarcerated in Burg and in Magdeburg for more or less long terms of imprisonment, from nine to twenty-one months. The captive officers were not actually ill-treated, but their nervous state verged on insanity. When the sister complained that many of the orderlies had been bitten by dogs the Commander looked quite astonished. 'Why they cannot have any objection to that, for they get twenty pfennig for every bite; you see we are training police dogs.' The worthy Teuton evidently considered twenty pfennig ample compensation to a Russian soldier for having his flesh lacerated by a German dog.

The German doctors encourage the Russian officers to take

---

[1] The Cossack maiden.

morphia, and several of them have become hopeless drug takers. The reading-rooms in the prisoners' camps are provided exclusively with revolutionary books; one of them contained a book of anecdotes about the Emperor Nicholas II. The Little Russians are separated from the rest of the prisoners, and they are lectured upon the advantages of severing their connection with Russia and having their own government. The same system is applied to the Caucasian prisoners.

When the sister had to give a formal account and sign the report of the Danish delegate, who had accompanied the Russian sister in her visits to the prisoners' camps in Germany, she felt miserably helpless. What could she do! She was obliged to sign a formal statement of what she had seen, but how could she express all that she had felt and lived through in each camp? It was the last straw ... the sister's nerves and her self-control gave way. In the presence of two German officers and of the Danish delegate she gave vent to her pent-up feelings and in a torrent of reproaches she let them hear the plain truth about the inhuman punishments – beating with an India-rubber stick is one of the favoured forms of modern German torture – of the jeering and mockeries the prisoners were subjected to, of the depressing moral atmosphere of the prisoners, to whom no rights were conceded in the 'cultured' country of the Germans. The German officers felt the policy of silence was best and held their tongues. What could they say in reply? ...

Commentaries are useless. Nothing can be added to the poignancy and horror of all this suffering. Can such acts as those of which the Germans have been guilty for over two years ever be condoned or consigned to oblivion? Can it ever be forgotten in Russia that every German is at heart an executioner?

Chapter XIII

THE PRESS

IF I were to follow an old tradition and place a motto at the head of each chapter, I should choose for this the inscription that is to be found in luminous letters at the entrance of hell – 'Leave hope behind all ye who enter here.'

Unfortunately Russia is entirely lacking in men whose obvious vocation is journalism. Furthermore she has no powerful organ in the press wielding influence and really representative of public opinion, an organ whose view would have to be taken into serious consideration. These two shortcomings are greatly to be deplored.

Last century, when half the people were illiterate, when Russia had only half the number of newspapers she now possesses, when the censor's yoke was felt by the press of all shades of opinion; at that time we had Aksakoff, the great tribune of the *Moscovsky Viedomosti*, to whose voice the Government of Alexander II listened with attention and respect, and Prince Vladimir Mestchersky, whose articles sometimes had power to change the direction of Government affairs and to decide the fate of ministers. This was likewise the epoch when the talent of Alexis Souvorine was in full bloom; it is to him that the *Novoe Vremia* owes its success. These were journalists who felt the divine call of their profession; men of vivid critical intellect, who knew how to conquer by virtue of their own gifts. Now, when life itself presents so many urgent problems, when all the European nations are making history and the deliberation of all questions of state and politics in general has become permissible for the Russian press, we lack the right men. We have only artisans of the pen, who fill the sheets of the daily papers with their writing, without being able to find either words or thoughts to electrify people, or to ensure the realisation of an ideal.

If by any chance you enter the editorial office of a Russian paper, no matter of what views, thinking the decency of your outward appearance and your polite manners will prove sufficient to secure a polite reception and amount of attention, you will immediately be forced to acknowledge that your hopes were delusive, and you will be made to feel that you have stepped over a boundary behind which reign peculiar laws and customs, where an outsider is only admitted to pay a subscription, or to hand in an advertisement, in a word, to bring money. Under all other circumstances his presence is plainly not desired. The customs of this journalistic world seem to require the exercise of particular discourtesy towards people belonging to society whose names have not a plebeian sound. A lady, for instance, will be kept waiting for some time before she is received, and, if she has the patience to wait for this belated admittance, she will frequently find herself greeted by the editorial divinity, sprawling in a chair and unmercifully puffing his cigarette the whole time.

It would be wrong to ascribe the blame for such ways and manners, which would not be tolerated in any decent company, solely to the want of breeding of the representatives of Russian journalism – the freest of all free professions. The unwritten rule appears to be 'newspaper offices for newspaper men'. There seems to be a fear in the hearts of Russian journalists of those from outside learning the inner secrets of their craft, or of giving new ideas to 'the Chief' and thus undermining the position of his subordinates. Unfortunately Russian journalism exists on a much lower level than is the case in England, for instance, where journalists are recruited from a vastly different class. In Russia it has always been a refuge for the unsuccessful, and in consequence it embraces a very mixed class of men, whose educational advantages are not all they might have been. When it is remembered that the journalist is speaking to the nation every day of the week and has the power to elevate or debase, particularly with a people so trusting and simple as the Russians, the danger of a press such as ours is manifest.

A great hue and cry was raised in press circles, a few years ago, when it was known that the Government intended to include a clause in the new press laws, requiring every editor of periodical publications to be provided with certificates showing that he had at least passed through a middle-class college. There was great excitement at the turn matters were taking, and a crusade was started, demonstrating the impossibility of putting such limitations on the activities of an open profession; that for a journalist education is secondary and only talent is required, etc. The wonder is why in other open professions an educational census is not considered an insuperable obstacle to freedom, but a man having the pretension to express daily and publicly thoughts and reflections representative of public opinion, and who has thousands of readers, must keep the doubtful privilege of writing illiterately, as well as preserve the intellectual outlook of an acrobat.

Education cannot ruin talent – it merely polishes it. After all, genuine talent is a power that will be acknowledged in all conditions, and the projected law would have been valuable, if only to combat the intellectual poverty of recent years. It is clear that the protest of the press was not inspired by conviction, but was merely the outcome of an anxiety felt by the present representatives of our debilitated journalism for themselves and their friends.

This anxiety explains the reason why the editorial office is so jealously guarded from the intrusion of anyone not guaranteed to have subscribed to the professional *credo*, or assured of sharing the ruling convictions of their organ on political and social matters, lest he should tell tales out of school.

When an article is received in the editor's office, be it by the great man himself or by a junior, attention is given not to its literary quality, nor to the degree of interest it may represent to the public, but to the personality of the writer. If the article is written by one of the usual press clique, or even by a new man who has been introduced and supported by one of the old members of the editorial staff, it will be sent to the printer frequently without perusal, even if it is badly written, or repeats for the hundredth time some old and jejune reflection, without interest and occasionally without an idea in the background. Nevertheless the article will appear the next day. But if the article is written by an outsider, it will receive a different treatment. The more talent it shows the less chance of its appearance; especially if it reflects the interests of the moment. The members of the staff will take good care that it shall disappear in the office wastepaper basket, and should the author hazard a personal appeal they will so manage that the opposition he meets with will effectually discourage his further efforts.

Every issue of a newspaper is composed of a fixed number of lines, divided into different sections. In each section appear the articles and paragraphs of one or several of the permanent staff, and every Saturday they receive a salary in proportion to the quantity of printed lines that have flowed from their respective pens in the course of the week. The more printed lines, the more money on Saturday! These writers consequently grow accustomed to look upon the printed lines as their own possession, and scent an adversary in anyone whose literary production might take up part of their columns, and so abbreviate the space at their disposal and thus diminish their weekly wage. Even Russian journalists are human.

The system is wrong. In England the press is always eager for new blood; in Russia it is always the old blood growing daily more impoverished. The present leaders of the Russian press like to regard themselves as the representatives of public opinion; they frequently emphasise their love of Russia, their jealousy of the public weal, but the melancholy fact remains that they close their doors against innovation, and a closed door means an impure atmosphere within. 'Such as the birds are, so will their songs be,' says a Russian proverb, and we in Russia hear many false notes from our press.

The integrity of the leading newspapers in Russia is, I consider, beyond question. Their existence in most cases is solidly guaranteed by the capital interest of the editors, or of a company of editors. They look carefully after the members of their staffs, and no shady transactions are tolerated. It is clearly understood among their employees that dishonesty means disgrace and dismissal. The smaller fry, however, are not so squeamish, and some of their contributors do not scruple to increase their meagre salaries by any means that come their way. Some content themselves with gratuitous refreshments at the buffet of those theatres that they write about, and with small sums, in the guise of loans, from an impresario or an actress craving for advertisement. Others use more energetic means to invade their neighbours' pockets. The following characteristic fact was related to me last summer: The chief of a small paper, widely spread among the lower classes, was taking his annual holiday and was represented in the editorial office by his assistant, Mr. X. The latter was a Jew, and a few days after having attained the summit of editorial power, a new reporter – a Jew likewise and a friend of Mr. X. – turned up in the office. The temporary chief gave him pleasant work to do, and amongst other things commissioned him to write reviews about a new summer theatre, which had been recently opened.

A series of articles appeared, full of praise and admiration, but, when the old editor returned, the director of the theatre came to him with the complaint that the Jewish reporter had extorted five hundred roubles from him, threatening in case of refusal to give his readers an unfavourable impression of the new theatre. The old editor called the reporter and ordered him to refund the five hundred roubles immediately. The despair of the unfortunate man was comical: he screamed and tore his hair, declaring excitedly that he had robbed nobody, but that someone was trying to rob him, a poor hardworking man, he would find ways and means, however, to circumvent them and would appeal to the law. When he was quieted, the situation cleared up, revealing the fact that out of the five hundred roubles paid by the theatrical director, four hundred and fifty had been kept by the temporary editor, Mr. X., leaving only fifty roubles to his friend, the reporter. And now the latter was called upon to return the whole sum – five hundred roubles! Was not that robbery? This incident was considered a good joke, and caused the members of the editorial staff much amusement – as for the impresario nothing remained for him but to join in the general laughter.

The indifference displayed by the proprietors, the extremely mixed elements of which the editorial staffs are usually composed, as well as the doubtful morals and manners of this 'milieu', deter people of breeding and education from devoting their leisure and talents to journalism, and, if by chance a man of the world makes the attempt, he surrounds his work with impenetrable mystery.

It will be a long time before Russian ladies and gentlemen will consent to contribute to certain parts of a newspaper or magazine under their full name, as is done in England, and before editors will realise the beneficent influence that such people, with more cultured intellects and refined tastes, would have on the general tone of their publications. If the editors would adopt a broader view and more modern methods they would not be confronted with the difficulty they feel nowadays, when the necessity presents itself of attending some pageant, or interviewing some eminent foreigner, or finding a suitable writer, who, in his language and manners, would be able to uphold the dignity of the press – this eleventh Great Power of the World – when its work is carried out with tact and self-respect. Such representatives do not exist and their 'interviews' give rise to no end of funny episodes.

An amusing story is that of a journalist belonging to a small paper. A grand ball was to be given in the ancestral halls of the late Mr. Basil Narischkine, an eccentric man, enormously rich, afflicted with a passionate temper. The journalist arrived intent on collecting some details about the coming festivity and writing a flourishing account of the ball. On being made aware of the object of his visit, Mr. Narischkine got into a frenzy of rage and had the poor fellow kicked downstairs. It must be admitted that this journalist was a little exigent; still, such a violent exit was too severe a chastisement. Since that memorable day the victim has become a wiser man and now uses the telephone for interviewing!

I must mention the name of the one modern journalist in whom public opinion recognises talent. Mr. Menschikoff is extremely popular, and he receives very high fees from editors. His articles on various aspects of external and internal politics are often astonishing by their force of analysis and clever arguments; his style is always good, though sometimes it appears a little heavy. Still, Mr. Menschikoff is not a journalist by vocation. In his youth he was an officer of the Russian navy. Clever, educated and well read, he can write on any subject, but always remains cool and dispassionate – and so do his readers.

At the present moment the newspaper that draws the greatest number of readers is the *Russkoe Slovo*, published in Moscow; it is at the same time the most flourishing publication in Russia.

Every Russian who loves his country must incline with deep respect before the bright memory of Alexis Souvorine, who, without capital or connections, rose from a master in a provincial National School to become a man of world-wide renown and created a business of national importance worth many millions. Alexis Souvorine was the embodiment of three magnificent qualities: talent, industry and honesty. Souvorine senior left a widow and four children, the outcome of two marriages. Before his death, he turned the *Novoe Vremia*, which belonged to him, into a company of shareholders; each share being valued at 5,000 roubles. Part of these shares Souvorine presented to his oldest and nearest assistants, who for so many years had helped him to build up success. The majority of the shares were distributed among the members of his family, thus securing to them the decisive voice in the company's council. The *Novoe Vremia*, with its many ramifications, spread all over the country with a branch in Paris.

Perhaps the war, from which we all expect so much, will produce a newer and a better journalism in Russia. Some editorial genius may arise who will see the folly of making an instrument such as the press a mere parochial baton. He will see the advantage of throwing open his columns to those with aims and aspirations and the power of expressing them. The result will be the conferring of a great blessing upon our beloved Russia.

Chapter XIV

SOCIETY OF PETROGRAD

I DO not think my account of Russia will be quite complete if I do not give my English readers a glimpse, however slight and superficial, of our Petrograd society.

As in every great capital, there are numbers of sets, coteries and circles, each of them leading a separate life, but I will limit my descriptive efforts to the Upper Ten, who represent the 'High Life' of Petrograd. I have already had occasion to mention that for the last twelve years the Imperial Court has taken no active part in the social life of the capital. There is, consequently, nothing in the nature of a social centre of gaiety and pleasure. Everyone recognises this as a great drawback. In former times the tone of society was set by the Court itself, and society had a standard to live up to. At present this is not the case, and the result is that society has acquired a casual tone and is becoming extremely 'unconventional', especially the smart set of very young women. Even the war, with all its horrors and misery, has failed to quench their insatiable craving for continual gaiety and excitement, and during the winter months of last season (1916) in a certain set of ten or twelve young married women, who shall be nameless, dancing went on every night. Balls and parties could not be given, but these irrepressibles assembled every evening at the house of one or the other of their number, and the night was spent in dancing. The husband of one of these ladies, coming home from the front for a short rest, reached his house late at night whilst the gaiety was at its height. Fresh from the scenes of bloodshed and suffering which he had so recently witnessed, and to which he might have been a victim had not a kind Providence protected him, he was shocked to the extent of deciding not to enter his own house under such circumstances. The next day a stormy interview ensued between him and his featherbrained wife, and the couple is now said to be on the eve of a legal separation.

The Countess Kleinmichel was considered the best hostess in Petrograd before the war; in fact notwithstanding her nearly seventy years the Countess was the mainspring of society. The Countess Marie Kleinmichel, by birth a Countess Keller, is the sister of General Count Keller, one of the heroes of the Russo-Japanese war, killed in the battle of Jan-Zelin. A woman of brains, highly cultured and very talented, the Countess is extremely fascinating. In her youth she was exquisitely pretty, in the pocket-Venus style. Her entertainments were always lively, her balls and dinner-parties great successes. She has the gift of making everyone feel at their ease in her presence, and the irresistible charm of her manner when she is acting as hostess is wonderful. She seems to electrify the whole company and compel them to enjoy themselves and feel happy. She has a sweet smile or a pleasant word for all, and not one of her guests, be he ever so unimportant, feels himself neglected.

Being well read, clever in discussions and smart at repartee, the Countess Kleinmichel is much appreciated as a conversationalist, and was a valued guest at all important dinner-parties, for no one knows better how to start and maintain the interest of a conversation. Her *salon* was a very interesting one: foreign diplomatists, ministers, high officials, clever people, artists and pretty women could always be met there. It used to be considered a political *salon*, because of the many influential people who met there, and because all new Government measures, political or social events and incidents were freely discussed at her house.

The Countess Kleinmichel has travelled a great deal, and part of her life has been spent abroad. Thus she has many intimate friends amongst foreigners, and on several occasions in passing through Berlin she has been invited to Potsdam to take tea with the German Kaiser and his Consort.

Being such a cosmopolitan, the Countess's house was a great resort of foreign diplomatists or distinguished travellers visiting Petrograd, for they were always sure of finding a warm welcome and congenial society. She was on friendly terms with all the ambassadors and resident ministers and their wives living in the

SOCIETY OF PETROGRAD

Russian capital. The Countess is very wealthy, her house in the Serguievskaia is a marvel of comfort and artistic luxury. She strictly follows the Western fashions, and her dinner-parties are always served in the latest Paris or London style.

The Countess's unbounded tact and *savoir-faire* are great points in her favour. It is said that the Countess keeps a diary containing a full record of all the events she has witnessed during her lengthy life. She paints a great deal in *gouache* and in watercolours, but her great achievements are her caricatures – she has a big scrap-book full of such drawings, some of them remarkably clever and full of wit. This album, however, is only shown to a very select circle of intimate friends.

When the war broke out a sudden blight seemed to fall on Countess Kleinmichel. Her intimacy with the German Ambassador, Count Pourtales, and with General Count Dolma-Schlobitten (the military plenipotentiary in Petrograd who preceded General von Helius) was acidly alluded to by extreme patriots. Her visits to Potsdam were remembered. However, her *salon* still continues to attract a number of people.

One of the ladies of Petrograd who has actively and generously come forward in her country's hour of need is the Countess Carlov. She has organised several war hospitals in Oranienbaum and in town, where she and her daughters are in daily attendance.

Countess Carlov is the widow of the late Duke of Mecklenburg-Strelitz. Her marriage was a romantic one. Nathalie Feodorovna Vanliarsky belonged to a good old but impecunious family. Through the influence of connections she obtained the post of lady-in-waiting to the late Grand Duchess Catherine Mikhailovna, the widow of Duke George of Mecklenburg-Strelitz, senior, and the mother of two sons and a daughter, born and educated in Russia. The two sons George and Michael remained German subjects, but were officers in the Russian artillery. Since the war the only surviving brother, the Duke Michael of Mecklenburg-Strelitz, has become a Russian subject.

I must now take my readers back a quarter of a century. At that time Nathalie Feodorovna Vanliarsky was past her first youth, she was not pretty, and no one thought of any danger from that quarter; but she was clever and fascinating, and her charm of manner was attractive, so the elder Duke fell violently in love with his mother's maid of honour. The Grand Duchess Catherine was indignant at the turn affairs had taken; Mlle. Vanliarsky was immediately sent away from Court, and things remained in this unsatisfactory state till one day, or rather one night, the old Grand Duchess Catherine, who was ill at the time, had a dream which partook of a vision. Her Imperial Highness saw the Holy Virgin, just as she was represented in her favourite ikon, approach her with two gold rings in her hand. 'Why do you prevent your son's happiness?' inquired the Virgin. 'Let them wear these rings; consent to their marriage, you shall never regret it.' The vision vanished and the Grand Duchess awoke, deeply impressed by the vividness of her dream, which she looked upon as a sign from Heaven.

She sent for her former lady-in-waiting, to whom she had always been much attached, called her son, and they were thus affianced at her bedside. A few weeks later the wedding was celebrated with due solemnity in the private chapel of the Mikhail Palace in the presence of the Grand Duchess and all the Imperial Family. The bride received the name of Countess Carlov for herself and any children that might be born to her.

After her final surrender the Grand Duchess Catherine became a very kind mother-in-law and treated her son's wife like a daughter, with affection and generosity. She died four years after the marriage and left her daughter-in-law a great part of her rich collection of laces and jewels.

Countess Carlov is likewise on the best of terms with her sister-in-law, the widowed Princess Helen of Saxe-Altenburg, and with her brother-in-law, the Duke Michael of Mecklenburg-Strelitz.

As long as her children were small the Countess led a very quiet life; she and her husband were devoted to each other. They lived a great part of the year in their beautiful palace an hour's distance from Petrograd. The Duke was a good musician, and they had musical Wednesdays, but only intimate friends and serious music-lovers were admitted to these weekly receptions. About seven years ago the Duke died suddenly, leaving his widow and children a very large fortune. When her daughters grew up Countess Carlov came out of her retirement, and during the season gave brilliant parties. Her eldest daughter, Catherine, is married to Prince Emmanuel Golitzine, an officer in the Chevalier Guards, and quite lately the engagement has been announced of her second daughter Marie to Prince Boris Golitzine in the Imperial Hussars. The youngest and prettiest of the sisters, Countess Nathalie, died about three years ago from an attack of pneumonia. Count George Carlov, the Benjamin of the family, has recently attained his eighteenth birthday.

One of the most important society leaders in Petrograd is Countess Elisabeth or, as she is more generally known, the Countess Betsy Schouvalov. By birth a Princess Bariatinsky, she was married to one of the richest members of the Schouvalov family, Count Paul Schouvalov, who died about fifteen years ago, leaving his childless widow a life interest in one of the richest estates in Russia.

The Countess lives in one of the handsomest houses of Petrograd, on the Fontanka Quay, palatial in its dimensions and artistically luxurious in its arrangements. One must have seen and felt the magnificence of the receptions given here by the Countess Schouvalov, for otherwise it would be difficult to give an adequate description of them.

An imposing white marble staircase branches up in two flights of steps, with a white marble gallery running round leading into a long suite of different-sized drawing-rooms, with stuccoed walls covered with beautiful old brocade. Empire style predominates everywhere, and the furniture is somewhat old-fashioned and ponderous, which corresponds perfectly with the large size of the rooms. The walls of the lofty white ballroom, with its enormous windows, are covered with sculptured bas-reliefs. At the end of the room is a good-sized stage (occasionally the Countess lends her state apartments for amateur theatricals got up for a charitable object). When supper-time comes the folding-doors of another neighbouring suite of brilliantly lit-up rooms are opened, and a row of marvellously laid out, flower-decked supper tables is exposed to view, with beautiful old china, cut glass and antique silver on all the tables, prepared sometimes for over six hundred guests.

At the present moment this magnificent mansion is turned into a hospital for wounded soldiers, and the rooms where dancing and rejoicings went on have been transformed into wards. The Countess herself has been absent from Petrograd for over two years, at the head of her own hospital-train at the front, and has devoted herself entirely to nursing.

The Countess's private apartments, arranged in a more up-to-date style, are on the ground floor.

Being one of the richest women in Russia, the Countess Schouvalov considers it her duty to use her income judiciously for the benefit of her fellow-countrymen as well as for her own satisfaction. In the course of the season she generally gives several brilliant festivities, because she thinks she owes it to her position in society; she likewise deems it indispensable to support various kinds of philanthropic and charitable institutions. The benevolence of the Countess is well known; she is energetic and generous, and has acquired the art of helping wisely. In one part of her immense house she has arranged a warehouse for Kustari goods, made by peasants on her estates, and work-rooms for poor women, who have been instructed to become model seamstresses. Over a hundred work here. The Countess sends for dainty lingerie models from Paris, and has them copied and sold for half the price they would fetch in a shop. Two aims are attained by this system: it gives well-paid work to numerous poor women, and to ladies who are not rich the possibility of getting well-made garments at a moderate price. The activity of the workshop has lately been widened, and at present one can also get frocks, coats, mantles, etc., copied from Paris models, which are just as smart and much cheaper than in an ordinary fashionable shop.

When the Countess is in town she spends hours in this workshop, and all the work is done under her personal guidance.

Countess Schouvalov is a very independent woman, and her position in society is quite an exceptional one. As has already been said, she is kind-hearted and generous, and she can be very charming; but if occasion demand, she will not hesitate to be severe. She is a staunch friend, but hates pushing people, and no amount of flattery will cajole her into admitting anyone to her parties if she does not wish to do so.

Very tall, with an exquisite figure that has retained its youthful lines in all their purity, the Countess is a very fine woman, and in evening dress, with her magnificent diamonds scintillating all over her, she is a most imposing figure. There is something in the expression of her face that makes one think twice before asking a favour of her, but people who are intimately acquainted with her know that she is the kindest-hearted of women if you approach her in the right way. One thing is absolutely certain: there is nothing petty or small in her nature.

A strange rivalry of long standing exists between the Grand Duchess Maria Pavlovna senior and the Countess Schouvalov. Nobody exactly knows the reason of this antagonism. Some people

SOCIETY OF PETROGRAD

affirm that it dates back to the days when the late Count Paul Schouvalov was the aide-de-camp of the Grand Duke Vladimir, and when the draft of a letter written by the Grand Duchess to some friend suddenly and mysteriously disappeared. This letter, said to contain slighting allusions to her brother-in-law the Emperor Alexander III, was by some means brought under the Sovereign's notice. The Emperor's retaliation consisted in forwarding the letter to his brother Vladimir without any comment. The incident was ended; but about the same time Count Paul Schouvalov unexpectedly quitted the Grand Duke's suite and was immediately made an aide-de-camp of the Tzar. This may only have been a coincidence, and the ill-feeling between the two ladies may in reality have another reason.

From time to time little incidents occur that give rise to a lot of gossip. For instance, at a very smart party the Grand Duchess approached a group of ladies, greeted each one of them with affability, pointedly omitting to shake hands with the Countess Schouvalov, who was one of the group. On the next occasion, seeing the Grand Duchess approaching her with extended hand, the Countess is said deliberately to have turned her back upon her. For some time there seemed to be a sort of truce between the two antagonists, and outwardly friendly relations were established, but the climax came just before the war. Some remark of the Grand Duchess made in a Paris restaurant angered the Countess, all the more so as the latter was taken at a disadvantage and did not parry the remark in her usual sharp way. Now, nothing is more aggravating than being displeased with oneself and regretfully thinking of all the smart repartees one might have made; the sting was therefore still rankling in the Countess's breast when she returned to Petrograd.

During the last season in Petrograd before the war the feud seemed to have reached a climax and gave rise to several piquant incidents. Great preparations were made by the Countess for three grand receptions. The first was a black and white ball, given in January, 1914. All the ladies had to be dressed in either black or white, or in a combination of the two. All the flowers for the cotillon were pure white, and the other items, such as scarves, tulle bows, etc., were in black and white. The whole of Petrograd society was at the ball – over six hundred guests. The members of the foreign diplomatic corps were present, several members of the Imperial Family graced the occasion by their presence, but the Grand Duchess Maria Pavlovna senior had not been invited, and no one of her particular set dared to appear.

The second ball was even more brilliant than the first; though the guests were less numerous they were more select. All the ladies were in coloured wigs – it was the first introduction in Petrograd of this new fashion, and the effect created was marvellous.

The Schouvalov mansion was graced by numerous members of the Imperial Family, eager to witness the novel sight of elegant women in evening attire wearing their hair in all the colours of the rainbow.

The Grand Duchess Maria Pavlovna was not present – the Countess had omitted to invite her.

I am reminded by this ball of an incident which occurred recently to a very smart member of Petrograd society. Last season she went to a fancy-dress ball in a costume designed by Mr. Bakhst the painter à la mode and the arbiter of ladies' fashions. No one ever understood what the costume was intended to represent; it was a costly and amazing mixture of myrtle-green and cobalt-blue. The lady had the shape of a turnip, pointed at the top and getting very wide at the hem of the short skirt, from under which peeped two daintily shod feet, the legs being clothed in silk bladder-shaped trousers. A blue wig, green gloves and costly gems completed the costume. Green roses were painted by M. Bakhst on the higher part of the lady's arms, but truth compels one to add that the heat of the ballroom sadly affected this over-modern art production: the paint melted on the warm skin and trickled down in ugly green streaks.

On the last day of Lent, Countess Schouvalov gave her last reception, which was to surpass all the rest in its magnificence. The festival was to commence with a short French comedy, and character dances beautifully organised, followed by a ball; but the distinguishing feature of the party consisted in the honour conferred on the Countess by the Dowager Empress, who had promised to be present at the entertainment. The Empress's two daughters and several other members of the Imperial Family were also expected. On that same day the Grand Duchess Maria Pavlovna gave a *folle-journée*, commencing with an early banquet, followed by dancing till the stroke of midnight. The Tzar and his two elder daughters came over from Tzarskoe Selo, the Dowager Empress and all the members of the Imperial Family were invited as well as the richest cream of society. This coincidence caused a great deal of heart-burning, for, though Her Majesty kept her word, her august appearance and that of her two daughters at the Countess Schouvalov's reception was a belated one; moreover, the Countess was thwarted in her desire to secure the presence of the Emperor and his daughters, and many members of the smart society could not be present because the guests of the Grand Duchess dared not risk her displeasure by leaving early to go on to the Countess Schouvalov. Consequently the party which was to have been so brilliant fell rather flat. The Grand Duchess had her revenge.

This reminds me of a similar incident in the past and how differently things were regarded in those days.

The late Chief Chamberlain, Emmanuel Dimitrievitch Narischkine, one of the richest and most important noblemen in the reign of Alexander III, and his wife Alexandra Nicolaïevna Narischkine gave magnificent entertainments in their somewhat old-fashioned but sumptuous house on the Palace Quay, at which the Imperial Family was generally present. A few years prior to the death of the late Tzar, M. and Mme. Narischkine gave a ball; the Sovereign and the members of the Imperial Family were invited as usual, but the Grand Duchess Marie Pavlovna had in some way incurred Madame Narischkine's disapproval, which she tactlessly manifested by omitting to invite the Grand Duke Vladimir and his wife, thinking that this act of independence would find favour in the Sovereign's eyes, for she was aware that there was scant sympathy between the Imperial couple and their sister-in-law. In this matter the strait-laced Madame Narischkine was grievously mistaken. When the Tzar noticed the omission and realised that an intentional slight had been put on his sister-in-law, he was very angry and showed his displeasure by leaving the ball with the Empress before the regulation hour, and without having sat down to the elaborate supper prepared for them. Moreover, when Madame Narischkine came to the Anitchkoff Palace to thank the Empress for the honour of her august presence at the ball, she was not admitted, and no invitation from the Narischkines was henceforth accepted by the monarch and his consort. The only time His Majesty crossed the threshold of their house again was when he went to see M. Narischkine during the latter's last illness.

'Tempora mutantur et nos mutamur in illis.'

The Narischkines are of very illustrious descent; they have no title in their family and would not accept one if it were offered, for they are too proud of their old and distinguished lineage to require a handle to their name, which has frequently figured in Russian history. One of our most sympathetic Tzaritzas, the wife of Tzar Alexis Romanoff, the mother of Peter the Great, belonged to this family and was known by the name of 'Tzaritza Nathalia Kyrillovna'.

The late husband of the Empress's Mistress of the Robes belonged to a collateral branch of the Narischkine family. The Chief Chamberlain, Emmanuel Dimitrievitch Narischkine, was the head of the family; when he died he bequeathed all his wealth to his childless widow, and she has a life interest in all his entailed estates, thereby making her one of the richest women in Russia. Since her widowhood Madame Narischkine has retired completely from society and seldom comes to Petrograd, dividing her time between Tambov and her country seat, 'Bykovo', close to this town.

Madame Alexandra Nicolaïevna Narischkine, née Tchitcherine, belongs to the rough diamond order of human nature.

A childless, benevolent woman, with more money than she knows what to do with, energy, brains and practical common sense, she spends her princely income in good deeds. In return for her many generous donations the distinction of 'lady of honour' has been lately conferred on her. Madame Narischkine was the first to introduce all kinds of handwork amongst the peasant men and women. The so-called 'Kustari' owe their origin and development to her. She engaged efficient workmen, and had the peasants taught all kinds of trades. The first well-organised lace works were established by her. She sent for patterns to Venice, France, Belgium, etc., and had the old designs reproduced. The result was a brilliant success, and the peasant women now make a good income from this trade. She also established a variety of workshops for the men. Madame Narischkine's example has since been widely followed, and the 'Kustari' work has spread all over the country. The latest exhibitions of peasant handicrafts have excited genuine admiration. In Petrograd Madame Narischkine was the founder of the society of 'Help to Poor Women' with its many branches. She has also organised on one of her estates in the province of Riazane an institution for practical instruction in agriculture. The manor-house is turned into a boarding-house for

SOCIETY OF PETROGRAD

young women wishing to learn farming or gardening under the tuition of a skilled agriculturist, who at the same time is the matron of the establishment.

Madame Narischkine's munificence, when any worthy purpose presents itself to her notice, is wonderful. During the Russo-Japanese war she gave one million of roubles for the Russian Fleet, and notwithstanding her age and failing health the old lady personally superintends her numerous institutions and hospitals both in Tambov and Bykovo.

The late Count Witte's adopted daughter married a nephew of that benevolent lady, M. Cyril Narischkine, an attaché of the Russian Embassy in Paris. Mlle. Vera Witte, young and handsome, with lovely Oriental dark eyes, was of Jewish origin. Her own father, M. Lyssanevitch, was fonder of racing than society. He and his wife, a handsome Jewess, were divorced, and later Madame Lyssanevitch married M. (afterwards Count) Witte, the Russian Minister of Finance. She was clever enough to secure M. Cyril Narischkine – a member of one of the most illustrious Russian families – as a husband for her daughter. This was a nine days' wonder, and the wedding was celebrated with the utmost pomp and solemnity in Count Worontzov-Dashkoff's private chapel. Count Witte was the great force at the time and very powerful.

The marriage ended in a legal separation, and the two offspring of this ill-assorted union – a boy of twelve and a little girl of four – have remained with their mother. Count Witte doted on the boy; he was the apple of his grandfather's eye, and nothing was too costly for Master Leo Narischkine. When the title of Count was conferred on M. Witte, both he and his wife were delighted, and the dream of Count Witte's last years was to bequeath his name and title to his adored grandson; but the boy's father would not hear of the arrangement. At the time of Count Witte's death it was said that he had left a letter to the Tzar imploring His Majesty to have the title of Count Witte passed on to his stepdaughter's son. But nothing has been heard of the title since. Count Witte's death occurred at the very moment when the public mind was occupied with tragically weighty matters. The treason of Colonel Miassoyedoff had just been discovered, and the close investigation of this crime brought forth appalling disclosures and the names of the Colonel's confederates. It was a dreadful time, and the general demoralisation led to unlimited and wholesale distrust.

In Count Witte's mansion all was confusion and consternation, for Count Witte, who had been slightly indisposed, died quite unexpectedly. The fact that the Emperor sent no message of condolence to Countess Witte on the occasion of her bereavement and no wreaths of flowers were deposited on the Count's coffin was much commented upon at the time. But everything was in chaos, and the Emperor, occupied with such a terrible tragedy as the Miassoyedoff affair, can be excused for forgetting both the flowers and the title.

Since the reign of Peter the Great the Scheremeteffs have always been considered one of the first families in Russia. Two Count Scheremeteffs are the present representatives of this noble family. The elder, the Chief Master of the Hounds, Count Serge Scheremeteff, was a personal friend of Alexander III. He owns a magnificent palace on the Fontanka Quay, one in Moscow with a private chapel in which all the male members of the Scheremeteff family are married, several large estates, and a beautiful place near Moscow, 'Mikhailovskoe'.

Count Serge Scheremeteff is a highly cultured man, who loves art and takes a deep interest in science. He is married to a Princess Catherine Wiazemsky, a granddaughter of the poet, Prince Peter Wiazemsky. Count and Countess Scheremeteff have never led a worldly life and seldom appear in society. Their happiest time is spent in their country place 'Mikhailovskoe' surrounded by their children and grandchildren. They have two married daughters, Countess Goudovitch and Madame Sabouroff, and four sons; the fifth, Count Peter, died a few months ago.

The younger stepbrother of Count Serge Scheremeteff, Count Alexander Scheremeteff, is even wealthier than his brother, for besides the legal part of his father's fortune he inherited all the money his mother had accumulated during her lifetime. His position is that of General of the Emperor's suite. He is married to Countess Marie Heyden, a remarkably clever woman. They have a beautiful mansion on the French Quay and their receptions are always magnificent, though since the marriage of their children these have almost entirely ceased. The family spend the early part of the summer in 'Oulianka', a luxurious place they have close to Petrograd. Their married daughters and daughters-in-law often stay with them there, and life in Oulianka is very animated.

On Sundays numerous officers, including the sons of the host

SOCIETY OF PETROGRAD

and hostess, motor over to Oulianka from Krasnoe Selo, where the Guards' camp is quartered in summer. Besides these weekly informal dinners, the Count and Countess Scheremeteff have two grand festivals in the course of summer, one on the 10th of June, the anniversary of their wedding, the other on the 22nd of July, the name-day of the Countess. This day is most brilliantly kept.

After a religious service held in the morning in the presence of all the assembled members of the family and household, the Countess receives the congratulations of the numerous retainers and functionaries attached to their household and estates. A lunch is served for everyone present, followed by the arrival of friends, neighbours and acquaintances, who motor over from the different country places in the vicinity. During the dinner, which is for over fifty people, two orchestras play alternately. As soon as it begins to get dark, the whole park is suddenly lighted up with a magnificent illumination. Fireworks and a torchlight procession wind up the festivity.

The Count Alexander Scheremeteff has the soul of an artist. Music is his favourite art; he plays the piano and the 'cello and is a very talented conductor. He has his own orchestra and chorus of singers, who are second only to those of the Imperial Chapels. The Count has spent large sums and taken a great deal of trouble in founding and furthering the development of a musical-historical society in Petrograd. The concerts given by this society are of great interest to all lovers of music. Some of these concerts are dedicated to national music, others to French music of the seventeenth or eighteenth century, old Italian, Scandinavian, etc.

The season before the war this musical society, with the help of Count Alexander Scheremeteff, organised the representation of Wagner's *Parsifal*, which took place in the Hermitage Theatre of the Winter Palace. The scenery, decorations and costumes were magnificent, the orchestra, conducted by Count Scheremeteff, perfect, and the voices of the singers, considering they were amateurs, very good. It was a great treat to music lovers.

The first representation of *Parsifal* took place in the presence of the Emperor and all the principal members of the Imperial Family. Invitations were issued from the Imperial Court. The representation commenced at six o'clock. At half-past eight, after the first curtain drop, all present were invited to a banquet, which was laid out in the Hermitage ballroom and gallery. When dinner was ended the representation continued.

After this gala representation, *Parsifal* was repeated about a dozen times, the public being freely admitted by invitation tickets, which were in great demand.

Count Scheremeteff has a fire-engine equipment, beautifully organised at his own cost, with the best fire-extinguishing apparatus and all the latest improvements.

The Countess Marie Scheremeteff is a very clever and energetic woman. Her activity is simply wonderful. She is the businesswoman of the family, and the great wealth of her husband, under her wise and able administration, has steadily increased. She is at the head of numerous philanthropic institutions, and being very benevolent, generously and wisely gives her help to those who need it.

Thanks to the Countess's energy and generous help, a home for girls who are studying has been greatly enlarged. The home, which is called St. Xenia's, and which was founded on the day of the Grand Duchess Xenia's birth, possesses at present its own well-constructed house, with a garden, roomy bedrooms, large refectory, cosy sitting-room, wide corridors and many bathrooms. A girl coming from the country or the provinces to study in Petrograd can here meet with a comfortable home and full board for the trifling sum of thirty shillings a month.

Both sons of Count Scheremeteff are at the war; the two daughters are married: Madame Elisabeth Derfelden and Madame Alexandra Scheremeteff.

The Scheremeteff family have always been known as staunch and devoted adherents of the Imperial monarchy.

The Countess's favourite institution is St. George's Red Cross Sisterhood of Nurses. She goes there daily and is indefatigable in organising hospital-trains and sending them to the front. Part of her town house is turned into a hospital for wounded officers, and a separate ward for wounded soldiers in the hospital of the St. George's Sisterhood is maintained from the private purse of Countess Scheremeteff.

One of the richest heiresses in Russia is the young Countess Marie Orloff-Davidoff. She is the only daughter of Count Alexander Orloff-Davidoff and of his wife, née Zographo, known in society as 'Countess Maisie'. If the war had not interrupted all gaiety she was to have come out last winter. The young Countess is a dainty little lady with a well-poised head, crowned by quantities of soft fair hair, a sweet face and a charming, well-bred manner. She does not in any way resemble the up-to-date young woman of today. Her father worships her: nothing is good enough for his darling. One of the richest prizes in the matrimonial market, her fate is supposed to be settled and her destiny ordained in the person of one of the younger scions of the Imperial Family.

The name of Orloff-Davidoff has lately attracted an unusual amount of notice, and been the theme of ceaseless gossip on account of a trial in which the young Countess's uncle figured as plaintiff. Count Alexis Orloff-Davidoff prosecuted his second wife for simulating the birth of a son and having him fraudulently registered as his offspring, whilst, in reality, the baby had been acquired from a poor girl-mother for the sum of thirty shillings. This trial will remain a cause célèbre in the annals of the law courts. It was a case of real life being stranger than fiction, for if all the circumstances revealed in the course of the trial were brought forward in a novel, the author would be accused of laying on the colours too thickly. The most astounding facts were disclosed by the evidence. Princes and counts, spiritualists and mediums, necromancers and palmists, lawyers, actors and detectives filed in procession before the bewildered jury. Nothing was lacking to enhance the interest of the case.

The summary of the story was as follows: About fifteen or sixteen years ago Count Alexis Orloff-Davidoff contracted an alliance with Thécla de Staal, the only daughter of the late Russian Ambassador at the Court of St. James's. Baroness Thécla was brought up in England. A high-bred, well-educated girl with artistic tastes, she had nothing in common with her rich suitor, and was not at all attracted by him, but her mother was very eager for her daughter to marry well, and the eligible partner seemed to the maternal eye a very suitable one. Baroness de Staal believed that her husband possessed no private means, and that they all lived on his salary. He was getting old and weak, his health was visibly breaking, and she naturally felt very anxious for the future of her child. A romance with an impecunious Englishman had been nipped in the bud, because of her want of a dowry.

Baroness Thécla adored her mother, and to relieve her anxiety she resolved to marry Count Alexis Orloff-Davidoff.

A few months after her marriage her father died, leaving a large fortune amounting to two million roubles (£200,000).

The Countess Thécla Orloff-Davidoff, however, enjoyed a brilliant position: she had a magnificent house on the English Quay in Petrograd, a beautiful country seat near Reval, estates all over the country, superb family diamonds and the most costly pearls in Russia. Everything that wealth can give was hers, and to complete her felicity a son and daughter were born to her.

The Countess is said not to have been very tactful in the treatment of her husband. At length the Count appeared to find the situation unbearable. About two years ago, whilst Countess Thécla had gone to Berlin to fetch her mother home, her husband had all her belongings carefully packed up and sent over to her friend the late Princess Nellie Bariatinsky. To his wife he sent a wire, delivered to her at the frontier station, desiring her not to return to her conjugal home. He had not the shadow of right to act thus, for his wife had always led a blameless life, but the Countess made no objection and accepted his decision. When, however, some months subsequent to these events, he wished for a divorce, she only consented to have the marriage dissolved on condition of having the guardianship of both her children. Since then the Countess has taken a house on the Serguievskaia and lives there very contentedly with her mother and children, giving much of her time to her favourite art, portrait painting. Her position in society has remained unimpaired and she is surrounded with esteem and sympathy.

Not long ago the Count Alexis Orloff-Davidoff married again. His choice this time fell on a very talented actress, past middle age, Mme. Marousina-Poirré, the sister of the well-known caricaturist, 'Caran d'Ache', who had the reputation of being fatal to those who love her.

She was not a pretty woman in the strict acceptation of the term, nor was she then young, being on the wrong side of forty when she first met the Count, but she was vastly fascinating, full of life and gaiety; she could dance any fantastic step, sing songs, compose songs to music, write verse, was a clever mimic, and altogether very amusing and much appreciated in the gay world. Notwithstanding this joyful existence, her life had been a long series of dramas.

She began by becoming the Count's friend and confidante. She studied his weaknesses and inclinations. Observing his penchant for the occult, she acted as a medium and surrounded the delighted Count with manifestations and signs from the other world.

The Count sorrowed deeply for his little daughter, and the spirit of little 'Sophy' would come imploring Mme. Poirré to save her father and saying that he was to leave his family. Crystal gazers assured him of the devoted love which one woman bore him, predicting also his divorce and second marriage and the birth of a beautiful healthy boy.

When the divorce was pronounced, Mme. Poirré informed the Count of her approaching motherhood (at fifty-four years of age!). The marriage was then solemnised in order to ensure the legitimacy of the 'Heaven-sent infant'. A few days later, in the absence of the Count, his second wife pretended to have given birth to a boy, and soon after that event father, mother and child went abroad, intending to remain there for several years. But the war broke out and they returned after a few months' absence. Here ends the success of the scheme. Having gained her ends, the new Countess Orloff-Davidoff's adoration for her husband seemed to wane, and she manifested an indifference to the long-expected son that excited the Count's suspicion.

He made investigations and discovered the fraud. This is the substance of the case. The Countess pleaded guilty and candidly confessed how she had carried out the trick. The Count unflinchingly faced the fiery ordeal and quaffed the bitter cup of ridicule to its dregs. The Countess was after all acquitted by an overindulgent jury, but the boy – now two years old – the innocent victim, was officially deposed from his position and stripped of all his rights. On hearing the verdict those present, consisting mostly of the accused Countess's friends, pelted her with flowers and carried her to the motor-car that was awaiting her.

One of the most original members of Petrograd society is Nicolaïevna, the widow of the late Admiral Capitolina Makaroff.

Makaroff is a man who would in all probability have done great things for Russia if his life had not been so suddenly cut off. The wreck of the *Petropavlovsk* at the time of the Russo-Japanese war was caused by a fatal accident, and Makaroff died the death of a hero. It was a great blow to Russia's hopes when it was known that Makaroff had perished with the *Petropavlovsk*. The country felt his death deeply. At the time of her bereavement his widow was naturally made much of by the Emperor and Empress, and the members of the Imperial Family in general showed her great attention. She received a handsome pension of 20,000 roubles £2,000) a year; her daughter was made a maid of honour and her son educated at the expense of the State. Statues were erected, scholarships founded, and a battleship was named after the Admiral. After the expiration of ten years a grand memorial service was held for him. Madame Makaroff received the order of St. Catherine. She proudly wears the order on all possible and impossible occasions, and unkind people say that she sometimes even sleeps with it carefully pinned on her night-gown.

Madame Makaroff calls herself the 'babuschka' (grandmother) of the Russian Fleet. When the British Squadron was in Cronstadt, Madame Makaroff took a prominent part in all the festivities that took place in honour of Sir David Beatty and the English officers. She was invited to all the State and official dinners.

An amusing story was lately current about her. Madame Makaroff at one of the last sessions of the Duma went to the wrong entrance door. A young official informed her politely that this was the private entrance of the members, requesting her to step a little further to the right, where she would find the door for the general public. 'My name is Makaroff,' was the lady's retort, without flinching from her evident resolve to use this entrance. The unfortunate official tried to expostulate, but was withered by a haughty glance. 'Young man, you evidently don't know the history of your country'; and with these words the irate lady swept past the intimidated youth and effected her entrance through the prohibited door.

The members of the Kourakine race have honourably figured in all the phases of Russian history. The Princes Kourakine have a pedigree that dates back to Guedemine, Prince of Lithuania in the fifteenth century, and the dynasty of the latter reigned in that country from the year 840.

The characteristics of their race are astute cleverness, penetration, sharp-wittedness, energy and firmness of purpose. A strain of cruelty lies in the blood of the Kourakines, modified and softened by culture and civilisation; still one must not expect much kind-heartedness from any member of that family, even in the present day.

Two of their ancestors are especially known in history as having been distinguished diplomatists. One was Prince Boris Kourakine, the brother-in-law of Peter the Great (married to a Lopoukhine, the sister of Queen Eudoxia, the first wife of Peter I, whom he repudiated because she opposed the reforms he was introducing in the country). He was sent as the Tzar's Ambassador to London in the reign of Queen Anne, and was the first propagator of the wisdom of an alliance between Great Britain and Russia.

His great-grandson, Prince Alexander Kourakine, was the Russian Ambassador in Vienna and in Paris in Napoleon I's time, and as Russia's representative signed the treaty of Tilsit.

The present scions of the Kourakine family are Prince Anatole and Prince Boris. Prince Anatole, a member of the Upper Chamber, is a clever and amiable man, with a wonderful head for business. Under his able management his fortune has considerably increased. His wife, by birth a Princess Wolkhonsky, is a charming, kind-hearted old lady who still continues to love society and is an ardent bridge player. The Princess and her husband have led an exemplary life for over half a century; they are devoted to each other, and the Prince considers his wife the mascot of his existence. Their bridge parties, followed by exquisite suppers, are always well attended. That this venerable couple is one of the most popular in Petrograd society was adequately proved in the spring of 1914, when nobody foresaw the coming horrors of the war, on the occasion of their Golden Wedding, celebrated with the utmost solemnity. It was *the* event of the spring season of 1914.

The festivities began with a religious service in St. Serge's Cathedral in the presence of the bridal pair and all the members of the Kourakine family, many of whom had arrived purposely from the country or abroad. The priest from Prince Kourakine's principal family seat came specially to Petrograd to be one of the officiating clergy. After the religious ceremony, when the family had regained their apartment, followed a *defilé* of deputations and a Golden Wedding breakfast for over a hundred guests. After that there was a reception for all who wished to congratulate the happy pair. Everyone in society vied with each other to show some attention to Prince and Princess Kourakine on the occasion of such a rare anniversary. Presents and flowers were showered on them; most of the former were either of gilded silver or of gold, and all the flowers were yellow. The handsomest present was given by the children and grandchildren and consisted of a set of dinner plates of solid gold.

The next day the Prince and Princess Kourakine gave a brilliant rout for about five hundred people.

The Princess wore a dress of gold brocade and her daughters and granddaughters were dressed in white and gold.

The elder brother, Prince Boris Kourakine, is a widower and spends most of his time in the country. A smart and remarkably handsome officer of the Chevalier Guards, in his youth he had the reputation of being a lady-killer.

One of the oldest families in Russia is that of the Princess Dolgorouky, which dates from Rurik, over nine centuries ago. The race is nearly extinct at present, for the sole male representatives are: the Emperor's aide-de-camp, Prince Serge Dolgorouky and his brother, Prince Peter Dolgorouky, who has only one little girl, and their uncle, a childless old man, married to an English lady, Miss Fleetwood-Coleridge, and who divides his time between London and Paris.

In the reign of Alexander II the Dolgoroukys were very powerful in Court circles. The late father of the above-named young Princes and the brother of the old Prince, Prince Alexander Dolgorouky, already referred to as Sandy Dolgorouky, held the post of Chief Marshal of the Imperial Household in the reign of Alexander III and remained in this position to the day of his death, which occurred about three years ago. His elder unmarried brother, Prince Nicholas Dolgorouky, was the Russian Ambassador in Rome. All three brothers were perfect specimens of an old race of boyars, transformed by breeding and culture into grand seigneurs of the old school: tall and imposing in appearance, very handsome, with a somewhat haughty bearing and old-fashioned, courteous manner. Brought up by an English tutor, they were quite English in their ways and customs and spoke the language like natives. Prince Alexander Dolgorouky was an art-lover and a great collector. The picture-gallery in his lordly house on the English Quay in Petrograd contains several masterpieces of the old and modern schools. The whole house is a regular museum and full of valuable artistic gems. The Dolgorouky collection of snuff-boxes is unique.

His widow, the Lady of Honour, Princess Olga Dolgorouky, born Countess Schouvalov, enjoys the possession of this house during her lifetime. She was never quite so popular in society as her husband, and since his death, and the marriage of her daughters, limits her appearance to intimate gatherings in her own set. One of her daughters, the Princess Olga Dietrichstein, is married to an Austrian peer, who at one time was the military attaché of the Austrian Embassy in Petrograd. The other three daughters are: Countess Sophie Fersen, the wife of Count Fersen, already mentioned, Princess Mary Troubetzkoy and Madame Barbara Koschouby.

The Princess Olga Dolgorouky's eldest son, Prince Serge Dolgorouky, will some day be one of the wealthiest men in Russia, for he will inherit the Schouvalovs' entailed property, which is very great.

The Dolgoroukoff branch of the family is not rich and is more numerous than the above-mentioned Dolgoroukys. The late popular Governor-General of Moscow, Prince Vladimir Dolgoroukoff, belonged to this family, as well as the Serene Princess Yourievsky. The family of the latter is not much esteemed in Russia. The inauspicious part played by Princess Catherine Dolgoroukoff during the lifetime of Alexander II's Consort, the Empress Maria Alexandrovna, and the latter's moral martyrdom, endured for so many years, has not been forgotten.

When the Empress Maria was suffering from ill health, the children of Princess Catherine Dolgoroukoff, who occupied an apartment in the Winter Palace just above the private rooms of the Empress, used to trample over the poor invalid's head, making a terrible noise, without any deference to the Empress's feelings. The latter was too gentle and unobtrusive to put her foot down and assert herself, as she should have done. One day, when the noise was louder and the Empress more ailing than usual, the maid of honour attending on the Sovereign was so exasperated that she exclaimed: 'Why is there no one to check those unruly little bastards?' The next day this phrase had spread all over town.

How differently Mademoiselle Nelidoff, the favourite of the Emperor Nicholas I, behaved under similar circumstances! She tried to efface herself, never forgot what was due to her Imperial Mistress, the Empress Alexandra, and when she used her influence with the Sovereign, she was prompted by unselfish motives. After the death of Nicholas I, Mademoiselle Nelidoff, who really was deeply attached to the Tzar, retired from the world, and to the day of her death led a very quiet life, seeing only her intimate friends.

The Princess Yourievsky, on the contrary, after a theatrical show of despair, soon recovered her spirits. She could not well remain in Petrograd, so she elected to live in France, where she surrounded herself with semi-royal state. Her sister, the Countess Berg, who had at one time also enjoyed Alexander II's favours, established herself there likewise. Both the sisters led a very gay life and some piquant adventures are ascribed to them.

There was even a time when the Princess Yourievsky wished to contract a second matrimonial alliance with the late Doctor Loubimoff, a very handsome and sympathetic man, much younger than herself. Only she wanted the marriage to be a morganatic one, and to keep the name and title granted to her by her first husband the Tzar.

She wrote to Alexander III explaining her wishes. The reply of her Imperial stepson was a masterpiece. The Emperor wrote that he found her wish to contract a second marriage quite natural, begged leave to convey his felicitations to her, wishing her joy in her new happiness, but he was of opinion that every wife should bear her husband's name and that he felt convinced that the wife of such a worthy man as Doctor Loubimoff should feel honoured to take his name.

This put a stop to all future matrimonial attempts.

A great favourite of the late Grand Duke Vladimir and of the Grand Duchess Maria Pavlovna is Dmitry Benckendorff. He has no official position, but is continually at the Palace and is always invited to the houses where the Grand Duchess is expected.

Years ago Benckendorff was a diplomatist. He is a very good linguist, and speaks French like a native; he is always entertaining and can be witty and very amusing. At dinner-parties he is invaluable: he sets the ball of conversation rolling and by his unfailing verve animates the dullest guests. These qualities are greatly appreciated at Court.

As a talented aquarellist, Benckendorff has achieved a well-merited success, and his pictures are always noticed at exhibitions. Smart afternoon teas are given by him in his studio, which is most tastefully arranged, and full of various artistic gems. The Grand Duchess and her set have often visited his studio and inspected his latest pictures and statues.

The Taneiefs are one of the most influential families at the Imperial Court. Alexander Sergievitch Taneief is the Director of the Emperor's private Chancery, a post he occupied during the lifetime of Alexander III. Taneief's attraction for the latter was his great musical talent, as pianist and composer. At one time, before his career as a courtier commenced, Taneief was a professor in the Petrograd Academy of Music.

SOCIETY OF PETROGRAD

Alexander III loved music and was himself a very good performer on the violoncello. During his reign an orchestra of amateurs was formed, in which the Emperor took part. It used to be his favourite relaxation, and intimate musical evenings, to which no invitations were issued, took place at regular intervals in the Anitchkoff and Gatchina Palaces. In those days it was considered particularly lucky to be endowed with a musical talent and have the chance of being included amongst the musicians of the Emperor's orchestra.

Taneief was fortunate enough to win the sympathy of the young Empress Alexandra; the bond between them was again music, for Her Majesty has a cultivated taste for this art, a good voice and, when in congenial society, used during the first years of her husband's reign to sing a great deal. Mr. Taneief's eldest daughter, Anna, became one of the Empress's maids of honour. As a rule the post of maid of honour to the Empress Alexandra is a difficult one, and in former years there were continual changes in the Imperial Household. Miss Taneief, however, overcame all difficulties and succeeded in becoming her Imperial Mistress's favourite; they read and sang and drove together, with the ultimate result of her becoming quite indispensable to the Empress.

Some years ago Miss Taneief married Lieutenant Vyrouboff, but after a few months of wedded bliss the marriage was suddenly dissolved, and Madame Vyrouboff resumed her duties at Court; she has no official position and her sole title to public consideration is the fact of her being the Empress's friend. Her Majesty is greatly attached to her and Madame Vyrouboff is always in close attendance on her Imperial Mistress.

The youngest and prettiest Miss Taneief is married to A. E. von Pistohlcorse, the son of Countess Hohenfelsen by her first marriage.

The Troubetzkoys were ever a powerful family in Russia. Different members of the race have figured at various epochs in various characters on the pages of history, as likewise in influential *salons*. Napoleon III's half-brother, the Duke of Morny, was married to a Princess Troubetzkoy. During the Presidency of M. Thiers one of the most influential *salons* in Paris was held by the Princess Lise Troubetzkoy. It was a political *salon* where all Government measures were freely discussed. Most of the President's decisions were at that time inspired by his Russian friend. The Princess wielded a well-balanced influence, and for a time swayed the destiny of France.

Prince Serge Troubetzkoy was a prominent politician; he was a member of the Duma, belonging to the Liberals. His sudden death before the opening of the second Duma was considered a heavy loss to his party and put an end to all the hopes that the Liberals had centred in him. His brother, Prince Eugene Troubetzkoy, is an eminent professor, highly esteemed in the scientific world.

Clericalism never was a feature of Petrograd society, but gradually and somewhat mysteriously a clerical tendency is getting to be the fashion, and, strange as such an assertion sounds, it is supposed that the Empress is inclined to encourage it. At the present moment we can boast of a bona fide clerical *salon*, although the war, which makes every other interest appear remote, has rather weakened its importance. The leader of this clerical salon is the Dowager Countess Ignatieff, by birth a Princess Mestchersky. The widow of a member of the Upper Chamber, former Governor-General of Kiev, the Countess was never contented merely to reflect the importance and consideration of her husband's position. She constantly struck out a personal line. Since the Count's death by the hand of a revolutionist in 1906, the Countess has had full scope, and for several years she has gone in for clericalism. She is very well known and rather feared in Petrograd society, for her tongue is sharp and can be very cutting. Being in close touch with the most important members of the Holy Synod, the nomination of archbishops and bishops is said often to have been brought about in her drawing-room. Her Monday evening receptions are specially dedicated to Church matters, and are the meeting-place of people interested in such questions. The former Procurator of the Holy Synod, M. Sabler (since the war his name has been changed into Dessiatovsky), was a constant visitor at these weekly gatherings, and bishops and influential priests are to be met there. The late editor of the *Grazhdanine*, Prince Vladimir Mestchersky, a staunch adherent of the Russian Orthodox Church, used also to frequent these assemblies, which at one time were very influential. Since M. Sabler retired, and since the death of Prince Mestchersky, the interest in these 'clerical Mondays' has somewhat abated. The new Procurator of the Holy Synod, M. Raïeff, is, however, an old friend of the Countess – it is believed she furthered his nomination

– so probably the 'Mondays' will soon regain their former importance.

The Countess represents that type of the old-fashioned dowager whom one so rarely meets nowadays in society. Tall and rather awe-inspiring in appearance, she discards new fashions and attends balls and evening parties in a high-necked, dark silk gown with a black lace handkerchief pinned over her hair. She has retained the stamp of a great lady.

During the season Countess Ignatieff, whose youngest daughter is unmarried, holds a reception every Sunday evening, which differs entirely from her 'Mondays', being eminently worldly, full of fun and animation.

In the reign of Alexander III the Ignatieffs were a powerful family. The most important of its members, Count Nicholas Ignatieff, the Russian Ambassador in Constantinople, and the author of the treaty of San Stefano, as well as his brother, Count Alexis, the late Governor-General of Kiev, are both dead. The widow of the first-named, Countess Catherine Ignatieff, by birth a Princess Golitzine-Osterman, has completely retired from the world and hardly ever quits the country. Her youngest daughter, Catherine, was a sister of mercy. Her third son, Count Paul Ignatieff, has just been appointed Minister of Public Instruction. All the Ignatieffs are clever, and it was always supposed that Count Paul, the most gifted of the brothers, who like his father is very capable, full of talent and enterprise, would make a brilliant career!

The cotillons of Madame Serebriakoff's balls are lovely, they consist only of flowers, but the luxury displayed in them is simply astonishing. At one ball, for instance, three enormous green tubs, filled with sheaves of La France roses, were brought into the ballroom and, as if by the touch of a fairy wand, the room was turned into a rosary. The beauty and fragrance of this huge quantity of roses delighted everyone. At a signal from the Grand Duke Boris, the guests began to applaud and the amiable hostess was the object of a gratifying ovation.

Madame Serebriakoff is a pretty, fair little woman, with starry sapphire-blue eyes. Some time ago a tragi-comic incident happened in consequence of Madame Serebriakoff's partiality for Imperial Highnesses. Madame de Peters, who has been mentioned in a preceding chapter, has lately been an invalid, suffering from heart attacks. To have more air she moved into a villa on the islands. One afternoon Madame Serebriakoff motored over to call on her. A few minutes later enters the Grand Duke Andrei Vladimirovitch, intent upon inquiring after the health of his mother's friend. Madame de Peters was much better, and the joy of receiving the Grand Duke made her quite animated. She very much wanted to have her Imperial visitor all to herself and secretly wished Madame Serebriakoff would depart. Madame Serebriakoff, on the other hand, was too exhilarated at the sight of the Imperial guest to sacrifice her opportunity and take her leave whilst the Grand Duke's visit lasted. A silent psychological duel was fought; blood was not shed, but a good deal of it was acidulated. One was wishing the other far away, and the other would not budge. The consequence of this mischance was that poor unfortunate Madame de Peters had another heart attack, brought on by irritation.

Madame Serebriakoff's entertainments during the season are numerous and sumptuous.

Amongst the smart ladies of Petrograd we have several Americans who by marriage have become members of Russian society. American women have a knack of adapting themselves to circumstances and of becoming easily familiarised with their surroundings. They never clash with those among whom they live, never put forward the superiority of their own country, and seem to merge their nationality into the new one acquired by marriage. They attentively study all Russian customs and strictly follow them to the best of their ability. This makes them perfect wives and gains them popularity in society with surprising facility. It has been observed that, up till now, there has not been a single case of divorce amongst the Russo-American intermarriages.

American women do not chum together as would seem natural for compatriots, moving in the same set in a strange country. On the contrary, the sentiments that some of them cherish towards each other are the reverse of cordial, and one must be careful to ascertain on what terms they are before inviting two American ladies to meet at a small party.

One of the most elegant of these ladies is the Princess Susie Belosselsky-Belosersky, formerly known as Miss Whittier. She has developed into a *grande dame* and has acquired a courtly manner and a dignified bearing that are much admired. Beautifully dressed, she always looks smart and has an individual style, of extreme neatness, looking as if she had just come out of a band-box. On the eve of becoming a grandmother, the Princess still looks quite a young woman, and her figure is perfect. She lived for several years in Kovno, where her husband's regiment was quartered, and she used to be called at that time 'the Queen of Kovno'. Her husband, Prince Serge Belosselsky-Belosersky, is now a general and attached to the Emperor's suite. He is fighting at the Caucasian front, and their elder son is likewise in the army. Prince Serge's parents are still alive; they are both of them old and seldom seen in society. The Belosselskys were very rich at one time, but having spent their money too royally they were obliged to retrench. Their magnificent palace on the Nevsky had to be sold, and became the residence of the late Grand Duke Serge and of his widow the Grand Duchess Elisabeth Feodorovna, when she comes to Petrograd.

Since the sale of their town mansion Prince Constantine Belosselsky and his wife, née Skobeleff, have retired to the islands. One of these, 'Krestovsky' by name, belongs to them entirely, and they possess a beautiful manor house there, which used to be only their summer dwelling but has now become their permanent residence. Two of their sons live there too.

The old General aide-de-camp, Prince Belosselsky, was the brother of the Princess Lise Troubetzkoy. A few years ago he became a Roman Catholic, but his family has remained faithful to the Orthodox Church.

For years the Belosselsky family have been considered infected by Anglomania; they always speak English amongst themselves, and lead an English life, strictly adhering to all British customs. They are great adepts at sport. Most of the fashionable English games have been introduced by them to Petrograd society. They have beautifully organised golf links on their Krestovsky island; a perfect tennis ground, and a superb ground for polo, football, cricket, etc. The polo matches are considered especially elegant, and at one time it was quite the thing for ladies of fashion to have afternoon tea in the polo pavilion and sit on the terrace watching the game.

A prominent place in Petrograd's highest circles of society must be allotted to the Countess Lili Nostitz of American origin. She was the widow of a German officer, von Nympsh, when she made the acquaintance of Count Gregory Nostitz, the Russian Military Agent in Berlin, and fascinated him to such an extent that he, who up to that day had been considered an invulnerable bachelor, who for years had escaped from the most warily planned matrimonial snares, finally succumbed to the fascinating widow.

The marriage created a sensation, for Count Nostitz was looked upon as the beau-ideal of an eligible suitor. For days the feminine tongues of society wagged – mammas of marriageable daughters were aghast to find this coveted prize escape from their grasp – and the marriageable daughters themselves likewise were not pleased to see their maiden charms outstripped by those of an unknown American. Consequently when the happy pair arrived in Petrograd, and Count Nostitz introduced his bride into society, the outward urbanity with which she was received was only skin deep. Society was eager to pick a hole in the pretty Countess, and mischief makers tried to ferret out something unfavourable in her past. But all malignant efforts were in vain; the Countess carried all before her, disarming everyone by her tact, her charming manner, her never-failing amiability and her magnificent receptions. At present she is quite acknowledged as one of the most important leaders of society.

Her receptions are sumptuous, and the lavish luxury they display is of the most refined style.

Everyone who is anybody is only too glad to be admitted to these festivities; the Grand Duchess Maria Pavlovna has frequently accepted her invitations, and so have numerous other members of the Imperial Family.

The Countess was the first hostess in Petrograd to introduce at her parties character dances performed by society ladies. Last year she had several such entertainments, one of them specially devoted to 'Furlana', which found such favour in the eyes of the late Pope Pius X. An Italian from Venice, a master in this art of graceful national dancing, was invited to show the assembled ladies and gentlemen the intricacies of the step.

The Countess Nostitz is a very handsome woman with a queenly figure and very graceful movements. She is always beautifully gowned. One of the most sympathetic traits in her character is her amiability, which is not artificial or put on for the occasion, but is the outcome of real kind-heartedness and the wish to please and give pleasure. She is staunch in her friendships and counts many sincere Russian friends.

Another fascinating American is Madame Marian Artzimovitch, the wife of the Assistant Minister of the Foreign Office. Madame Artzimovitch is very good to look at, with her lovely hair,

SOCIETY OF PETROGRAD

the colour of burnished gold (due to nature and not to her hairdresser's skill), beautiful complexion and graceful figure. Unfortunately she does not speak French, the language mostly spoken in society, nor Russian, so one must know English in order to fully appreciate how charming she is. It is difficult to realise that Mme. Artzimovitch has a grown-up daughter, and when they appear together they look like sisters.

The Princess Julia Cantacuzene-Speransky is the daughter of Mr. Grant, the former Ambassador of the United States in Rome, where she made the acquaintance of her present husband, Prince Michael Cantacuzene-Speransky, the Prince being Military Attaché at the Russian Embassy. The wedding took place in Rome, and when the lovely bride reached Petrograd her beauty made a conquest of all who saw her. The Princess Julia is much more reserved than her compatriots generally are; she must be given time for the thin coating of ice to melt before she becomes her natural amiable self.

The Baroness Hoyningen-Huehne was the daughter of Mr. Lothrop, the former American Resident Minister in Petrograd. Dowagers remember her as a charming girl, very lively and full of spirit, but since she has become the wife of a Baltic baron, whose ancestors fought in the wars of the Crusades, she deems it necessary to be more 'Livonian' in her bearing. This new, grand air does not sit well on so charming and debonair a personality. Her husband is one of General von Grünwald's prime favourites. After leaving the Chevalier Guards regiment he secured a good post on that General's staff and has received likewise the nomination of an Imperial Equerry.

Baroness Fanny Ramsay, the wife of an Imperial M.C., is a very pleasant woman much liked in society. By birth a Miss Whitehouse, she greatly resembles the Empress, and not unnaturally seems proud of a likeness that ranks her amongst the beauties of Petrograd.

Our most renowned *gourmets* are dead. The late Mr. Netchaeff-Maltzev's luxurious banquets, with dishes of strawberries in January, have not yet been rivalled, and the recherché dinner-parties of the deceased Prince Abamelek-Lazareff will be missed in society.

The best dinners at the present time are given by the French Ambassador, M. Paléologue. He has an excellent chef and is very hospitable. The entertainments at the British Embassy are not so frequent, but they are always extremely distinguished. Sir George Buchanan is a genial host, and Lady Georgiana has the knack of putting everyone at their ease. As to their pretty daughter, Miss Meriel Buchanan, she is charming and a great favourite in Petrograd society.

Most of our pretty women have now become sisters of mercy. The Countess Marie Golenistchev-Koutouzoff, one of the loveliest, nearly lost her life in nursing the wounded. Among the beautiful women of Petrograd society one must include Baroness Tatiana Medem, Baroness Stella Meyendorf (an Englishwoman, formerly known as Miss Whishaw), Madame Olga Yourievitch, Madame Irene Rodzianko. The daughter of the late Duke Eugene of Leuchtenberg, Baroness Daria Graevenitz, is still one of the most attractive women in Petrograd.

It would be impossible to give an account of society in the capital without mentioning one of its favourite forms of entertainment – the singing of the Tzigane, or Gypsy, choruses. To go in *troikas* on a calm moonlit winter night to the islands (the principal haunt of the modern Gypsies), stop for an hour or two at a small restaurant, drink champagne and listen to their weird singing is one of the chief winter pleasures which Petrograd offers.

Since the fifties of last century the fashion for the Tziganes has somewhat died out, but there was a time when men went mad about the pretty Gypsy singers. Pushkine immortalised them in a beautiful poem, and other gifted poets tuned their lyre at the Gypsy's shrine; large fortunes were squandered, foolish marriages took place, and the Gypsies of that period represented a real danger to the young nobility and the officers of our crack regiments.

Few know the origin of the Tzigane choruses. More than a century ago, one of the serfs of Count Orloff-Tchessmensky, a Gypsy named Ivan Sokoloff, organised a chorus of his countrymen and women and taught them to sing and dance. This chorus appeared at all the Count's entertainments and had a wonderful success.

In the Empress Catherine II's reign, one of her field-marshals took a Gypsy chorus with him to divert his leisure hours during the campaign.

Chapter XV

LOOKING FORWARD

THE unanimous will of the Russian nation, aided by the sincere and unlimited support of her Allies, will achieve complete victory over Germany. The Allied Powers will emerge from this conflagration revived and liberated from the incrustations of Atheism and Socialism with which an unprincipled and over-practical age covered them. The old traditions of the past will be resuscitated in new forms of life.

It would be impossible not to put one's faith in this regeneration, when even now one witnesses such marvellous deeds of self-sacrifice and nobility, which seem to come out of pages yellow with age, of an old and forgotten romance of chivalry. For instance: what an ideal figure, in its greatness, is that of Lord Kitchener, calmly going to his doom, continuing to smoke his pipe on the deck of the sinking cruiser. The brief report from the Staff of the death of a colonel in command of one of the regiments of the Russian army reads like a wonderful legend: 'The colonel led his regiment on to attack a German trench, when a bullet hit him full in the breast; dying from loss of blood, the colonel, with the last effort of his strength, shouted: "Forward, regiment!" and fell back dead.'

Has not a miracle been effected in France, restoring her to Christ, after the lamentable epoch of Godlessness, the destruction of ancient abbeys, the persecution of priests and nuns? What the patriot nationalists incarcerated in republican prisons, or, like Paul Deroulêde, dying in exile, could not achieve; that which the subtle diplomatic wisdom of the late Pope Leo XIII could not attain, has come about naturally by means of the tempest of war.

The Alliance, based on perfect trust between enlightened

France, Christian Russia and the iron-willed Ruler of the Seas, must become closer still, not only for the weal of their own countrymen, but for the prosperity of mankind.

Serious thought must be given to the development of future relations to be established when the war comes to its inevitable end. On no account must Russia drift back to her former dependence on Germany. These last two years have brought Russia and Great Britain into close contact with each other; the two nations have fought and suffered in the same cause. The English have learnt to understand and appreciate the Russians, and the latter are proud of their English friends. The veil of misconception and distrust that for so many years impeded friendly dealings between the two countries has been torn asunder and even the last shreds have been blown away. It now remains to consolidate these good feelings into a lasting friendship after the war has ceased. The peace that will be concluded in due course must give Great Britain the same advantages as it does to Russia. No ill-feeling must be nurtured in that respect. This thought must be uppermost in the minds of Russian and English diplomatists at the forthcoming Peace Congress. But that is not enough – England and Russia must be bound by commercial interests to the equal benefit of both countries.

One of the first and most important reforms in Russia will have to be the perfecting of professional and technical education. It is a well-known fact that no other country can vie with Russia as regards her natural riches, but notwithstanding this abundance Russia (relatively to products) was mostly provided from without. Our raw materials were sent abroad, at a very low rate, returning to us at high prices from foreign lands. This was hardly noticed prior to the war. The difference was scarcely felt at first, but with the protraction of this war we began to feel the want of many things, commencing with trifles required for household necessities, and ending with important objects indispensable to our manufactories. This was the time to realise our backwardness in comparison to foreign countries, and to recognise our serious lack of specialists. The root of this evil lies in the inertness of the Russians and their unwillingness to work their own riches. The urgency of establishing professional colleges and schools is evident. These reforms, however, cannot be accomplished in a day, and we shall continue for some time to be provided from abroad. Nevertheless, Russia must on no account drift back into the former grooves. The Russian market, which used to be flooded with German wares, must henceforth be closed to German merchants. A commercial alliance with Great Britain would be the best safeguard against letting the Germans take their former stand in Russia. The German merchants are fully aware of the risk they are running of losing the Russian market, and their anxiety to avert this calamity is so keen that several of them, even at the present moment, are making persevering endeavours to renew relations with Russian firms. Commercial travellers (mostly Jews) with samples of German wares have been arrested and sent out of Petrograd; circulars have been received with all kinds of alluring offers. The following letter which I am quoting textually is a convincing proof of German brazenness. The recipient is one of the most important chemists in Petrograd; the writer a Berlin druggist, who used to supply the Russian chemist with all kinds of drugs, several hundred thousand roubles' worth at a time. Loath to lose such a profitable customer, the German druggist sent his client the following epistle, which was received in Petrograd from Sweden in July, 1916:

'We were not the instigators of this murderous war, which has already lasted two years. The war was thrust on us and has cost us unheard of sacrifices, but the feud cannot last for ever. We did not seek territorial advantages from our good neighbours, and the time is not far off when our enemies shall be convinced of Germany's invincible might, and will cease this aimless bloodshed.

'We hope that the whole world is now aware of what we knew long ago, that the strife between nations in the twentieth century does not take place on the battlefield or in bloodshed, but in technical supremacy, in the superior degree of culture and in commercial prosperity. Our enemies cannot deny us the possession of these qualifications. The world could not exist without German culture, or without the colossal development of German industry. The cheapness and good quality of German wares and the integrity of German tradesmen cannot be altered by the war.

'We therefore suggest the renewal of your esteemed orders to our firm, for we have reason to know that the war will come to an end in November of the current year and you will thus be able to receive our wares with the first transport.'

The German industrials evidently imagine that their wish is sufficient to put an end to the European strife. Inflated with insolent presumption, they even go so far as to predict the exact time when the war will end. The German firm whose letter I have quoted belongs, it is true, to a syndicate of important manufacturers who, as the *Berliner Tageblatt* asserts, profit by the extensiveness of the war, and keep up the strife against the wish of the rest of the German nation. One may conclude consequently that it remains with them to influence the Kaiser to lay down his arms. Still, it is to be hoped that the fate of Europe will not be ruled by German industry, and that the writer's boast of conquering the world without bloodshed will be a vain one.

The British merchant, as a rule, is not over-conciliatory in his dealings with foreign firms. The great obstacle to commercial transactions with Great Britain consisted in the unwillingness of the English firms to give credit to Russians. The Russian tradesmen are used to credit, and are thoroughly convinced that no business can be transacted without it. In their dealings with German firms they had no difficulty in this respect. Another formidable impediment is the high price of British wares, whereas those of the German are cheap. How will it be possible to instil into a stubborn Russian merchant's mind that he must henceforth import, let us say, pencils from England at the rate of two roubles a dozen, when he can get them from Germany for half the price?

The following incident will make my meaning quite clear.

The best jute-bags are made in Scotland. As an agricultural country Russia uses such bags in enormous quantities, and used to get them from Hamburg. A friend of mine had seen the Scotch bags and was able to judge of their infinite superiority to those imported from Germany. He had the idea of starting an agency in Petrograd for Scotch jute-bags, feeling confident in the success of his scheme, and of spreading the sale of them all over the Empire. With this aim in view, he entered into communication with several of the largest firms in Edinburgh and Dundee. The best references were given, but the conditions were such as to make all competition with Hamburg impossible. The agent was given no credit; the money for the bags was to be handed over to the captain of the merchant vessel in return for the bills of lading. No reduction of price was accorded to the agent acquiring the bags wholesale, only a percentage from the bags disposed of. Taking into consideration the expense of duty, etc., the Scotch bags turned out much more expensive than the German ones. Nevertheless, if the agency could have had facilities granted to it, the evident superiority of texture of the bags and their one-seamed shape would have undoubtedly appealed to the farmers and tradesmen in quest of bags; but in order to ensure the success of the enterprise, a six months' credit would have been indispensable.

After the war Russia will afford many openings to enterprising Englishmen, Americans and companies of rich shareholders, keen to lay out their money in the most profitable way. The organisation of the magnificent watering-places and health resorts in the Caucasus offers immense possibilities and would be a capital investment. It would also put an effective stop to the yearly pilgrimage of thousands and thousands of Russian and English travellers in search of alleviations of their ailments to the German and Bohemian baths. When the war broke out these places were over-filled with foreign tourists who were shamefully ill-treated by the German authorities. The most suitable punishment that could overtake these health resorts would be a strict boycott in the future. The numerous watering-places in the Caucasus offer the same advantages; they even surpass the German and Bohemian baths. Medical men have long since recognised the superior quality of the boiling springs of Essentucky to those of Carlsbad and Marienbad. The cure at Piatigorsk is more efficacious than that of Aix-la-Chapelle. The percentage of iron contained in the waters of Zelesnovodsk greatly exceeds that of the springs of Schwalbach and Franzensbad. Kisslovodsk is a beautiful place with most bracing air, and the waters there are even stronger than those of Nauheim. Sufferers from cardiac diseases benefit immensely from a sojourn in Kisslovodsk. The climate of the Caucasus is beautiful, the scenery magnificent, reminding one in its picturesqueness of some parts of Switzerland. The above-named health resorts have been crowded during the last two years, and even foreigners have been amongst the visitors. The French General Pau, suffering from gout, was much benefited by a course of waters and baths taken in Essentucky. But – the everlasting Russian But – the general accommodation and bath establishments leave plenty of room for improvement. In the reign of Alexander III a Belgian company offered the Russian Government to take the Caucasian group of watering-places on a long lease, build first-class hotels, magnificent casinos, bath establishments, according with the modern standards of comfort and hygiene, colonnades, etc.; in a word, to provide them with all the indispensable accessories which well-managed health resorts should possess. The Belgian company made only one stipulation; they wanted to have a *salle de jeu* in the Casino of Kisslovodsk, similar to that of Monte Carlo; but the Russian Government objected to gambling.

Sakki, in the province of Kherson, not far from Odessa, is renowned for the efficacy of its mud-baths. Many wounded and crippled officers and soldiers have been sent to Sakki, and the most wonderful results have ensued from a course of these baths.

On the shores of the Black Sea there are wonderful places, such as Gagry, Sotchi, etc., which are eminently suitable for rest cures. A lovely climate, combined with the beauties of nature and the richness of the Southern flora, make them delightful resorts. The balmy air is impregnated with the perfume of magnolias, daturas, roses and other flowers.

If all these places were properly arranged with comfortable accommodation for tourists, good hotels and restaurants, they would be certain to attract travellers from foreign countries and in time become the fashion. The Prince of Oldenburg possesses a lovely country seat near Gagry; in fact nearly the whole place belongs to him. His Imperial Highness is one of the best organisers in Russia, and has had a magnificent hotel built there, which is perfectly managed. All the rooms are of one size and one price, comfortably furnished, with a balcony adjoining them. There is a bathroom to every two bedrooms. The price of each room was three roubles a day (about six shillings). The food was excellent, everyone ate *à la carte*, each dish costing thirty-five copecks. The price of lunch and dinner depended entirely on the number of dishes selected.

The want of a first-class hotel is greatly felt in Petrograd. Moscow is better provided in this respect. We have nothing approaching the Savoy in London, the Ritz in Paris, or even the Adlon in Berlin.

If the same unity of all parties could be maintained after the war, it would be much easier to wrestle with the German influence. There is no use in blinding oneself to the fact that the most strenuous efforts will be made to put the intercourse of the two nations on to the old footing. Our fierce and belligerent neighbours will turn sweet as honey in order to gain their own ends; all concessions will be made, for what will they do if the Russian market remains closed to German wares? But Russia must be firm, and England, our true and valued Ally, must remain our friend, and help us in the moral struggle that will ensue after the war between Russia and Germany, which, though less injurious than the present conflict, will still be of the greatest importance.

Meanwhile, we are all agreed to defend Holy Russia, and to expel the enemy from our native soil. From the Arctic Ocean to the Black Sea, from Vladivostock to the Baltic, the Russian people have but one aim, one wish, one aspiration: to fight for their Tzar and their country till the last drop of their blood. They must be victorious!

Available as a companion volume

THE FALL OF THE ROMANOFFS
With an introduction by Alan Wood

Written in 1917 between the February and October revolutions, this book is a highly subjective account of the demise of the Romanov dynasty which had ruled Russia for 300 years. The author, an anonymous aristocrat, attaches most of the blame for events to the Empress Alexandra and the clique of German sympathisers surrounding her who were thought to be undermining the country's efforts in time of war.

A leading character in the story is the *staretz* (or travelling holy man) Rasputin, whose baleful influence on the Empress was a major factor in alienating much of the political establishment from the royal family. The 'traitor's' rise to power, his period of dominance and his eventual murder are described by the author in elaborate detail.

A host of other personalities take the stage in the course of the narrative – members of the court circle, military leaders and politicians of various persuasions. In the latter part of the book there appear the 'Lenintzys', or Bolsheviks, whose growing influence among workers and soldiers is noted by the author with unease but whose cataclysmic role in the months to come he fails completely to foresee.

RUSSIAN PORTRAITS

CLARE SHERIDAN

Edited by Mark Almond

In late 1920 the sculptress Clare Sheridan, cousin of Winston Churchill, clandestinely left England bound for Soviet Russia. She departed, without telling family or friends and without the knowledge of the British Government, in the company of the Bolshevik Kamenev, who had offered her the opportunity of modelling busts of the revolutionary leaders.

This book, a diary of that remarkable journey, recounts how Sheridan abandoned her aristocratic English background and arrived in a country which was entirely alien to her and whose leaders had been portrayed in the West as monsters. It then describes her meetings with some of the most important figures in the Revolution, such as Lenin, Trotsky and Dzerzhinsky. Although Stalin is missing from her gallery of portraits, many of those who would later fall victim to his purges are presented here, for once, without his awful shadow.

Based in Moscow, Sheridan did not glimpse much of life beyond the city, but she did enjoy a unique access to the Bolshevik leaders which makes *Russian Portraits* a fascinating picture of events at the very heart of an embattled revolution.

THE ARGONAUTICA EXPEDITION
THEODOR TROEV
Foreword by Tim Severin

The legend of Jason and the Argonauts, and their quest for the Golden Fleece, has long fascinated classical scholars. Intrigued by the discovery of a curiously shaped golden ingot in the Black Sea, which led to a new theory concerning the origins of the myth, Bulgarian writer and explorer Theodor Troev suggested a voyage following the route of the Argonauts to the land of the Golden Fleece, Colchis – present-day Georgia. The aim of this expedition was to investigate the possibility that maritime and cultural links had existed between what is now the Bulgarian coast and other points in the ancient world and also to establish what it really was that Jason and his crew had sought on their journey.

In this book Theodor Troev describes his research into the story of the Argonauts, the preparations for the expedition, the voyage itself, and the discoveries that he and his crew made in Georgia and along the northern coast of Turkey on their homeward journey. He also tells of his team's encounter with the expedition led by the renowned British explorer Tim Severin which at the same time was tracing Jason's voyage in the replica galley Argo. The book will delight all those interested in Greek mythology, archaeology, travel and adventure, and the new hypotheses that emerge from it will make a valuable contribution to the study of the ancient world.

CHARLES KNIGHT – A FORGOTTEN GENIUS

DEREK STOW AND JUDITH HUNTER

Charles Knight – writer, publisher, editor, historian, reformer, critic and commentator – made a major contribution to the history, literature and art of the England of the nineteenth century. Yet to most people his name is unknown.

Working within the 'Society for the Diffusion of Useful Knowledge', Knight aimed to bring the world of learning and education to the Victorian masses. In the process he produced and largely wrote the publication for which he is best remembered, the *Penny Magazine*. Appearing between 1832 and 1845, and achieving a huge circulation, this was a magazine of quality and integrity, illustrated by the work of some of the country's finest engravers, on sale at a price that made it available to all. Among Knight's numerous other publications were a pictorial Shakespeare in eight volumes, *London* in six volumes and his magnificent two volumes of *Old England* which contained over 2,500 engravings, some of which are reproduced in this book.

Charles Knight's story is also a chronicle of a period of great social change which witnessed the revolution in industry and travel caused by the dawning of the steam age. Knight actively worked with many leading politicians and reformers of the time and journeyed throughout the country in a constant effort to encourage the regard for fairness and people's rights which formed the basis of his beliefs. He also developed a friendship with Charles Dickens and appeared on stage with him.

Forming a unique record of Knight's life and achievements, the book has been written by Derek Stow, author of *Charles Knight's London*, and Judith Hunter, Curator of the Royal Borough Collection at Windsor. Their text is complemented by extensive material from Knight's memoirs and those of his grand-daughter Alice Clowes.